Authentic Blackness | "Real" Blackness

Rochelle Brock and Richard Greggory Johnson III
Executive Editors

Vol. 26

The Black Studies & Critical Thinking series
is part of the Peter Lang Education list.
Every volume is peer reviewed and meets
the highest quality standards for content and production.

PETER LANG
New York • Washington, D.C./Baltimore • Bern
Frankfurt • Berlin • Brussels • Vienna • Oxford

Authentic Blackness | "Real" Blackness

Essays on the Meaning of Blackness in Literature and Culture

EDITED BY MARTIN JAPTOK AND JERRY RAFIKI JENKINS

PETER LANG
New York • Washington, D.C./Baltimore • Bern
Frankfurt • Berlin • Brussels • Vienna • Oxford

Library of Congress Cataloging-in-Publication Data

Authentic blackness/ "real" blackness: essays on the meaning of
blackness in literature and culture / edited by Martin Japtok,
Jerry Rafiki Jenkins.
p. cm. — (Black studies and critical thinking; v. 26)
Includes bibliographical references.
1. American literature—African American authors—History and criticism.
2. Blacks—Race identity. 3. African Americans in literature.
4. African Americans in popular culture. I. Japtok, Martin.
II. Jenkins, Rafiki.
PS153.N5A93   810.9'896073—dc22   2011012665
ISBN 978-1-4331-1509-7 (hardcover)
ISBN 978-1-4331-1508-0 (paperback)
ISSN 1947-5985

Bibliographic information published by **Die Deutsche Nationalbibliothek**.
Die Deutsche Nationalbibliothek lists this publication in the "Deutsche
Nationalbibliografie"; detailed bibliographic data is available
on the Internet at http://dnb.d-nb.de/.

FSC

Mixed Sources
Product group from well-managed
forests, controlled sources and
recycled wood or fiber

Cert no. SCS-COC-002464
www.fsc.org
©1996 Forest Stewardship Council

The paper in this book meets the guidelines for permanence and durability
of the Committee on Production Guidelines for Book Longevity
of the Council of Library Resources.

© 2011 Peter Lang Publishing, Inc., New York
29 Broadway, 18th floor, New York, NY 10006
www.peterlang.com

Printed in the United States of America

Contents

Introduction

We are living in an age concerned with identity, both cultural and personal. Ironically—since it is a major cause of that concern in that it tends to erode identity—it is especially commercial popular culture that exhorts us "to keep it real," especially those of us who are African American. But what's to keep real? Why is there concern over keeping "it" real? The concern itself has real, legitimate causes. On the one hand, signs of "blackness" are all over the place: Snoop Dogg is on the Tonight Show and everything from raisins to cars is sold with rap. To be associated with "coolness," everyone—from politicians to professors, from suburbanites to country youths, from ad executives to ad consumers—tries to show his or her knowledge of some facet of "blackness," usually a facet associated with the entertainment world. With "blackness" spread so thin, and globally so, no wonder people who actually are black and others who are not wonder what it means—both being black and the sudden ubiquity of "blackness." Thus the admonition to "keep it real," thus books exploring "black identity"—from a renewed interest in "passing" narratives, both autobiographical and fictional, to books on pop culture, the meaning of "black leadership," and countless books asking "whither black culture?"—and thus this collection of essays, which intends to shed some light on these developments by explicitly focusing on concerns over and debates about "authentic blackness".

Questions about authenticity tend to arise when culture is under assault—as it is everywhere as a consequence of economic globalization and the commercialization of every area of life that is one of globalization's major consequences. In his 1996 Jihad vs. McWorld: How Globalism and Tribalism Are Reshaping the World, Benjamin Barber explains that the forces of economic globalization tend to level out differences between cultures; after all, if we all can be made to desire and consume the same things, markets are increased and so is economic efficiency—fewer kinds of movies, cars, fashions, etc. for everyone. Such commercially induced pressure to become similar is often countered by what Barber calls, somewhat unfortunately, "jihad," by which he means resistance (in all its forms) to the sameness of globalization, such as a refusal to surrender local customs or an insistence on local music and TV content. The ensuing irony: authenticity itself has become commodified, as one can see, for example, in the widespread use of the phrase "keepin' it real," which was originally meant as a sort of reminder of the importance of (a kind of) authenticity.

Authentic Blackness/"Real" Blackness is a response to such trends. The idea for this essay collection grew out of countless and recurring discussions both editors have had over the years involving, implicitly and explicitly, the meaning of blackness as trends in everyday life, in popular music, in politics (think of the questions surrounding Barack Obama's "blackness" or supposed lack thereof early in his campaign), on TV, in literature, and on campus seemed to be weighing in on what being black is or is not supposed to be. The ensuing call for papers yielded many responses—none, curiously, interestingly, and indeed regretfully, from the Afrocentric side of the spectrum of takes on authentic blackness (why that is so we leave to readers to contemplate)--though the call for papers stressed that we were open to all ideological perspectives on the question of authentic blackness, notwithstanding our own skepticism concerning "authentic group identities."

Nonetheless, the essays that follow cover a wide range of contemplations on the idea of authentic blackness as it is reflected, commented on, implied, or critiqued in the culture at large. The essays do not necessarily agree with each other, as we did not intend that they should; some take it as a given that there is such a thing as authentic blackness, others aim, implicitly, to define it, others categorically reject the concept.

We start the collection with an introductory essay that attempts to put discussions of authentic blackness into some cultural and historical context. How and in response to what did the idea of authentic blackness develop? We give a selective overview of that part of the discussion that occurred primarily among African Americans and in other parts of the African Diaspora—though the pressure of the debate over the meaning of blackness among Euro-Americans makes itself felt in that discussion. Our introductory "What Does It Mean to Be 'Really' Black? A Selective History of Authentic Blackness" serves to provide a historical context for the essays that follow and to introduce readers to the various twists and turns the discussion of blackness has taken from the time Africans arrives in the Americas. Three essays on hip hop follow this historical overview as hip hop has assumed an almost dominant role in discussions of contemporary blackness, especially, but not only, in relation to youth culture, thus giving us a glimpse of where "authentic blackness" is headed in the future.

Dara Byrne and Jean-Jacques Rousseau's "The 'Defining' Problem of Black Authenticity in Canada: Real Slang and the Grammar of Cultural Hybrity" reminds us that "racial authenticity" is never inherent but always socially constructed. In Canada, even the language of "blackness" is a matter of geography (English or French/Creole) and authenticity is often measured by its closeness to Caribbeanness. Dara Byrne and Jean-Jacques Rousseau take Canadian rap music as their point of departure for this discussion but move to a debate between Rinaldo Walcott and George Elliott Clark over what blackness in Canada means. In contrast to the U.S., Canada lacks a unifying (hi)story that gives and outline to a potential Canadian blackness. The authors believe that the multilingual, multicultural, immigrant backgrounds of many black Canadians offer a chance for developing a "nonessentialist position on black authenticity."

In "Privileging the Popular at What Price? A Discussion of Joan Morgan, Hip Hop Feminism, and Radical Politics," David M. Jones embarks on a meditation of the uses of black popular culture as a basis of judgment for what is considered "authentically black" by way of a critical reading of Joan Morgan's writings on hip hop culture. While he shares and sympathizes with Morgan's fondness for black popular culture and recognizes its cultural impact, both positive and negative, he is skeptical about using pop culture, as a way to understand African American culture, given that pop culture, especially hip hop, has become a market commodity, making it difficult to ascertain how much "folk spirit" can actually be attributed to it—or how much political change it an affect.

What happens to an idea of black authenticity that is closely associated with hip hop when Fillipino DJs make the claim that they, too, are "keeping it real"? Tony Tiongson explores that question in "Claiming Hip Hop: Authenticity Debates, Filipino DJs. and Contemporary U.S. Racial Formations." Tony Tiongson is sympathetic to arguments that asserting hip-hops exclusive blackness is in and of itself a social construct, since, according to a number of music and culture critics. Hip hop has had a variety of points of origins and multicultural influences—and, though hip hop clearly is a African "Diasporic expressive form," the near-exclusive African Americanization of hip hop emerges along with its commercialization. With this commercialization and globalization, however, hip hop opened itself up to practitioners anywhere. Filippino DJs. as Tiongson shows, claim their legitimacy by their devotion to hip hop and their respect for its African American originators, by 'de-racing' it through claiming its universality, but also by seeing themselves as "raced," and, to some extent, marginalized. Tiongson calls for more attention to dynamics of societal power and how they relate to who can or will take postures of authenticity when practicing hip hop.

The section on hip hop is followed by two personal encounters with "authentic blackness," one in the American South, the other in Jamaica.

Wendy Rountree offers a journey through her encounter with authentic blackness in "Faking the Funk: A Journey Towards Authentic Blackness." Finding herself marginalized in adolescence by her African American peers for "trying to act white." As they perceived it, she develops and "intra-racial double consciousness," leading her to wonder, in her essay, about the power and sources of the equation of blackness with working class status. At the same time, she also probes into the ways in which middle class upbringing may instill doubts about blackness, as log as blackness is defined in such class-bound ways. Her essay implies, though, that such definitions of blackness may ultimately be provincial, and that a broader, internationalist outlook on black identity and politics might well be the cure for parochial definitions of blackness.

"Brown Boy Blues. . . Inna Jamaica" by Gregory Stephens is a personal, engaged, and searing critique of racialism, and of black-white binarisms, as the author encounters them in his years in Jamaica. Arguing that too many Jamaicans define authentic blackness merely through its opposition to whiteness, and thus authenticity also acquires colorist elements (black is valued over brown, or rather brown is suspicious because of its closeness to white) Gregory Stephens shows how such a definition of blackness then necessitates the rejection of former culture heroes, such as Bob Marley, once too many white people embrace them. As an alternative to ideas of racial authenticity that are ultimately beholden to whiteness and give it too much power, Stephens proposes looking to the larger America in which the concept of "mestizaje" offers a potential way out of racialism.

Joy Viveros's "Black Authenticity, 'Racial Drag,' and the Case of Dave Chappelle mixes personal observations and critical discourse to come to an assessment of the meaning of "blackness." Arguing that "race" is both social construct and "real," she shows that the "realness" of race is nonetheless always performative and unstable. Because of this instability, it makes sense that comedy and satire have become more and more prominent in approaching the paradoxes of "race"—Joyce Viveros and Cynthia Willett implicitly agree on satire being an appropriate mode for explorations of "race." Viveros makes that case in a detailed analysis of a number of Dave Chappelle's sketches, showing that the absurdist mode they often employ means to undercut any certainties an audience might have about "race."

The final four essays of the collection show how the debate over authentic blackness in the culture at large is reflected in literary works—and how literary works themselves weigh in on that discussion. In "Peculiar Irresolution: James Baldwin and Flanerie," Monika Gehlawat explores whether group-based authenticity and marginality in that group can simultaneously exist and argues that "flanerie" is a life posture enabling such a feat. The flaneur observes, is vagrant, unrooted, but this very position gives him, James Baldwin, a vantage point of exceptional clear-eyedness, and his insights are of value in the fight against racism in which Baldwin took part; thus, Monika Gehlawat defends Baldwin from critics accusing him of lacking "racial commitment."

Clarence Major's literary work does not merely critique racial authenticity or advocate for certain kinds of racial authenticity, it does away altogether with notions of group identity that limit and circumscribe the actions of individuals—thus argues Benjamin Carson in his "'Many forces at work': Clarence Major's Early Fiction and the Critique of Racial Economy." The postmodernist and experimental form Major has chosen for much of his work assists him in arguing for a post-racial world in that it stresses the indeterminacy and openness of writing—and the difficulty in interpreting people's actions based on one interpretive category. Benjamin Carson contrasts Major's work to some critics who, he claims, make "race" the bedrock of their analysis even while critiquing racial essentialisms, and he compares Major's approach especially to Paul Gilroy's Against Race.

If there is such a thing an authentic blackness, in what language does it express itself? I. Reilly's "'Isn't the whole point of writing to escape what people not me think of me': Wideman's Decolonization and the Failure of Language in Philadelphia Fire and God's Gym" explores the struggle over this question that is a thread winding its way through John Edgar Wideman's work. According to I. Reilly, Wideman's search for Afrocentric expression in a Eurocentric cultural seeing is illustrated by his characters' failure to take into account the colonizing forces of language. Reilly reads Wideman's prose fiction as an on-going decolonizing project in that it searches for a communal voice countering the loss of the individual to the larger, negating racism that surrounds him or her.

In "How Black Do You Want It? Countee Cullen and the Contest for Racial Authenticity on Page and Stage," Jonathan Shandell defends Countee Cullen against charges of racial self-hatred and "inauthenticity" by challenging the notion that authenticity has to find a specific artistic expression. Jonathan Shandell's essay shows that Cullen, both in his poetry and dramatic work, not only staked his claim as an African American artist in European-derived poetic modes and genres but re-invented them to serve African American purposes, not least to challenge contemporary ideas of white supremacy.

Taken together, these essays provide an in-depth examination of many of the facets of "authentic blackness." While many of the authors voice some skepticism as to the very concept of racial authenticity, they are also aware of the forces that have prompted discussions about authenticity in the first place.

The irresolvable irony that emerges is that while African Americans are engaged in a legitimate struggle to define themselves, self-definition, both of groups and individuals, does not take place in a vacuum, and thus what others think of one and what one thinks of oneself result in a dynamic that makes group authenticity an on-going process. The essays collected here give further insight into the elements that make up that process and point to directions a successful struggle for cultural self-definition might take.

What Does It Mean to Be "Really" Black? A Selective History of Authentic Blackness

Martin Japtok and Jerry Rafiki Jenkins

According to The Oxford Dictionary of Word Histories, the word "authentic," since its first usage in the late Middle English period, has been used to refer to something as "genuine" (Chantrell 35). The word acquired a great deal of social value as "a notion in museum curatorship" in which the "museum" (which initially referred to "a university building") refers to a place where "authentic" things are kept and where the "curator" (the "custodian of a museum") functions as the authority on what is or is not authentic (Heath and Potter 269; Chantrell 130-31, 336). Thus, as John L. Jackson, Jr. argues in Real Black: Adventures in Racial Sincerity, "[a]uthenticity presupposes a relation between subjects (who authenticate) and objects (dumb, mute, and inorganic) that are interpreted and analyzed from the outside, because they cannot simply speak for themselves" (14-15). One of the "crucial tests" used by the one who has the authority to authenticate is "the absence of commodification: truly authentic things are made by hand, from natural materials, for a traditional (i.e., noncommercial) purpose" (Heath and Potter 269). According to this understanding of authenticity, to establish something as "authentic," the curator must determine who made it, how it was made and why. That is to say, "authentic" things must be made by "authentic" people, people who make things solely or primarily because they want to use them, not because they want to sell them. The question of authenticity arises when an original has been copied. In the words of Walter Benjamin, "[t]he presence of the original is the prerequisite to the concept of authenticity" (220).

The concept of authenticity thus arises with urgency when boundaries between the "real" and the "fake" or the "copy" are blurred—an endemic cultural condition after the Industrial Revolution. In the nineteenth and twentieth centuries, advancements in technology made it possible to reproduce an original at a faster pace and on a wider scale than ever before. In this context, the reproduction or copy "jeopardize[s]" the "authority" and "value" of the original by making it available to people outside the sphere in which it was produced (Benjamin 220-221). Under these conditions, the search for the "authentic" becomes essentially futile because the original can be reproduced endlessly and, as today's advertisements about the wonders of high-definition television proclaim, the reproduction can now be made to look "better" or "clearer" than the original. Less and less importance is being placed on something being handmade in a world in which the machine-made is often regarded as superior, and thus Walter Benjamin has argued that the concept of authenticity has become less important in determining the value and function of a work of art. Therefore, today, a work's "authenticity" and, therefore, its "authority" and "value" do not depend on how the original was made, who made it, or why it was made. Instead, questions of authenticity are now often focused on whether the reproduction is "better" than the original (as in the "remakes" of pop songs).

In the social sphere, however, questions over authenticity still revolve around the concept of uniqueness, on being an "original." Existentialism, a philosophical and literary movement popular in Europe, especially in France, immediately after World War Two, focuses on "the uniqueness of each human individual as distinguished from abstract universal human qualities," implying that to be "authentic" is to resist conformity or what some called "anonymity" (Audi 255). Thus the authentic person is one who is not "contaminated" by culture, especially the economic system in which a culture is grounded. Existentialists such as Sartre, Camus, and de Beauvoir celebrated the individual who is true to oneself regardless of what society says about his or her beliefs and actions. However, since humans beings are "thrown" into the world and "exist without justification," we are always tempted to choose "inauthenticity" over "authenticity"; that is to say, we are always tempted to define ourselves or make decisions about our lives based on "public preoccupations" that encourage us to "drift along with the crowd, doing what 'one' does, enacting stereotyped roles, and thereby losing our ability to seize on and define our own lives" (Audi 256, 318-19)—in other words, if we conform to societal expectations, we become copies rather than originals.

The existentialist notion of the authentic human is further developed in the 1970s. In Nation of Rebels: Why Counterculture Became Consumer Culture, Joseph Heath and Andrew Potter argue that for today's "countercultural rebel," one who believes that the repression of the individual by "the system" can be countered by "reclaiming our capacity for spontaneous pleasure," to be authentically human is to adopt a pre-capitalist worldview in which use value is privileged over exchange value, and "having fun" is viewed as a revolutionary or anti-capitalist practice because it is presumed that "[p]leasure is inherently anarchic, unruly, wild" (9). They note that the publication of Lionel Trilling's 1972 book Sincerity and Authenticity ushered the term "authenticity" into the vernacular and defined it as "a thoroughly modern value that emerged in direct response to the alienating effects of technocratic life." If "authenticity" is associated with "the unity between self, society and others that gives a sense of wholeness or reality to our lives," the "inauthentic" represents consumer capitalism's repression of the needs and desires that reflect our "true selves" (Heath and Potter 269-270). In this light, part of our society's current concern with "keeping it real" is about a conscious or unconscious search for a pre-market Self that is defined from within, not from without.

The problematic link between authenticity and consumer capitalism described by Heath and Potter is especially pronounced for those of us who are African American. Many of the signs of "blackness" that we see all over the place, especially in mainstream media, can be interpreted as signs of "black success," usually (though not always) defined by the amount of money one has made. One might think here, obviously, of such icons of black success as Oprah Winfrey and Barack Obama, of the many prominent African Americans in the entertainment industry (from Will Smith and Denzel Washington to Jay Z and Mary J. Blige), or of the Williams sisters, of countless African American basketball, baseball, and football greats, or of Tiger Woods (whose "blackness" has been questioned by the media, fans, and himself, but whom ESPN once declared as the most popular athlete inside and outside the sports world). However, that black financial and cultural success is still so often tied to areas of achievement admissible even at the height of white supremacy in the late nineteenth and early twentieth century—entertainment and sports, e.g. minstrelsy or boxing—raises questions about whether blackness continues to be assigned a specific cultural "box." Who, in other words, gets to define what "blackness" is or means? And who is to say what is "really" black?

Black Authenticity before the Mayflower—and After

The question of black authenticity starts, in a New World context, with the trans-Atlantic trade: people from various linguistic, ethnic, and cultural groups are forged together, compelled to speak European languages for communication, and their status in New World societies is defined from the outside. The beginnings of New World racism are also the beginnings of questions of "black authenticity." Forced into this new framework, African identities and self-understanding give way to new, hybrid cultural constructs woven from African, Native American, and European strands. One's condition as a marginalized outsider, often enslaved, becomes the framework within which the meaning of blackness has to be established. What, in such circumstances, does it mean to be black? The concept of black solidarity must of necessity arise against the hostility of one's captors, even though one must guard against a monolithic image of the always hostile white antagonist; but in a wider sense, in the sense that New World society in the budding U.S. and elsewhere is founded on white (European) privilege, African and Native American labor, and Native American dispossession, antagonistic whiteness which seeks to define blackness as subservient is a bitterly ironic ingredient in this newly forming sense of blackness. Other distinctions—of language, culture, shade of color, of position within the larger hostile surrounding, of degrees of freedom—exist, but it is the shared fact of racism that creates a sense of shared blackness. In many ways, contemporary notions of "authentic blackness" reflect such beginnings, often in complicated ways. The sense of blackness that was developing in the fledgling New World, especially in the U.S., emerges similarly in the context of European colonialism in the Old World–in both instances, defining "blackness" is a process that is not entirely controlled by black people. That is to say, "blackness" is partly a product of what Stuart Hall refers to as the "gaze of Otherness" in a discussion of the famous Martiniquean psychoanalyst and writer Frantz Fanon. According to Hall, "[i]t is a fantastic moment in Fanon's Black Skin, White Masks when he talks of how the gaze of the Other fixes him in an identity. He knows what it is to be Black when the [French] white child pulls the hand of her mother and says 'Look momma, a Black man.' And he says, 'I was fixed in that gaze.' That is the gaze of Otherness" ("Ethnicity" 345). Implicit in Hall's comments is that the search for an "authentic" racial self or identity is futile precisely because "most of the identities that [we] have been [we've] only known about not because of something deep inside [us] the real self but because of how other people have recognized [us]" (344). Thus, "blackness," like all other identities, is defined from without as well as from within.

Though one has to be wary of retroactively importing current notions and ideas of "race" into the ancient world, it is instructive to see that the question of who gets to define whom as "black" does have antecedents. In ancient Egypt, for example, identifying blackness with Egyptianness was a response to the invasions by the Persians who emphasized "the value and moral superiority of lightness" and linked lightness with themselves and the paler Lower Egyptians (Bernal 80). In an intricate interplay of internal and external definition, the Egyptians thus embraced as positive what was meant to be a negative ascription. According to Martin Bernal, before the arrival of Persian conquerors in sixth century BCE, ancient Egyptian artists attempted to convey "'Egyptianness" by representing a more or less homogenized population of red-brown men and yellow-white women" that did not emphasize or place any hierarchical social value on the differences in skin color among ancient Egyptians (77). Bernal reminds us that "Egyptian Pharaohs and slaves alike could be black, brown, or olive with Negro, East African, or Mediterranean features" (78). The purpose of artistic renderings of Egyptians as "red-brown men and yellow-white women" was "that Egyptians should not be confused with southwest Asians, who were stereotyped as pale, and Nubians, who were generally portrayed as black with broad noses and tight curly hair" (77). Thus, blackness became meaningful in ancient Egypt only when the invaders, through their preference for lightness, assigned social value to skin color. As Bernal puts it, "[r]esistance to the Persians and later to the Greeks involved a cultural 'return' among Egyptians to African blackness, to the art of the great southern dynasties in Upper Egypt, and to an image of a dark Nubia as a source and refuge for true Egyptian culture" (80).

The notion of blackness that emerged in the fifteenth century AD in Europe, however, was defined by non-blacks who believed that blacks and non-blacks could only coexist in a relationship of domination and subordination because nature or God predetermined one's place in the social universe. Indeed, "caste racism," especially that which developed in Iberia during this period, "is not merely an attitude or set of beliefs; [....] It either directly sustains or proposes to establish a racial order, a permanent group hierarchy that is believed to reflect the laws of nature or the decrees of God" (Fredrickson 6). This naturalization of the link between skin color and socio-economic status spread in the West in the fifteenth century; the Portuguese started claiming that Africans were "slavish by nature" to justify their kidnapping and selling of West Africans (Bernal 82), though the origin of such ideas was the Muslim world. According to Fredrickson, in fourteenth and fifteenth-century Spain "the association of blackness with slavery was apparently already being made [....] [I]t was during this period when Christians and Muslims coexisted in Iberia that the former learned from the latter to identify blackness with servitude" (28-9). While medieval Arabs and Moors had white and black slaves, it appears that "the Islamic world preceded the Christian in representing sub-Saharan Africans as descendants of Ham, who were cursed and condemned to perpetual bondage because of their ancestor's mistreatment of his father, Noah, as described in an obscure passage in Genesis" (Frederickson 29).

Although the notion of blackness that came into existence in ancient Egypt in 500 BCE is qualitatively different from the one that emerged in Iberia roughly 2,000 years later, both notions were significantly shaped by outsiders to the group being defined, and the power of outsiders impacted how insiders of the group came to see themselves; therefore, a search for an "authentic blackness" should not be understood as a search for a "true" racial self but as a search for power. As Patricia Williams explains, "racism is a gaze that insists upon the power to make others conform, to perform endlessly in the prison of prior expectation, circling repetitively back upon the expired utility of the entirely known" (74). In this light, the question of "black authenticity" is more about who has the power to define "authentic blackness," what blackness "really" means, than it is about what constitutes "authentic blackness." In fact, a crucial link between the sense of "blackness" that slowly crystallized in Europe from the fifteenth century onward and "New World blackness" is that they are both products of racism, of a relationship in which whites use their power advantage to impose their definitions of blackness on black people as well as to treat those who they identify as black in cruel and unjust ways (see Fredrickson 9).

One must be careful not to focus solely on the "contribution" of racism to racial identity, however. In spite of the shared experience of racism, the notion of authentic blackness has been a historically and passionately contested concept within the African American community. Ironically, one could argue that the debate over "black authenticity" within the African American community has largely been about intra-racial differences rather than inter-racial differences. Debra Dickerson makes this point in The End of Blackness (2004), arguing that one of the "most fundamental revelations" that black people who are "analyzing" their "past" and "claiming" their "future" will learn is that "[i]t is other blacks whom blacks spend their lives trying to please, not whites" (13-14). This intra-group conflict is highlighted in E. Patrick Johnson's suggestive and selective sketch of moments in American history when the meaning and content of being black was in dispute. According to Johnson,

> if one were to look at blackness in the context of American history, one would find that, even in relation to nationalism, the notion of an "authentic" blackness has always been contested: the discourse of the "house niggers" vs. "field niggers"; Sojourner Truth's insistence on black female subjectivity in relation to the black polity; Booker T. Washington's call for vocational skill over W.E.B. Du Bois's "talented tenth"; Richard Wright's critique of Zora Neale Hurston's focus on the "folk" over the plight of the black man; Eldridge Cleaver's caustic attack on James Baldwin's homosexuality as "anti-black," "anti-male"; urban northerners' condescending attitudes toward rural black southerners and vice versa; Malcolm X's

militant call for black Americans to fight against the white establishment "by any means necessary" over Martin Luther King Jr.'s reconciliatory "turn the other cheek"; and Jesse Jackson's "Rainbow Coalition" over Louis Farrakhan's "Nation of Islam." (3-4)

What is implied by Johnson's brief sketch is that the search for authentic blackness within the African American community has not been too concerned with finding a "balm for something sitting at the heart of the African-American consciousness: a sense that at the end of the day, black people are inferior to whites" (20), as John McWhorter implies in Authentically Black: Essays for the Black Silent Majority (2004). Instead, the debates over black authenticity reveal, as Guthrie Ramsey, Jr. argues, that "[t]he diverse and sprawling processes we think of as 'African American culture' did not develop simply as a response to hegemony, racism, and social oppression. Recent academic studies and populist discourses reveal a feisty intrablack dialogue over the representation of blackness in the public and scholarly arena" (24). While a concern over representations of blackness relates to the way in which such representations may affect the lives of black people in a racist society, the very disagreements over how to represent oneself also bears witness to black participation in defining blackness. In addition, "the metaphor of a representation 'contest' within African American culture challenges the notion of a static sense of racial authenticity within African American communities" (Ramsey 24). Indeed, this representational "contest" is informed by the ways in which "blackness" is experienced in different places, by different people, at different times, and for different purposes. As Beverly Tatum explains, "how one's racial identity is experienced will be mediated by other dimensions of oneself: male or female; young or old; wealthy, middle-class, or poor; gay, lesbian, bisexual, transgender, or heterosexual; able-bodied or with disabilities; Christian, Muslim, Jewish, Buddhist, Hindu, or atheist" (18).

Authentic Blackness and the Discourse of "House Niggers" vs. "Field Niggers"

It is noteworthy that Johnson begins his history of "feisty intrablack dialogue" with the "house niggers" versus "field niggers" debate because this discourse points to the moment at which discussions over "authentic blackness" in the (yet-to-be) U.S. emerged: when African servitude became African slavery. However, it appears that such debates did not initially take place among blacks in colonial America but among white colonists. The twenty Africans who landed in Jamestown in 1619 became indentured servants rather than slaves. During Virginia's first half-century of existence, black indentured servants were being assigned land in much the same way as their white colleagues after their period of service was completed (Franklin and Moss 56). However, the infamous John Punch trial of 1640, when a court handed out different sentences to black and white runaway servants, signals the moment when an "official" definition of blackness begins to appear in the record of the fledgling U.S. The judge in this trial ordered the white runaways to serve their master for an additional year while he ordered the black runaway "to serve his said master or his assigns for the time of his natural life here or elsewhere" (qtd. in Franklin and Moss 57). By 1661, the year the first statutory recognition of slavery in Virginia was passed, it seems that two types of "black" people were already developing in the white colonial mind as a result of a rising mulatto population. To deal with this crisis over the meaning of "blackness," laws were passed to authenticate one's free or slave status. In 1662, the Virginia House of Burgesses declared that a child's status as free or slave was determined by the status of his or her mother (Hine, Hine, and Harrold 57). A 1681 Maryland law declared that "black children of white women and children born of free black women would be free" (Franklin and Moss 58). Laws and rulings seeking to distinguish African Americans in bondage from free African Americans and the growing equation of blackness with slavery represents white colonists' attempt to define the role of African Americans in society. Increasingly, from then on, since freedom is racialized as white in colonial logic, it becomes difficult for one to be both "black" and free.

Thus, the first debates about authentic blackness in the English colonies began among whites and were later conducted between blacks and whites. By the middle of eighteenth century, however, it seems that the debate shifts to differing notions of black liberation within the emerging African American community. For many critics, the person whose writings seem to embody the issues that inform the "house niggers" versus "field niggers" discourse is Jupiter Hammon (1711-c. 1806?), who became, in 1760, the first African American male poet to be published in the U.S. For some critics, Hammon's writings are significant because he is the first African American to acknowledge in print that a shared sense of blackness existed among the slaves in colonial America before the writing of the Declaration of Independence. For other critics, Hammon is significant because they see him as the first "house nigger" to be published in the US. Faith Berry defines Hammon as an "atypical slave who willingly conformed to slavery" and as the "'first contented slave' in Afro-American literature" (50). According to Berry, Hammon, like Phillis Wheatley (the first African American female poet to write and publish a book of poetry and whom Berry refers to as "Hammon's spiritual soul mate in human bondage") "barely spoke of the tyranny of servitude" that defined the slave's life and tended to define Africa as a "dark abode" (50-51). In his infamous 1787 piece, "An Address to the Negroes in The State of New York," Hammon claims that slaves should obey their masters without complaint because God demands it and because the slave's well-being depends on his or her obedience. In his words, "[God] has commanded us to obey, and we ought to do it cheerfully, and freely. This should be done by us, not only because God commands, but because our own peace and comfort depend upon it. As we depend on our masters, for what we eat and drink and wear, and for all our comfortable things in this world, we cannot be happy, unless we please them" (Hammon 53).

Like the notion of blackness developing in fifteenth century Iberia that held the link between biology (e.g. blood, skin color, facial features, and hair texture) and socio-economic status (e.g., master or slave, rich or poor, colonizer or colonized) to be natural or part of God's plan, Hammon appears to present black subordination to white domination as one of God's commandment and, therefore, an element of being black. While Hammon's words clearly represent the thinking of white slave owners and pro-slavery strategists of the period, one could also argue that Hammon's words represent the only type of "blackness" a slave could publicly display in order to get an education, to get published, or to survive another day. As Patricia Liggins Hill reminds us, Hammon's masters (the Lloyd family) and the larger white community would have had to approve Hammon's works before they were printed, distributed, or read to slaves because of questions of authenticity (validating the slave's authorship to the printer), of content (determining if the work can be construed as anti-slavery protest), and of black solidarity (colonists' feared the rise of a slave community network that extended beyond the borders of their localities). Consequently, if Hammon wanted to convey a subversive message or image of blackness within his writing, that message or image would have to be "coded" (Hill 71-2). As suggested by Hammon's use of words such as "we," "black," "African brethren," "Ethiopian" and "ancient" in his writings, a history of involuntary migration, perpetual servitude, and skin color are the elements that created a shared sense of blackness among the slaves and free blacks in colonial America. According to Hill, Hammon's constant reference to his "African brethren" as "ancient" attempts to "uplift" his enslaved brothers and sisters by locating them in a history older than that of their British masters, a history that has inspired "a recurring quest for authentic African history and culture" in the African American community (72).

Hammon's "Address" also suggests, on the other hand, that there was disagreement over what it meant to be authentically black within the emerging African American community. For example, it is important to note that Hammon was forty-nine years old when his first poem was published and around seventy-six years old when his "Address" was published because this raises the distinct possibility that Hammon's pro-slavery tone was also informed by a fear of being homeless. Many Northern slaveholders began to emancipate their elderly slaves by the middle of the eighteenth century because they could no longer work, which left these former slaves, who were forced to serve their masters all of their lives, "homeless and without food, income, or family" (Hill 73). In this light, Hammon's life and writings suggest that although slavery is a shared experience among Africans in America, the response to that experience was not universal because slavery was practiced differently depending on the type of labor the slave was expected to perform and because of the differences amongst African Americans such as age, gender, region, religion, level of formal education, and free or slave. To label Hammon a "contented slave," "house nigger," or inauthentic ignores the oppressive restrictions placed on the everyday lives of slaves in the North, especially the lives of elderly slaves who were born into slavery such as Hammon.

Authenticity, "Uplift," and the Role of the Folk

As suggested by Hammon's life and writings, the discourse about "appropriate blackness" is best understood as a conflict between survival strategies—at least certainly in the antebellum period—not as a conflict over who is or is not "real" or "authentic." In this view, a "house nigger" is a slave who (begrudgingly) accepts the system and attempts to create a survival space within it, whereas the "field nigger" is a slave who believes that rebellion is key to black liberation. There is a direct link between the question of how to achieve liberation and the late 19th century debate concerning "uplift." In Uplifting the Race, Kevin K. Gaines notes that African Americans attached "mixed meanings" to the term "uplift." One notion of uplift, which dates back to the "antislavery folk religion of the slaves" and flourished after Emancipation and during Reconstruction, can be viewed as a "liberation theology" in which education is regarded, with an "almost religious fervor," as the "key" to black freedom and social advancement. Another notion of uplift, which emerged after Reconstruction and prevailed throughout the era of segregation, links black solidarity and black progress with black class stratification through its emphasis on "self help, racial solidarity, temperance, thrift, chastity, social purity, patriarchal authority, and the accumulation of wealth" (1-2).   In many ways, the post-Reconstruction notion of uplift, as promoted by the fledgling black bourgeoisie and as resonating through texts such as Frances W. Harper's *Iola Leroy*, is an ideology not primarily interested in ideas of racial authenticity. One the one hand, this notion of uplift, summarized by W.E.B. Du Bois's 1901 essay, "The Black North," is a critique of white elites who saw blacks as a monolithic group: "A rising race must be aristocratic; the good cannot consort with the bad--not even the best with the less good" (qtd. in Gaines 165). On the other hand, Du Bois and uplift ideology also believed that the black elite was morally responsible for "saving" the black masses from themselves, as expressed in his well-known essay, "The Talented Tenth." This sense of moral responsibility, informed by Protestantism and the "Benevolent Empire" ideals of the various reform movements springing out of the Second Great Awakening in the first half of the nineteenth century, motivated the emerging middle class coming out of the historically black colleges founded before and after Emancipation to see as its mission to serve as an embodiment of such values and disperse them among the African American masses. Individual African American accomplishment and success was to help all African Americans and not be enjoyed hedonistically. Late nineteenth-century and early twentieth-century African American passing novels by Frances Harper (*Iola Leroy*), Charles Chesnutt (*The House behind the Cedars*) James Weldon Johnson (*The Autobiography of an Ex-Coloured Man*), and even Harlem Renaissance passing novels such as Jessie Fauset's *Plum Bun* show the influence of uplift ideology in that they portrayed passing by middle-class African Americans as a kind of betrayal from which only signing on to the mission to "uplift the race" could redeem the passer. Such an uplift ideology had little room for notions of "racial authenticity" as the values it embraced—excepting racial solidarity--were seen as universal values (that is, universally Protestant American values) and as the pathway to the American mainstream.

Kevin Gaines's definition of "uplift" ideology also describes to a large extent the ideology of the Garvey Movement of the 1920s, though the latter was far more politically charged and had black autonomy as its final goal rather than black incorporation into the U.S. Racial solidarity took center stage for Garvey, according to whom "race" defined individuals as well as groups. In His "African Fundamentalism" (1925), Marcus Garvey proclaims that "blackness" provides life goals and political programs:

> As the Jew is held together by his religion, the white races by the assumption and the unwritten law of superiority, and the Mongolian by the precious tie of blood, so likewise the Negro must be united in one grand racial hierarchy. Our union must

know no clime, boundary, or nationality. Like the great Church of Rome, Negroes
the world over must practice one faith, that of Confidence in themselves, with One
God! One Aim! One Destiny! [. . . .] . . .you can do no less than being first and always
a Negro, and then all else will take care of itself. (Clarke 158)

The tensions in such pronouncements are palpable: on the one hand, racial
authenticity appears inevitable: one simply has to listen to one's "blood," then
one's path is clear. On the other hand, the many command forms in the
passage show that racial authenticity cannot be taken for granted but must be
defined by someone (in this case, Garvey himself); in other words, racial
authenticity is an ideology, a plan of action to be embraced or rejected.
Possibly hundreds of thousands of African Diaspora followers joined or
contributed to his United Negro Improvement Association not least because
of the continued denigration of their racial identity by their societies;
embracing the identity others denigrate and asserting it proudly is a political
countermove--the actual "content" of such a racial identity was secondary and
something Garvey himself was usually vague about, beset as he was by his own
demons of authenticity stemming from the color hierarchy (who is black,
brown, red, etc.) of his native Jamaica and by the class and color tension
between himself and the NAACP leadership, whom he suspected of being a
sort of "'blue vein' aristocracy (Levering Lewis 41). Racial solidarity was, for
Garvey, a political rallying cry less in the service of a "racial authenticity" (the
outward trappings of UNIA marches, uniforms, titles, etc. were rather
Eurocentric) but in the pursuit of political and economic power.

During the Harlem Renaissance, which in some sense can be seen as the
artistic climax of the "racial uplift" movement, debates about "black
authenticity" centered on the arts and resumed center stage: the issue of
representation was at the heart of the Harlem Renaissance project. In his
foreword to *The New Negro*, the volume still regarded as a defining document
for the Renaissance, Alain Locke argues that "[o]f all the voluminous literature
on the Negro, so much is mere external view and commentary that we may
warrantably say that nine-tenths of it is about the Negro rather than of him, so
that it is the Negro problem rather than the Negro that is known and mooted
in the general mind" (xxv). Thus, the intent of the Harlem Renaissance
project was to wrest control of black representation from hostile forces, to redefine what "blackness" was in the eyes of the nation, and to present images of
black competency and genius to a wider public. James Weldon Johnson
maybe voiced best the hopes that accompanied the burgeoning of African
American arts in the early decades of the twentieth century: "The final
measure of the greatness of all peoples is the amount and standard of the
literature and art they have produced. . . . No people that has produced great

literature and art has ever been looked upon by the world as distinctly inferior." Therefore, Johnson believed that the most effective way to counter and reverse negative attitudes towards African Americans was "a demonstration of intellectual parity by the Negro through production of literature and art" (Johnson 861). To that end, in Du Bois's view, any questions of "authenticity" in art ought to be subordinated to the greater end of fighting for justice, since "[art] is part of the great fight we are carrying on and it represents a forward and an upward look—a pushing onward" (Du Bois "Criteria" 752). Going "forward" and "upward" thus meant depicting African Americans in ways in which racist white authors would not and to which white readers were therefore unaccustomed. The role of the artist is to expand the artificially limited horizons for black art. As Du Bois explains, "We can go on the stage; we can be just as funny as white Americans wish us to be; we can play all the sordid parts that America likes to assign to Negroes; but for anything else there is still small place for us" (Du Bois "Criteria" 756). It is for this reason that he deplored Claude McKay's Home to Harlem since he believed it would play into the very hands of those wishing to give Africans a particular place on the American scene: "That which a certain decadent section of the white American world, centered particularly in New York, long for with fierce and unrestrained passions, it wants to see written out in black and white, and saddled on black Harlem" (Du Bois "Two Novels" 759-60). McKay's novel, according to Du Bois, fulfilled the wishes of the "primitivists," those who saw African Americans as living out the primal urges white Americans were too "civilized" to engage in. While Du Bois's critique has often been maligned, in view of the more recent debates about rap and hip-hop videos it has acquired a renewed relevance.

But then as now, the question of who was to represent African Americans and how created some intellectual divisions. Ironically, all the participants in the debate could be called "bourgeois" in the wider sense of the word, but it was these very bourgeois intellectuals who debated the role the "folk"—which everyone from Du Bois to Hughes agreed were the ultimate source of racial authenticity—should play in African American representation. According to James Weldon Johnson, the folk provide the artist with his or her material: "The fact is, nothing great or enduring in music has ever sprung full-fledged from the brain of any master; the best he gives the world he gathers from the hearts of the people, and runs it through the alembic of his genius" (Johnson 865). Artistry thus does not spring from the folk spontaneously, but it is the artist who filters folk material and refines it. Alain Locke agreed with such a conceptualization of the relationship between folk and artist, but also warned against taking the folk as the only measure of African Americans as a whole—as the measure of authentic blackness: "with the Negro rapidly in process of class differentiation, if it ever was warrantable to regard and treat the Negro en masse it is becoming with every day less possible, more unjust and more ridiculous" (Locke 6). Indirectly, Locke argues here for middle class artistic representation, on which many Harlem Renaissance novels and short stories focused, not least as a counterbalance to distorted folk representations by white authors, the musical theater, and film (e.g. the notorious 1915 Klan movie Birth of a Nation by W.D. Griffith). Among those who objected to a focus on the middle class was Langston Hughes:

> But then there are the low-down folks, the so-called common element, and they are the majority—may the Lord be praised! The people who have their hip of gin on Saturday nights and are not too important to themselves or the community, or too well fed, or too learned to watch the lazy world go round. . . . Their joy run, bang! Into ecstasy. Their religion soars to a shout. Work maybe a little today, rest a little tomorrow. Play awhile. Sing awhile. O, let's dance. These common people are not afraid of spirituals, as for a long time their more intellectual brethren were, and jazz is their child. They furnish a wealth if colorful, distinctive material for any artist because they still hold their own individuality in the face of American standardizations. (Hughes 1268)

Hughes engages in an idealization of the folk at the same time that he stereotypes them hardly less than the plantation lore of the later decades of the nineteenth and early decades of the twentieth century (e.g. Gone with the Wind). Earlier sections of his famous 1926 essay "The Negro Artist and the Racial Mountain" had depicted the black bourgeois as insecure, self-hating, and white-identified, and his folk-idealization serves as a counterpoint to such lacking "racial authenticity." For him, then, it is the folk alone who fully embrace their blackness and thus represent the "race." Ironically, the artist stands somehow above them, as the folk furnish "material" for him or her. To that extent, Hughes's conceptualization of the artist is identical to Johnson's.

However, Hughes identification with the folk stands in a somewhat tense relationship to the goal of artistic freedom as he enunciates it at the end of his essay:

> We younger Negro artists who create now intend to express our individual dark-skinned selves without fear or shame. If white people are pleased we are glad. If they are not, it doesn't matter. We know we are beautiful. And ugly too. . . . If colored people are pleased we are glad. If they are not, their displeasure doesn't matter either. (Hughes 1271)

The irony here is that Hughes's radical individualism is in many ways far more bourgeois than Locke's or Du Bois's insistence on the political role of art. Indeed, Hughes's view of the role of the artist emphasizes the values of artistic self-realization and autonomy even as it supports the politically-committed idea that the artist springs from the folk and should create a distinctive art related to the distinctive spirit of the folk.

For all their differences, Harlem Renaissance artists saw the folk as embodying the "authentic" spirit of the "race," even if it was left to artists to distill this spirit into something else, to make art out of folk art. For Hughes, such art should express folk authenticity, if the artist was so inclined, rather than pander to white tastes; for Du Bois, Locke, and Johnson, questions of authenticity could not be separated from questions of the potential socio-political usefulness of art; therefore, the artist should choose what (authentic) material to present so as to assure a beneficial political impact of black artistic representation. In that choice, though, the artist was to be partially guided by what would serve the political and socio-economic interests of African Americans best. One could therefore question why critics have generally been sympathetic to Hughes as the supposedly more progressive Harlem Renaissance artist as opposed to the "stodgy" bourgeois pronouncements of Du Bois and Locke. As far as their commitment to African American collective advancement and the political responsibility of the artist compared to Hughes individualism, one might well regard them as progressive and Hughes as bourgeois. But whether by the bourgeois or by the progressive, if indeed these are or need be juxtapositions, in the wake of Du Bois's *The Souls of Black Folk*, the folk came to be regarded as a source for "racially authentic" art (following the precedent of European Romanticism which had posited as much) and thus, implicitly, as a source of black authenticity—"implicitly" because despite their acknowledgment of folk culture as the most important source of black art, Harlem Renaissance artists did not feel they needed to depict the folk and only the folk in order to create (black) art. Even Zora Neale Hurston, probably the most emphatic of all Harlem Renaissance writers when it came to a focus on African American folk, felt free to write *Seraph on the Suwanee*, a novel revolving around a white Southern family.

Authenticity after the Harlem Renaissance

The Great Depression brought class concerns into the foreground and marked a leftward shift among many African American intellectuals. W.E.B. Du Bois, Claude McKay, Langston Hughes, and many others began to be sympathetic to socialism and gave Marxism serious intellectual attention. At the same time, the nineteen thirties and forties also brought on a new wave of African American nationalism (in the wake of the Garvey movement, which had by

and large subsided by the late 1920s) and saw the founding and growth of
several small nationalist organizations, the most important of which was to
become the Nation of Islam under Elijah Muhammed (Essien-Udom 46 ff.).
W. E. B. Du Bois symbolized both of these trends, embracing aspects of
Marxist analysis and combining them with nationalist thinking. While Du
Bois was curious about and appreciative of the Soviet re-organization of society
of the 1920s and early 30s, he did not believe that working class consciousness
could unite black and white workers in the U.S., arguing that white racism
prevented such a possibility (Levering Lewis 310). As a result, he argued for a
cultural nationalism in which African Americans were to focus on their own
economic and social development while not abandoning the long-term goal of
a global humanism. To that end, black colleges, he argued, should focus on
instruction informed by "racial authenticity" and "[acknowledge] the real-
world particularity of the black experience in America," as David Levering
Lewis explains (313). Carter G. Woodson, founder of the Association for the
Study of Negro Life and History, came to similar conclusions when
proclaiming, in his landmark The Mis-Education of the Negro (1933), that the
"program for the uplift of the Negro in this country must be based upon a
scientific study of the Negro from within to develop in him the power to do
for himself what his oppressors will never do" (144). Such pronouncements
were based on the recognition of the limited success that the struggle for
recognition and human rights had had up to this point and postulated as
solution that African Americans should focus on themselves rather than on
Euro-Americans and develop institutions appropriate to African American
conditions.

What did not change was that African American intellectuals, still
influenced by "racial uplift" ideology, pronounced the racial solidarity of the
better-off and educated with the downtrodden. The protest novels of the
1930s and 40s can indeed be seen as an expression of such solidarity as
African American writers turned to depicting the plight of the urban folk;
protest novels complete the momentous shift in the locus of racial authenticity
that had been under way since the migration of African Americans from the
rural South to Southern, Northern, and Midwestern cities before and during
World War I and again before and during World War II. From the 1930s
onward, much African American art regards the "folk" as urban, not as rural,
and novels such as Ann Petry's The Street, Chester Himes's If He Hollers Let
Him Go, and Richard Wright's Native Son dramatize the effects of socio-
economic marginalization brought on by racism. The focus here is not on
racial authenticity, on defining who the "folk" are or what an African
American "folk spirit" is, but on protesting the condition of the "folk." As

Ann Petry told an interviewer in 1946 in response to questions about The Street,

> "In The Street my aim is to show how simply and easily the environment can change the course of a person's life. . . . For I am of the opinion that most Americans regard Negroes as types—not quite human—who fit into a special category and I wanted to show them as people with the same capacities for love and hate, for tears and laughter, and the same instincts for survival possessed by all men." (Ervin 71)

Protest novels focus on universalism and common humanity, and thus a focus on racial authenticity, stressing difference rather than similarity, could potentially allow a white readership—in many ways the implied readers of protest novels—to avoid the identification with African American characters that protest novels demand. Underlying this absence of an emphasis on racial authenticity is, however, a political goal underwritten by racial solidarity and the assumed connectedness of African Americans across class lines.

A similar trend towards an emphasis on universalism pervades Mary Church Terrell's 1949 letter, "Please Stop Using The Word 'Negro.'" Terrell, a founder of the National Association of Colored Women and founding member of the NAACP, calls for the editor of the Washington Post and "others willing to advance our interests and deal justly with our group" to use "African American" or "colored people" in place of "Negro" when referring to Americans of African descent. According to Terrell, Negro is a "misnomer" because it does not "represent a country or anything else except one single, solitary color. And no one color can describe the various and varied complexions in our group" (548). Moreover, Terrell suggests that "Negro" also implies that Americans of African descent are not really American. As she explains, "[i]t is a great pity that the word 'Negro' was not outlawed in the Emancipation Proclamation as it certainly should have been. After people have been freed, it is a cruel injustice to call them by the same name they bore as slaves" (549). Terrell's disdain for the word "Negro" suggests that, in mid-century, much of the African American community was less concerned with what defined African Americans as different from other Americans and more concerned with what defined them as American. However, this claim to Americanness should not be seen as a call for African Americans to sever the link between themselves and their African roots. Instead, it should be viewed as a result of what John Hope Franklin and Alfred Moss, Jr. refer to as the "new position of African Americans in the United States" that began at the end of World War Two. African-based notions of authentic blackness had not been strong in the U.S. since the height of the Garvey movement in the 1920s (Garvey died in 1940), and the claiming of Americanness was influenced by the "intensification of the drive, in several quarters, to achieve equality for blacks" (461) as Americans. For Howard Zinn, this "drive" to achieve racial equality was not only due to the anti-colonial movements in Asia and Africa, the emerging Cold War with the USSR, "matter[s] of conscience," and African American frustration with fighting racism abroad but allowing it at home; it was also influenced by an "economic reason": racism was beginning to be viewed by many of the white elite as "costly to the country, wasteful of its talents" (440). Not least among the costs was the fact that U.S. anti-black racism became a serious complication for American efforts to win allies in the Third World during the Cold War.

While there are many reasons why this "drive" for black equality emerged, it is clear that it influenced how African Americans in the post-war era defined what it means to be black. In particular, the discussions of folk culture by Ralph Ellison and Zora Neale Hurston assume that questions of authentic blackness are not about the Africanness of African American folk culture; rather, these questions are about the possibility of African Americans claiming Western culture, particularly American culture, as their own through the use of folk culture. For example, in his 1945 essay, "Richard Wright's Blues," Ellison argues that although Wright's use of "fictional techniques" in his autobiography *Black Boy* may have been influenced by writers such as Nehru, Joyce, or Dostoevsky, his "ways of seeing, feeling, and describing his environment" came from the "immediate folk culture into which he was born." According to Ellison, "the specific folk-art form which helped shape [Wright's] attitude towards his life and which embodied the impulse that contributes much to the quality and tone of his autobiography was the Negro blues" (129). Ellison suggests that folk culture is the issuing source the blackness of Wright's text. Ellison makes this point clear in a 1955 interview where he argues that African American writers should not be concerned with "plead[ing] the Negro's humanity" to a white audience because it is a "false issue." Instead, these writers should be concerned with "the specific forms of that humanity, and what in our background is worth preserving or abandoning? The clue to this can be found in folklore, which offers the first drawings of any group's character" (213). Since, according to Ellison and in keeping with the ideas of European romanticism and the nationalist movements embracing them, folklore contains the earliest ideas about what it means to be part of any community, it follows that the blues contains some of the earliest ideas about what it means to be authentically black in America. Moreover, because the blues provides a cultural space in which ideas and practices are interrogated to determine if they are "worth preserving or abandoning," Ellison suggests that authentic blackness is not unchangeable but specific to the social environment in which it is conceptualized, thus departing from Romanticist and nationalist conceptions of folk culture. According to Ellison, *Black Boy* shows that "Negro sensibility is socially and historically conditioned" and that "Western culture must be won" ("Richard Wright's Blues" 143). In this view, authentic blackness is never static because notions of blackness that were necessary during one historical moment may be dangerous or counterproductive during next. What is noteworthy about Ellison's description of the blues is that it emphasizes an individualist notion of blackness. In particular, Ellison's distinction between individualistic and the "pre-individualistic" black communities implies that while notions of authentic blackness are never static, pre-individualistic notions of authentic blackness can be oppressive. For Ellison, "the pre-individualistic black community discourages individuality out of self-defense. Having learned through experience that the whole group is punished for the actions of the single member, it has worked out efficient techniques of behavior control" (140). Although these "techniques" are performed out of "concern" and "love" and are a response to the white South's repression of black individuality, the cruelty and violence that tends to accompany these techniques prevents the black child from satisfying his or her "curiosity" and sense of "adventure" by punishing him or her for "reaching out for those activities lying beyond the borders of the black community." Moreover, when this child continues to seek out these activities, "the parent discourages him, first with the formula, 'That there's for white folks. Colored can't have it,' finally with a beating" (141). According to Ellison, Wright critiques these techniques of self-control in *Black Boy* by rejecting "that part of the South which lay within him" (142). This rejection is what makes *Black Boy* like the blues—the text not only "recognize[s]" the "essential cruelty" that derives from these techniques of behavior control, but it refuses to make "peace" with this cruelty. However, *Black Boy*, like the blues, falls "short of tragedy" because it offers "no scapegoat but the self" (143).

In contrast to Ellison, Zora Neale Hurston became critical of folk culture after World War II. In particular, Hurston argues in her 1950 essay "What White Publishers Won't Print" that there are very few novels about upper-class blacks because these blacks are viewed by white publishers as inauthentic. The main reason for this view is due to what Hurston calls "THE AMERICAN MUSEUM OF UNNATURAL HISTORY." This museum is an "intangible built on folk belief" in which "it is assumed that all non-Anglo-Saxons are uncomplicated stereotypes" (974). She argues that Western literary tradition's portrayals of black heroes or heroines from the middle or upper classes always "brings us to the folklore of 'reversion to type.'" According to this "doctrine," "[n]o matter how high we may seem to climb, put us under strain and we revert to the type, that is, to the bush. Under a superficial layer of western culture, the jungle drums throb in our veins" (975). For Hurston, by defining folk culture as the issuing source of authenticity, one is also implying that the authentic always and only comes from "below." Moreover, this celebration of the folk—to which Hurston had contributed in her own writing career—has a major pitfall: it treats race as a significant difference. And, as Hurston puts it, "difference to the average man means something bad" because, according to this logic, "[i]f people were made right, they would be just like him" (975). Consequently, for Hurston, non-African Americans tend to view African Americans as "folk," and middle and upper class blacks are not viewed as authentically black by mainstream American culture; for that reason, folk culture should not be treated as the only vehicle that will lead to a better understanding of what it means to be black in America in part because it only emphasizes difference, and such an emphasis on difference perpetuates racism.

While Ellison and Hurston disagree on the role that folk culture plays or should play in defining authentic blackness, they both seem to agree that being authentically black means being part of Western culture. For example, in defense of Wright's statement about "the cultural barrenness of black life," Ellison asserts that "Wright knows perfectly well that Negro life is a by-product of Western civilization, and that in it, if only one possesses the humanity and humility to see, are to be discovered all those impulses, tendencies, life and cultural forms to be found elsewhere in Western society" (143). Similarly, Hurston argues that "it is urgent to realize that minorities do think, and think about something other than the race problem. That they are very human and internally, according to natural endowment, are just like everybody else" (975). In both instances, African Americans' humanity—and implicitly their Americanness, not their Africanness, is their defining feature.

A consensus on the relationship between folk culture and the black middle class has not been reached, though. Being critical of African American folk culture was (and sometimes still is) viewed by many as a sign of inauthentic blackness. For example, in his 1957 work *Black Bourgeoisie*, E. Franklin Frazier argues that middle-class African Americans who emerged after World War Two were "uprooted" from their "'racial' traditions" or "folk background" (24) and thus "accepted unconditionally the values of the white bourgeois world" (26). The assumption that underlies Frazier's analysis of the black bourgeoisie is that African American folk culture is crucial to understanding what it means to be black in America. In its attempt to conform to the ideals and standards of the white bourgeois world, the black bourgeoisie, according to Frazier, has "rejected the folk culture of the Negro masses" (112). The black bourgeoisie's rejection of African American folk culture is most important for Frazier because, as he puts it, "[t]he folk culture of the American Negro developed out of his experiences on American soil" (115); that is to say, African American folk culture is largely defined by the "way of life" that developed as a result of black people's "social isolation in the rural South" (117). Frazier suggests that this tradition helped the Negro masses who left for the city during the two World Wars achieve a "spiritual emancipation" that allowed them to overcome "feelings of inferiority" (123) and to "escape the contempt and disdain of the white man" (145). According to Frazier, the black bourgeoisie is inauthentic not because middle-class blacks are less "African" than the black masses, but because they seek to distance themselves from the black masses. Thus, as our discussion of Terrell, Ellison, Hurston, and Frazier suggests, the rise of the "street" to authentic status, which we will discuss in more detail below, is related to debates about African American folk culture in the post-war era and reaches back even further to discussions about folk culture during and ante-dating the Harlem Renaissance.

Black Inauthenticity in the 1960s

In The Artificial White Man: Essays on Authenticity (2005), Stanley Crouch argues that viewing the "street brother" and his so-called "manifestations" (e.g., the Black Panther, the Rastafarian, and the thug) as icons of authentic blackness in the U.S. can be traced back to the 1960s, when Frantz Fanon's Wretched of the Earth reached U.S. audiences. According to Crouch, the "street brother" is an African American adaptation of Fanon's fellah, the revolutionary Algerian in revolt against French colonialism, or, as Crouch has it, "the pure, angry peasant, unawed by colonial power and standards" who symbolized the "human foundation of revolution." Embraced by a "naive and omni-directional American love of rebels," the fellah was transformed into the "street brother" who disdains anything "white" and treats everything middle-class as white (219). It seems, however, that the rise of the "street brother" to authentic status may have more to do with the migration of hundreds of thousands of African Americans from the rural South to northern urban centers in the last two decades of the nineteenth the first half of the twentieth century. The various stages of this "Great Migration" gradually transformed the image of the "folk" from agrarian to "inner-city." But if a book is to be credited with de-throning the African American middle class as icon of black respectability and as the status that all African Americans should aspire to, as was implicit in "uplift" ideology, then it might be E. Franklin Frazier's 1957 Black Bourgeoisie, with its searing critique of the African American middle-class, rather than Fanon's *Wretched of the Earth*. As noted above, Frazier argues that middle-class African Americans have "accepted unconditionally the values of the white bourgeois world" (26). The presumption that underlies Frazier's analysis is the familiar notion that the "folk" is the source of authentic blackness. By the 1960s, Frazier's views of middle-class blacks and racial authenticity were reinforced by images of black inauthenticity articulated by African American leaders, artists, and academics.

In his 1965 work, *The Black Anglo-Saxons*, Nathan Hare argues that the Black Anglo-Saxon is "an animal who can shuffle his feet and keep his eyes on the ground when he's talking to white people, and at the same time stand before colored people and demand immediate racial equality" (1). Although Hare states that not all Black Anglo-Saxons are middle-class (133), the focus of his criticism is overwhelmingly directed towards popular entertainers, professional athletes, political leaders, ministers, and college-educated professionals. This focus suggests that class and questions of inauthentic blackness are linked in such a way that middle-class blacks are more likely than working-class blacks to try to become "whiter than white" (129). It seems that the only difference between Frazier's "Black Bourgeoisie" and Hare's "Black Anglo-Saxons" is that the former refers to the black middle-class as whole, while the latter refers to specific members of the black middle-class. Nevertheless, both labels identify middle-class blacks as inauthentically black and as haters of blackness.

In the same vein as Hare, Malcolm X claims in a 1962 debate with Dr. James Farmer at Cornell University that pro-integrationist black men are monsters. As Malcolm explains, "the black man in America has been robbed by the white man of his culture, of his identity, of his soul, of his self [....] You have brain-washed him and made him a monster. He is black on the outside, but you have made him white on the inside" (364). Like Hare's Black Anglo-Saxon, the black monster is a product of anti-black racism in which the monster is brainwashed to believe that he should have the white man's "house," "factory," "school," and "woman," because whatever the white man has is superior to anything that black people possess (ibid.). Thus, although the black "monster" is hard to identify because the horror that he embodies is concealed by his black skin, his morals, canons of respectability, standards of beauty, and consumption practices are the traits that highlight his inauthenticity. In other words, his living in a predominately white neighborhood, his attendance of predominately white schools, his work at a predominately white corporation, and his marriage to a white woman supposedly illustrate the black monster's racial inauthenticity. Once inauthenticity is linked with "white" middle-class values and authentic blackness is defined not by "race" but by values that must be in opposition to middle-class "whiteness," "inauthenticity" becomes transferable to other contexts—and it becomes a versatile weapon. Thus, Eldridge Cleaver, Minister of Information of the Black Panther Party, links black homosexuality with inauthentic blackness in his 1968 collection of essays Soul on Ice. Cleaver claims that black gay men are contaminated blacks who, in their "sickness," believe that the only way for blacks to assimilate into American culture is to become white. According to Cleaver, the black gay man is a "white man in a black body." Cleaver opines that "it seems that many Negro homosexuals, acquiescing in this racial death-wish, are outraged and frustrated because in their sickness they are unable to have a baby by a white man" (102-103). Cleaver defines the "racial death-wish" as a "principle of assimilation into white America" driven by the belief that "the race problem in America cannot be settled until all traces of the black race are eliminated" (101). According to the homophobic logic of the racial death-wish, the black gay man is an icon of inauthentic blackness because his supposed desire to have a white man's baby symbolizes his sick and dangerous desire to erase all traces of blackness from himself and American culture.   The link between racial self-hatred and black inauthenticity is also expressed in the creative works of Amiri Baraka (formerly Leroi Jones), one of the founding figures of the Black Arts Movement. Baraka's view of art is based on the belief that politics cannot be separated from art and that there is "something identifiably black about African American artistic creations" (Smith and Jones 658). In this view, what makes an artistic work "black" is its politics, a politics in which middle-class blacks are portrayed as icons of black inauthenticity. For example, in Baraka's 1966 "Poem for Half White College Students," the speaker equates the "Half White" college student to a "ghost," a black man who cannot "swear" that he is not "an imitation greyboy" (664). Even if this student chooses a black woman as his significant other, that woman will be "full of Elizabeth Taylor" who is constantly "dreaming about dresses" (664). Baraka's 1969 poem "Black Bourgeoisie" attempts to provide some explanation for why these students exist. According to the speaker of this poem, the black bourgeoisie is defined by the black male who "dreams about Lincoln(s)," "conks his daughter's hair," and "sends his coon to school." Moreover, this black man "sees white skin in a secret room" and "does not hate ofays/ hates, instead, him self/ him black self" (663). These poems posit that being middle-class is being white and, therefore, a sign of one's uprooting from one's "racial" traditions and folk background. According to Baraka's poems, the black bourgeoisie has, using Frazier's words, "accepted unconditionally" the morals, canons of respectability, standards of beauty and consumption practices of the white bourgeois world. Because of this unconditional acceptance, Baraka argues, middle-class blacks and their children develop a hatred of themselves and anything or anyone who is black. Malcolm's black monster, Hare's Black Anglo-Saxon, Cleaver's queer black man, and Baraka's half-white college students, illustrate that concerns about inauthentic blackness in the 1960s revolved primarily around men. Malcolm X, Hare, Cleaver, and Baraka critique the pro-integrationist philosophies and practices of middle-class black men, and they agree on another issue: questions of black authenticity are essentially questions of masculinity. In her 1970 essay "The Liberation of Black Women," Pauli Murray observes that the main thrust of the contemporary literature on the "black revolution" is a "bid of black males to share power with white males in a continuing patriarchal society in which both black and white females are relegated to a secondary status" (189). Cynthia Griggs Fleming shares this view of black female marginalization and asserts that the accomplishments and character of black women activists were routinely tied to negative notions of black womanhood by the black community and the larger white society (575). Similarly, in Transcending the Talented Tenth, Joy James notes that black women activists such as Ella Baker, who resigned from the NAACP and criticized the SCLC for their talented tenth elitism and sexism, were "neither popularized nor vilified" by the mainstream press as Malcolm X and Martin Luther King were during the 1960s (86)—in other words, not much attention was paid to women.

As suggested by Murray, James, and Fleming, discussions of black inauthenticity in the 1960s were male-centered because race and liberation in the United States were gendered male. At the same time, their comments suggest that one of the major problems with male-centered discussions of inauthentic blackness is that they presume that a black woman's racial authenticity is solely defined by the man she chooses to be her lover, leader, and/or liberator. Moreover, as implied by Murray's comments, by adopting patriarchal notions of race and liberation, male-centered discussions of inauthentic blackness, despite their militancy, essentially amount to little more than discussions about how to produce darker-skinned versions of mainstream white patriarchs. That is to say, the militant "street brother" differs very little from the black bourgeois integrationist whom he criticizes because they are both engaged in a struggle to assume the (gendered) power predominantly held by middle and upper class white males. Similar to Murray, although arriving at the claim differently, Crouch asserts that bottom-up notions of authentic blackness, in which the street brother is celebrated as authentically black and middle-class blacks are treated as inauthentic, are ultimately "white in origin." Crouch derives the tendency to equate black authenticity with a street swagger from "the anti-intellectual rise of a 'common man's culture' that began after the War of 1812" and was designed to differentiate the "down-home" American from the over-refined European (218-19). In this view, there is nothing uniquely black about the "street brother" who sees himself as more "real" than the over-refined black bourgeois—he is following American precedent. Nevertheless, the street brother's transformation into the "nigger" during the post-Civil Rights era suggests that many African Americans continue to believe that there is something about being middle-class in the U.S. that makes one less "black." As Randall Kennedy observes in his 2002 work *Nigger: The Strange Career of a Troublesome Word*, "[s]ome blacks use nigger to set themselves off from Negroes who refuse to use it. To proclaim oneself a nigger is to identify oneself as real, authentic, uncut, unassimilated, and unassimilable—the opposite, in short, of Negro, someone   whose objection to nigger is seen as part of an effort to blend into the white mainstream. Sprinkling one's language with niggers is thus a way to 'keep it real'" (39).

N-word Authenticity, Afrocentricity, Masculinity, and Rap Music

One might assume that blaxploitation films are largely responsible for popularizing the N-word in black popular culture during the 1970s. While these films, especially the ones released in latter part of 1972 and afterwards, tend to define the street brother as an icon of black authenticity, blaxploitation films that used the N-word in their titles (e.g., The Legend of Nigger Charley and Boss Nigger) created too much controversy to be commercially viable (Pierson 150, n. 3). The medium of entertainment that seems to be largely responsible for today's fascination with the use and meaning of the N-word is comedy, particularly the comedy of Richard Pryor. Before the 1970s, the N-word was rarely used by professional comedians, especially in the presence of racially mixed audiences (Kennedy 30-31). Pryor's rise to celebrity status in the 1970s is partly based on his willingness to use the N-word before such audiences. However, what made Pryor a seminal figure in American popular culture, according to Mel Watkins, is that he "introduce[d] and popularize[d] that unique, previously concealed or rejected part of African-American humor that thrived in the lowest, most unassimilated portion of the black community" (qtd. in Kennedy 32-33). Although Pryor emphasizes the multiple meanings of the N-word, his use of it also implies that being middle-class means being white. The link between class and race that Pryor establishes in his standup performances defines the "nigger" as stemming from the "lowest, most unassimilated portion of the black community"--and as authentically black. Since Pryor's success is partly based on the desire by black and white Americans to "de-taboo" the N-word, his success reveals that by the end of the 1970s, many Americans had begun to make class as important as skin color in determining if one is really black.

Inspired by his three-week stay in Africa (mainly Kenya), Pryor announced in the early 1980s that he would no longer use the N-word on- or off-stage because it has been "misunderstood" by his audiences and himself (Kennedy 155-156, n. 86). Similar to Mary Church Terrell's call to replace "Negro" with "African American," Jesse Jackson declared in 1988 that black people in America should henceforth be referred to as "African American" because the term carries more "cultural integrity" than the word "black" (Norrell 320). Pryor's refusal to use the N-word and Jackson's call to replace "black" with "African American" are noteworthy because they point to the growing influence of Afrocentrism in the 1980s and early 1990s. In Afrocentricity (first published in 1980), Molefi Asante, who is widely recognized as the leading proponent of Afrocentrism, suggests that Pryor's trip and Jackson's call are part of a contemporary movement by African Americans to reconnect with their African roots. Asante claims (in 1980) that almost three-fourths of all African Americans who travel outside the US make Africa their first stop (68)—unfortunately, that is hardly true today. However, Afrocentrism does not call for a physical return to Africa, as some black nationalist movements (e.g. Garveyism) have done in the past. Instead, it calls for a cultural return (particularly to an ancient or pre-colonial Africa), a mental shift that allows one to see the world through African instead of European eyes. According to Asante, Afrocentricity is a critical theory and cultural practice that is concerned with liberating African Americans from the "intellectual plantation" of Eurocentric thinking that constrains their economic, cultural, and intellectual development ("Afrocentricity" 21). The Afrocentrist studies "every thought, action, behavior, and value, and if it cannot be found in our culture or in our history, it is dispensed with quickly. This is not done because we have something against someone else's culture; it is just not ours" (Afrocentricity 5). Since Afrocentrism places Africa and Africans at the center of one's consciousness, "black" and "nigger" are terms that should be discarded from African American culture because—contrary to their usage by those who see themselves as authentic--they represent an Eurocentric perspective of Africans, Africa, and the world.

What, then, is an Africa-centric view of the world and what is it to accomplish? According to Asante, "Authenticity finds its triumph in allowing people to realize themselves through their own history. Therefore, the man whose biological father was Obenga but who now calls himself Merleau, due to the interjection of an artificial history, must reclaim his historical name and, hopefully, in this process reclaim even himself" (Asante 125). While one applauds the anti-colonialism implicit in the illustration of what realizing oneself through one's own history means, it is based on a number of assumptions: for one, one wonders if the history of above mentioned man would be regarded as artificial if the usurpers of his group's land had been from another African nation. In addition, what history would not be artificial, since the history of any region of the world tends to be a history of migrations, invasions, conquests, etc.? The implication here is that it is "race" that makes his history artificial, that somehow something different happens when the invaders are of a different color. Was that then also the case when Berbers and Arabs invaded the medieval Malinese empire? Was a Soninke who adopted Islam and an Arab name as inauthentic as Obenga who becomes Merleau? A counterargument here might be that Arab invasions did not have the historical consequences the Middle Passage was to have—but that would be to ignore a thousand years of Arab slave trade and continuing anti-black prejudice in much of the Arab world. There mere fact that European imperialism eventually overshadowed Arab imperialism does not make the latter benign or harmless any more than European imperialism can attempt to make itself look better or less unusual by pointing to racism in the Arab world.

But authenticity is not just about culture in Afrocentricity—it is about "race" as well, "race" as a kind of symbolic marker: "Blackness is more than a biological fact; indeed, it is more than color; it functions as a commitment to a historical project that places the African person back on center and, as such, it becomes an escape to sanity" (Asante Afrocentricity 125). Blackness, then, is one aspect of authenticity as Asante sees it, but it is accompanied by ideological requirements and commitments without which a black person could be said to suffer from "false consciousness," or "Eurocentric consciousness," as Asante says. "Afrocentricity," however, is the cure for such false consciousness: "[n]ot only is it an individual or collective quest for authenticity, but it is above all the total use of method to effect psychological, political, social, cultural, and economic change. The Afrocentric idea is beyond decolonizing the mind" (Asante The Afrocentric Idea 125). In this definition, Afrocentricity is more than "placing African ideals at the center of any analysis that involves African culture and behavior" (Asante Afrocentricity 6). Of course, understanding the world around oneself based on concepts developed in one's own culture is no more than what most people take for granted, and such a goal is non-controversial at face value. What, however, is "one's own culture"? Or at what point does even the culture of an invader become one's own? Can a culture be one's own even if it denies or belittles one's existence? Can it become so if it stops engaging in such actions? How do "race" and "culture" interconnect, if they do? Are European cultures per se less compatible or more alien to African cultures than Arab ones? And can one really speak of "African ideals" in a monolithic way as if African cultures could be reduced to specific concepts and juxtaposed to "European," or "Arab" or "Asian" ideals? This ignores the fact that even the very concepts of "Africa," "Europe," or "Asia" as the terms tend to be understood now are relatively recent—and, ironically, of European origin. Asante's conceptualization of authenticity posits a kind of return, a return to an Africa prior to European contact, a purely "African" Africa, and thus an Africa that has never existed any more than a Europe without African contact has. What role would Egypt play in such a history, standing as it does at the beginning of both African and European civilizations? In other words, looking to Africa for black authenticity is a natural starting point, but not one without significant complications. Moreover, the problems that plagued discussions of black authenticity in the 1960s also plague Afrocentricity, especially its patriarchal, homophobic, and bottom-up visions of authentic blackness. Melba Joyce Boyd argues that Afrocentrism's rise to prominence in the early 1990s is not based on a counter-hegemonic explanation of or solution to the "chaos" that exists in black urban communities. Instead, Afrocentrism became popular because it provides a "conventional explanation" for why this chaos exists--the lack of an authentic black identity and the need for black male role models (26). In this view, the Afrocentric assumes that race is gendered male; therefore, what it means to be black for the Afrocentric is essentially asking what it means to be a black, heterosexual male. Indeed, none of the leaders whom Asante identifies in Afrocentricity are women. Furthermore, Afrocentrism's patriarchal vision of authentic blackness is reinforced by its homophobia. Similar to the homophobic logic of Cleaver's racial death-wish, Asante believes that homosexuality is a white thing and, therefore, "does not represent an Afrocentric way of life" (Asante qtd. in Nero 401). According to Asante, homosexuality is a "deviation" from the Afrocentric way of life because it is a social identity that is a direct result of "European decadence" (57)—a view also adopted by a number of African dictators.

In spite of evidence that dates homosexuality in the African American community back to the colonial period (Nero 403-404), Asante insists that queer black men are white men in black skin. However, Charles Nero has noted—and we have seen previously—that Asante is not the only intellectual who knowingly or unknowingly reinforces heterosexist representations of African American history: "With only a few exceptions, the intellectual writings of black Americans have been dominated by heterosexual ideologies that have resulted in the gay male experience being either excluded, marginalized, or ridiculed" (399). Kendall Thomas argues that the "jargon of authenticity" expressed in the writings of Asante and other black intellectuals reinforces the heterosexist notion of authentic blackness, a notion that does not reject, but "reincorporates white racism's phobic conceptions of black sexuality in the denigrated figure of the colored homosexual" (131). In this view, it is the black homophobe, not the black homosexual, who represents inauthentic blackness, the white man in black skin. In addition to its sexist and heterosexist assumptions about authentic blackness, Asante's Afrocentrism defines the black educated elite as Frazier defined the "Black Bourgeoisie": as black people who have been uprooted from their racial traditions and folk background, who have embraced the ideologies of the white bourgeois world, and who, therefore, have no place in the black or white world. According to Asante, the black "educated elite," whom he calls "assimiladoes," cannot be trusted to speak on the behalf of the "people" because they are "dead to the culture." However, the "death" of the educated elite does not mean that the "people" have no hope; rather, their "death" represents the first step towards destroying the "icons of mental enslavement" ("Afrocentricity" 22). The link that Asante makes between "death" and the "educated elite" reinforces the problematic assumption that one loses one's blackness as one moves up the socio-economic ladder because this move involves distancing oneself from the "people." Scrutinizing Frazier's critique of the black bourgeoisie and support of folk-based authenticity, Martin Favor explains the danger of static cultures:

> It appears as though one leaves 'the culture' if one attains a measure of class mobility. But aren't cultures in fact dynamic? Must not we be able to account for ways in which cultural practices transform over time and individuals maintain a relationship to their heritage while simultaneously exploring new territory? Positing too-concrete bonds between authenticity, culture, color, and class risks reliance on a vision of identity so dependent on marginality as its legitimizing feature that it can never effectively deconstruct the center. (Favor 8-9)

In other words, Asante's assumption about the educated elite is similarly problematic as Frazier's critique of the black bourgeoisie: both critiques call for static notions of blackness, a blackness locked into a "folk" position in terms of culture and class.

Ironically, the Afrocentric vision of blackness has been adopted by "gangsta" rappers to justify their use of the N-word, a word that the Afrocentrist detests. Gangsta rap as we know it began on the east coast (e.g., Afrika Bambaata, Kool Herc, Grandmaster Flash, Philadelphia's Schooly D, and New York's KRS One and Scott La Rock of Boogie Down Productions) in the late 70s and early 80s, but it was the music from the Los Angeles area, gangsta rap, that began to take "all the prizes for authenticity," partly due to the media frenzy engendered by the 1988 murder of a young Asian woman in Westwood, California (Cross 24). Moreover, although rap music was significantly influenced by Afrocentrism during the 1980s and early 1990s (as represented by such groups as Public Enemy, Queen Latifah, Jungle Brothers, Poor Righteous Teachers, X-Clan, and KRS One), gangsta rap music has been the most deeply commercialized genre of Hip Hop since the late 1980s. What makes gangsta rap's success important in this context is that the music represents, at the same time, what Afrocentrists claim to be fighting for and against.

According to Robin Kelley, the "'gangsta' aesthetic" has been a part of Hip Hop since its beginnings in the mid-1970s, and its roots can be traced back to "the blues, to the baaadman tales of the late nineteenth century, and to the age-old tradition of 'signifying'" (186-187). Part of this aesthetic is using the N-word to "distinguish urban black working-class males from the black bourgeoisie and African Americans in positions of institutional authority" (210). From an Afrocentric perspective, the gangsta rapper draws upon African and African American narrative traditions to show the ways in which whites, the black elite, and other so-called inauthentic blacks contribute to the oppression of the black working-class. On the other hand, the gangsta rapper's use of "nigga" is critical of the ideological practice of placing Africa at the center of African American consciousness. For example, Ice Cube, formerly a key member of N.W.A (Niggas Wit Attitudes), the group most responsible for mainstreaming gangsta rap music, suggests in "The Nigga You Love to Hate" that black diasporic identification does not address the problems faced by black people in America: "You wanna free Africa, I stare at ya'/ cause we ain't got it too good in America/ I can't fuck with them oversees/ my homeboy just died over keys." As expressed by Ice Cube's lyrics, "gangsta rappers implicitly acknowledge [in their use of the N-word] the limitations of racial politics, including black middle class reformism as well as black nationalism" (Kelley 210). For example, when asked in a 1992 interview if using the N-word in his songs and in the group's name is hurting race relations, Eazy E, a founding member of N.W.A and the founder of perhaps the first gangsta rap label, Ruthless Records, states that "as long as you're black, to anybody else you're a nigga. We call white people niggas. It's just a word like homeboy now" (Small 164). Never mind the contradictions. If one were bent on lionizing Eazy E, one would call them a dialectic. Unlike Pryor's use of the N-word, the gangsta's use of the word is based on the belief that anybody can be a nigger regardless of race. Confirming Eazy E's view,

Kennedy notes that in contemporary America "[b]lacks use the term with novel ease to refer to other blacks, even in the presence of those who are not African American. Whites are increasingly referring to other whites as niggers, and indeed, the term both as an insult and as a sign of affection is being affixed to people of all sorts" (137). As witnessed in the film *Training Day*, the belief that the N-word is no longer just a "black" thing seems to permeate contemporary American culture—after all, Denzel Washington received an Oscar for portraying Detective Alonzo Harris. Harris, a black narcotics officer, is essentially a gangster who refers to his white partner, played by Ethan Hawke, as "my nigga." This phrase not only helps to stabilize Harris as a gangster, but it also suggests that Harris is on some level helping to de-racialize the N-word by treating race as an insignificant factor in determining whether someone is indeed a "nigger." In this view, the nigger is not an icon of authentic or inauthentic blackness; rather, it represents anyone who is "real," anyone who comes from or identifies with the values of the most unassimilated. Against this background, some see critics who condemn the use of the N-word as not only too sensitive but as clinging to the past; such critics, some argue, potentially and unwittingly reaffirm the ideas of racial essentialism that they claim to challenge by implying that only black people can be niggers. Since the 1990s, however, there has been a strong and consistent effort to abolish public use of the N-word. Critics have argued that the "nigger" represents everything that is wrong with the African American community. For example, comedian Chris Rock stated in his 1996 standup performance *Bring the Pain* that he "love[s] black people," but he "hate[s] niggers." According to Rock, the differences between these groups of African Americans represent the two sides of today's black "civil war." "On the one side," according to Rock, "there's black people. On the other, you've got niggers. The niggers got to go" (qtd. in Kennedy 33). Like Rock, Stanley Crouch asserts that "black people do not celebrate ignorance, criminality, and lack of initiative," while "niggers" insist that "[t]he less you know, the realer a black person you are. The more removed from civilized behavior you are, the realer you are. The more inarticulate you are, the realer you are" ("Straighten Up and Fly Right" 256). Other critics of the N-word have argued that the word will always refer to black people because it is a term born of anti-black racism. As Rev. Otis Moss III, assistant pastor at Trinity United Church of Christ in Chicago, stated in his eulogy at the NAACP's 2007 "burial" of the N-word in Detroit, the N-word is "the greatest child that racism ever birthed" ("NAACP").Moreover, according to Jerry Herron, while other racial epithets have lost their potency over time, the N-word still conjures up feelings of hatred, inferiority, and violence that are "woven into the fabric of our society that we haven't yet fixed." Herron suggests that the N-word will begin to lose its power to conjure up these feelings only when the problems that are a direct result of America's racial past are resolved (Graham). In this view, even if whites and other non-blacks use the N-word to refer to themselves, it is used with the image of a black person in mind. At the center of the discussion about the uses and abuses of the N-word has been rap's celebration of the "nigger." Orlando Patterson argues in Rituals of Blood that the sports, music, and advertising industries have merged "the athlete, the gangster rapper, and the criminal into a single black male persona" that has become "the predominant image of black masculinity in the United States and around the world" (277). Patterson contends that mainstream culture's attraction to Hip Hop as a "Dionysian ethos" in which the "oppositional and self-destructive impulses" of the "cultural creations and athletic prowess of the Afro-American lumpen proletariat" are represented as authentic is leading African Americans to "largely [abandon] the authentic music of the blues and jazz" (217, 272-273). While Patterson's assertion that jazz and blues are self-evidently more "authentic" than Hip Hop is problematic, he rightly points to the fact that gangsta rap and the "Dionysian ethos" it is associated with are being used by the culture industries to market the "nigger" as an icon of authentic black masculinity. As Patterson compellingly contends, such a narrowing of focus has not only had negative consequences for black self-expression but also for the work black culture is made to do in the U.S. and thus for African Americans as a group:

> What has emerged is nothing other than a cultural division of labor in which those images and creations [of African American males] have now become the specialized Dionysian counterweight to the Apollonian discipline of the downsized, disciplined workplace. As I indicated earlier, one of the major achievements of the civil rights movement was to open to Afro-Americans the unfilled symbolic space of the Dionysian impulses of other Americans. My argument is that while this has been wonderfully functional for Euro-Americans and the broader mainstream culture, it has been nothing short of disaster for Afro-Americans. (272)

The irony of the rise of the N-word and its associated culture, then, is that that it has played, according to Patterson, a cathartic role for Euro-Americans but has pushed African Americans even further into the margins.

An associated effect of gangsta rap being identified as representative of authentic black masculinity is the emergence of a patriarchal and hetero-normative notion of blackness that insists, as Ice Cube does in "Horny Lil' Devil," "true niggers ain't gay." According to Kendall Thomas, the "jargon of authenticity" articulated by Ice Cube's lyrics is "best understood as a displaced expression of internalized racism" (123). However, black popular culture is not the only space where this jargon of authenticity is being articulated. Marlon B. Ross argues that this jargon is also influenced by the mainstream media's "sensationalist and noisy" focus on the "rivalry" between white homosexuals and the black community. According to Ross, "the media tends to characterize blacks as being more homophobic than nonblacks. Gay men are characterized by the media as preying on the black community, taking attention away from the racial struggle and exploiting the successes of black civil rights in attempt to parlay similar successes for themselves." In short, as Ross points out, "Gay people are always portrayed in this context as all white and as male; the only blacks the media tends to interview [on issues of homosexuality] are more socially conservative (male) ministers" (400).

Although Thomas and Ross present different reasons for why a discussion about the "black authenticity" of homosexuality exists in the African American community, they both suggest, as does Robert Reid-Pharr, that the production of black masculinity in late twentieth-century America has often involved marginalizing or excluding "the homosexual, the scapegoat, the sign of chaos and crisis." However, violence towards queer black men is not only about returning "the community to normality, to create boundaries around Blackness" (603). This violence also gives voice to the fear that "there is no normal Blackness to which the Black subject, American, or otherwise, might refer" (ibid.); if there is black homosexuality, then maybe black masculinity really does not differ from white or other masculinities, and if there is no normative black masculinity, a hyper-masculinity separate from other masculinities, then maybe there is no blackness either. In this instance, the "nigger" and the "black fag," even as they represent different notions of black masculinity, seem to serve similar functions in the "feisty intrablack dialogue" about authentic black masculinity in the late twentieth century: both figures are reminders that blackness is, using the words of Cecil Brown, "nothing and everything at once" (qtd. in Kelley 707). Both terms attempt to circumscribe what being black is about by excluding who gets to be black (homosexuals, the middle class, "Uncle Toms," presumably the opposite of "niggas"); neither "nigger/nigga" nor "black fag" ultimately offers substantive content for blackness but defines it by what it is not, and through this negational approach to black identity, both homophobic and gangsta rap notions of black authenticity leave a dangerous definitional vacuum, a vacuum into which popular culture has poured every conceivable stereotype.

How to Talk about Authentic Blackness Now?

"I argue that a collective identity is not a necessary condition for cultivating effective bonds among African Americans, and in fact that attempting to forge one would be self-defeating. I contend that we should separate the need for an emancipatory black solidarity from the demand for a common black identity"—Tommy Shelby, We Who Are Dark 11

"[T]here are ways in which authenticating discourse enables marginalized people to counter oppressive representations of themselves"–Patrick E. Johnson 3

Given current concerns and discussions over the meaning of blackness, how can one the approach this fraught terrain without getting tangled? One basic premise, often side-lined or undervalued in discussions over the meaning of blackness, is that "blackness" does not exist in a vacuum but derives much its meaning from a larger context. Indeed, the meaning of blackness is not fully controlled by people self-identified as "black." This is true on a macrocosmic, societal level as well as on a microcosmic, personal one. Orlando Patterson reminds us that "[t]he Afro-American lies at the heart of Euro-America's conception of itself as a 'race,' as a culture, as a people, and as a nation. 'Blackness' is the canvas against which 'whiteness' paints itself, the mirror in which the collective eye sees itself, the catalyst in which this great mass culture explosively creates itself" (240). To that extent, blackness, like all other identities, is meaningless without its other(s); that is, blackness is defined by what it is not as well as by what it is. Moreover, it could be argued that the question of what blackness is not may be more important than what it is because the former tells us something about the differences that a culture considers meaningful. In addition, the "dialogic relationship" (Hall 345) between blackness and its other(s) is not only a question of difference, but it is also a question of power—the power to define. Debates over what blackness is or is not, and even the very existence of the idea of blackness itself, originate in power struggles between groups which came to be defined as "races" by those who temporarily won those struggles. Subsequent debates still bear the traces of those origins, even if they take place within African Diaspora communities.

On the microcosmic, personal level, as Beverly Tatum emphasizes, "[t]he concept of identity is a complex one, shaped by individual characteristics, family dynamics, historical factors, and social and political contexts. Who am I? The answer depends in large part on who the world around me says I am. Who do my parents say I am? Who do my peers say I am? . . . . What do I learn from the media about myself? How am I represented in the cultural images around me? Or am I missing from the picture altogether?" (Tatum 18). Even outside of racial identity, who I "really" am depends always in part on who other people think I am. In addition to these foundations of identity—the place a group is assigned by other groups and how I as an individual am viewed in part based on my membership in that group—one cannot underestimate the reactive dynamics: a basic insight of ethnicity studies argues that ethnicity is more about the boundary it establishes to other groups than the content of ethnicity (e.g. Sollors 26 ff.). What form a racially-ethnically defined culture takes has to do as much with the external dynamics it finds itself in as with intra-cultural postulates. Tatum refers to a high school study conducted by Signithia Fordham and John Ogbu to make that point: "They observed that the anger and resentment that adolescents feel in response to their growing awareness of the systematic exclusion of Black people from full participation in U.S. society leads to the development of an oppositional social identity. This oppositional stance both protects one's identity from the psychological assault of racism and keeps the dominant group at a distance." This self-protection and distancing is key to understanding why "[c]ertain styles of speech, dress, and music, for example, may be embraced as 'authentically Black' and become highly valued, while attitudes and behaviors associated with Whites are viewed with disdain"(Tatum 60-61). Herein lies one explanation of the success of hip hop, especially in its gangsta rap incarnation. On the face of it, gangsta rap appears to draw a clear boundary line to the white suburban mainstream that rejects African Americans (as evidenced in the language of implicit housing codes, fear of losing property values when African Americans move into white neighborhoods, private schools sprouting up when public schools become predominantly Black and Hispanic, etc.). The irony: suburban white youth have embraced gangsta rap as a way of creating a generational boundary. Thus the high turnover of artists, especially in the gangsta rap genre: it represents a constant re-drawing of the boundary which commercial culture continually erases in using "rebellion" as a sales tactic—which illustrates how difficult a game authenticity has become in a hyper-consumerist and technology-framed culture.

Thus, Todd Boyd's analysis, while explaining the value if "authenticity," fails to account for the tension between commercialism and a search for authenticity:

> Ice Cube's emphatic demand that one stay "true to the game" has to do with cultural authenticity . . . Not only must one exist in a hostile world, but as the lure of financial and material success becomes real and the temptation to assimilate becomes stronger, it is necessary to remain true to one's cultural identity while existing in the mainstream. This is what is meant when rappers say, "Keep it real." Authenticity becomes a central issue. Those who have embraced the strongest sense of cultural authenticity have held the longest-lasting influence over the culture at large. It is the strength of this cultural authenticity, which is challenged but never fully

compromised by material possessions, mainstream recognition, or personal aggrandizement, that sets the production of certain Black males apart from those of cultural producers who simply get by on their pop appeal rather than really enhancing the culture. (Boyd 14-15).

It is difficult, of course, to say exactly what "game" Ice Cube has strayed "true" to other than the game of making money, or how he has enhanced "the" culture (*Are We There Yet?*), or which culture. Even Chuck D, one of the lead rappers for Public Enemy, states in "Welcome to the Terrordome" that he is a "hustler of culture." Thus, Boyd's assertion that authenticity is "never fully compromised by material possessions" is just that: an assertion in need of proof. Importantly, though, "authenticity," for Boyd, is apparently opposed to assimilation, which is the counter-term here and spells death to black authenticity. According to that standard, rap, assimilated as it has become, would have died long ago. Rap is enunciated here as a heroic male pursuit to stay separate from a mainstream characterized by financial success and larger cultural recognition—and as such, it bears an uncanny similarity to the quintessentially American myths of rugged individualism, of Western cowboys and gunslingers resisting the encroachments of East Coast modernity; indeed, gangster rap has heavily leaned on the "outlaw" modality of American individualism.

Becoming part of the mainstream, however defined, or "assimilating," becoming bourgeois, appears for Boyd the end to black authenticity. Such fear of the mainstream, whether defined by socio-economic status or color—and frequently those definitions are taken to be near-synonymous by those appealing the anxiety of being swallowed by the mainstream—is both related to and rooted in the now familiar privileging of the "folk" as the primary culture carriers and representatives of authentic blackness. The bourgeois mainstream supposedly alienates one from the folk and "disauthenticates" one. J. Martin Favor has some words of caution for those championing such a version of blackness: "If the uniqueness of African American culture lies in its folk forms," as Houston Baker and a host of other literary critics favoring a "vernacular" or "blues" approach to African American literature claim, "then the authenticity of folk identity is privileged in the discourse of black identity. This is a powerful model for scholarship, but can it also account for the presence and products of the black middle class? Does this particular vernacular also have room for, say, immigrants from Africa and the Caribbean and the vernaculars they bring along with them?" (Favor 4-5). Not all black folks have the same folk roots, and thus a monolithic notion of "folkness" may well exclude significant portions of the ("authentically black") African-descent population in the U.S.. But Favor also reminds readers that the privileging of the folk was never really a matter of empirical definitions or scholarly observation alone: "By maintaining the primacy of the folk and folk culture, Baker and Gates, among others, offer resistance to a crushing assimilationism and/or naturalization of African American cultural inferiority. Their work is not merely an arbitrary intellectual endeavor, but rather a strategic assertion of cultural pride and political power" (6). The emphasis on the folk is not least an expression of self-empowerment and a refusal to bend to the imposed definitions of those who might not have black folks' interests at heart. Nonetheless, can such an emphasis on the folk still work in the twenty-first century, when the nature and condition of the folk and of what goes as modern "folk culture" have changed significantly? One significant change here is that the "folk" of today are citified and that the ghetto is often seen as today's source of black folk culture, as discussed at length above. Such a ghettocentric view of blackness sits uneasily with many scholars of African American culture. For example, as Robin D.G. Kelley alerts us, exclusively folk-derived versions of black authenticity might simply not be accurate: "The way that ethnicity passes itself off as ancient, natural, stable, and self-evident should be treated with a healthy dose of skepticism. What is generally thought of as 'folk' culture—especially during the past century—is actually bricolage, a cutting, pasting, and incorporating of various cultural forms the result of which becomes categorized into a racially or ethnically coded aesthetic hierarchy" (qtd. in Ramsey 37). Bakari Kitwana drives this point home with reference to what today's sources of black "folk" culture are:

> Today the influence of these traditional purveyors of Black culture [such as family, church, and school] have largely diminished in the face of powerful and pervasive technological advances and corporate growth. Now media and entertainment such as pop music, film, and fashion, are among the major forces transmitting culture to this generation of Black Americans. Today, more and more Black youth are turning to rap music, music videos, designer clothing, popular Black films, and television programs for values and identity. Working diligently behind the scene and toward the bottom line are the multinational corporations [that] produce, distribute, and shape these images. (Kitwana 7-9)

What Kelley and Kitwana suggest is that corporatized popular culture is largely responsible for making ghettocentricity synonymous with black authenticity. In this view, the culture industries are as invested in defining authentic blackness as those defined as black. However, we should avoid the temptation to conclude that today's black youth always blindly consume what is fed to them by the culture industries as authentically black. In his assessment of Afrocentric curricula for black urban students, Shawn Ginwright notes that one problem with Afrocentrism is that it fails to address how other social identities, such as gender and class, inform black youth's understanding of blackness.   At a summer camp that Ginwright coordinates for African American high school students in the San Francisco bay area, a black female student gives a picture of the class distinctions that exist among her black peers.   When asked about the meaning of blackness, the student stated the following: "Do you mean ghetto black or just regular black? [....] Well I'm not ghetto, you know, but I ain't bourgie [meaning bourgeois] either" (Ginwright 91).   As expressed by this student, class, not color, is the social trait that separates "ghetto" blacks (poor and working-class blacks) from "bourgie" blacks (middle- and upper-class blacks).   The summer camp student also claims, however, that she is a "regular" black, a class of African Americans who are neither "ghetto" nor "bourgie."   In the same vein as Zora Neale Hurston, who once stated that the "best-kept secret in America" is the "average, struggling, nonmorbid Negro," the black person who is not "exceptional" nor "quaint" (976), this student's reference to these different types of black groups is based on the belief that there are more than two classes of African Americans: there are black people who are located above, between, and below the bourgie-ghetto divide.   While this student may imply that the "regular" black is the authentic black, her distinctions allow that none of the groups has the final say on what it means to be black.   In this view, contemporary discussions of black authenticity are problematic because they presume that a universal notion of blackness exist in the U.S.   Such an assumption ignores the social realities of everyday life in black America, realities not always defined by being black.

Nonetheless, despite recognizing what is problematic about seeing "blackness" as a unified cultural experience, Guthrie P. Ramsey, Jr. thinks that there continues to be something useful about the idea of blackness: "I must reiterate here that while I recognize and share, to a large degree, the recent critical stance against a monolithic conception of black culture, I do want to rescue from the critical guillotine the idea of a collective black critique, a collective sensibility, however contested it may be" (41).   He bases his support for the concept of a specifically "black" critical and collective sensibility on observed cultural practices: "Thus, for all our academic enthusiasm to deconstruct monolithic impulses in the name of a diverse blackness, we must recognize that some cultural markers have remained remarkably stable in practice, albeit not in their precise meanings" (41).   His discussion poses difficult questions: is a practice still the "same" if it shifts meaning despite retaining appearances?   If "sameness" signals a kind of continuity, how many shifts in meaning can a practice undergo, and by how many other people can it be adopted, maybe also with shifts in meaning, and still be called "black"?

Or at what point does a practice loose its "authenticity," if by authenticity one means here its rootedness and meaning in a specific culture? And while the idea of group authenticity, especially of a folk-based version of authenticity, has been an important tool in shaping a group solidarity that was and still may be nothing less than a necessity in an abated but not vanished onslaught on black cultural self-esteem, one should not underplay the fact that the idea of authenticity can also be limiting, both from the "inside"—if it is imposed by group members—and the "outside"—if demanded by non-members. Patricia J. Williams emphasizes this point when narrating the following recurring episode: "More often than I like to remember, I have been told that my opinion about this or that couldn't possibly be relevant to 'real,' 'authentic' black people. Why? Simply because I don't sound like a Hollywood stereotype of the way black people are 'supposed' to talk. 'Speaking white' or 'Talking black.' No in-between" (35).

***

The final questions then are, do we want or need to have a concept of blackness that is clearly circumscribed, so one can tell who and what is black and who and what is not, and if so, what function should such a concept play? The question of a clearly circumscribed notion of blackness, an authentic blackness, so to speak, is a political question, not a cultural, biological, or sociological one. The very disagreements over the question of what is an authentically black practice, the very disagreements even over who is black (as witnessed in different applications of the uniquely U.S. one-drop rule from state to state—see Davis), the questions over whether a cultural practice stays black when others adopt it, the "racial shifts" of cultural practices (e.g. Malcolm X regarding the lindy-hop as quintessentially "black," while its equivalent, swing dance, now tends to be regarded as "white"), the seamless commercialization and globalization of cultural forms once seen as uniquely black, all these bear witness to the impossibility of fixing someone or something as "authentically black" across time and space. The very wish to do so at any given point in time is motivated politically—that is not to say that there might not be legitimate reasons for doing so. When African American cultural practices have been turned into lucrative commercialized art forms by white entertainers who profited from the fact that African Americans did not have access to many cultural venues they did have access to, then questioning the white entertainer's authenticity or highlighting that of the African American performer is really less about whether they are capable of performing a certain art form and more about who should by right be making money from doing so. That is to say, the need and desire for a "true" depiction of the racial self are politically and economically motivated; they emerge primarily from pressures exerted on the black community from without–not from within.

Once we are honest about the purpose of "authentic blackness," the purpose it has historically served and continues to serve, we can then proceed to wonder about whether such a purpose is still useful and necessary. We can ask whether there are moments and circumstances that necessitate locking some people out from a group or a practice defined as "authentically black"– because locking out is always the effect, whether intended or not, of declaring a group or a practice as "authentic." We do not think there is–and even if there should be, we do not believe that such a strategy can bear fruit or further the well-being of the group that, under duress, might resort to "authenticating discourse." But that is naive, some might object. Every group struggling for liberation and/or for advancing its well-being in a given society cannot afford total openness–it needs to be wary of interlopers, people who might steer the group from its true path to liberation and advancement. But it is exactly here where the danger of authenticating discourse lies: it declares a true path, but by what authority or on whose behalf? "The People," is the usual answer here, uttered rarely by "The People" but by someone declaring him–or herself as the voice of the people. Declaring something to be "authentic," in other words, always happens in someone's interest, but interests are not monolithic, and even a marginalized group does not have homogeneous needs.

Thus, although declaring one's solidarity across class-lines in support of racial solidarity has been an important tool in the African American fight for human and civil rights, and although it has often taken on the form of a privileging of "folk authenticity" that was seen to provide a common cultural base, there is nothing intrinsically racial about such an approach–or there need not be. In an attempt to explain what he sees as common African cultural traits, for example, Jacques Maquet invokes an environmental and mechanistic argument: "Like every broad cultural synthesis, Africanity is based on similar experience of the world shared by various societies and on the dissemination of several culture traits among these societies. Two mechanisms are operating: the development of similar ways of adapting to the natural environment and the diffusion of culture traits" (Maquet 28). Though this approach frees one from linking race and culture, it also raises questions. Should not then people living in savannas have different cultures than people living in forest belts, or in deserts, or in mountains, or people living in urban areas from people in rural areas? And indeed they do. Maquet thus posits the isolation of Africa as an additional cultural unifier, arguing that "contacts within Africa were frequent, contacts with the world outside Africa were infrequent" (28). Similarly, in a U.S. context, or in any Western hemispheric culture that practiced racial segregation, the latter created a kind of isolation allowing for the development of a unique culture. Thus, one can explain African American cultural traits without recourse to a "racial mystique" which only too often hovers over "authentic blackness," over attempts to mark something as uniquely and exclusively "black." However, the unifying effect of authenticating discourse is still needed. Tommy Shelby proposes that we retain the effects without the discourse: "I argue that a collective identity is not a necessary condition for cultivating effective bonds among African Americans, and in fact that attempting to forge one would be self-defeating. I contend that we should separate the need for an emancipatory black solidarity from the demand for a common black identity" (11). Making the distinction between "need" and "demand" may define the future of black authenticity in America—and it may be seen to hint at the growing black class divide.

The bifurcation that such a distinction implies is already well under way. For some time now, it is becoming possible for some African Americans to become, almost, "post-racial"—their African Americanness is becoming ethnic, a cultural identity revealed through selective use of Black English and Black styles. Barack Obama, Will and Jada Pinkett Smith, and Oprah Winfrey are examples of such an ethnic Blackness which, as the selection implies, is at this point possible for upper and upper middle class African Americans. It is possible now, as the 2008 election has shown, even for people with racist reservations to (more or less cautiously) embrace such African Americans and cherish their displays of cultural blackness while simultaneously regarding the majority of African Americans with suspicion and wariness. As Charles W. Mills has argued, "race" may be "debiologized, making explicit its political foundation. The overall trend is toward a limited expansion of the privileged human population through the 'whitening' of the previously excluded group in question" (78). In this particular instance, it appears the dynamics are even further complicated by class: while upper middle class African Americans may now be regarded as fully American (though "Joe the Plummer's" campaign exhortation—in the presence of John McCain—in the final stage of the 2008 election to elect a "real" American, implying not too subtly that only white Americans were real Americans, was an attempt to call into question just such a development). What this expansion of full citizenship will mean for lower middle class and lower class African Americans remains to be seen. If "authentic blackness" becomes even more firmly associated with marginalized socio-economic status, then such authenticity may well become synonymous with locking lower class African Americans into place—the analogy here would be the wish, often expressed by well-meaning liberals, that indigenous populations around the world ought to retain their folkways. Such a wish ultimately also cements existing power relations, and we ought to be careful that a call for authentic blackness does not do the same.

Works Cited

Asante, Molefi Kete. *The Afrocentric Idea.* Philadelphia: Temple University Press, 1987.

—. *Afrocentricity.* Trenton, NJ: Africa World Press, 1992.

—. "Afrocentricity, Race, and Reason."*Race and Reason* 1.1 (Autumn 1994): 20-22.

Audi, Robert (ed.). *The Cambridge Dictionary of Philosophy.* Cambridge: Cambridge University Press, 1997.

Baraka, Amiri. "Poem for Half White College Students" and "Black Bourgeoisie."*The Prentice Hall Anthology of African American Literature.* Rochelle Smith and Sharon L. Jones (eds.). Upper Saddle River, NJ: Prentice Hall, 2000. 663-664.

Barber, Benjamin. *Jihad vs. McWorld: How Globalism and Tribalism Are Reshaping The World.* New York: Ballantine, 1996.

Benjamin, Walter. "The Work of Art in the Age of Mechanical Reproduction." *Illuminations.* Hannah Arendt (ed.). New York: Schocken, 1968.

Bernal, Martin."Race in History."*Global Convulsions: Race, Ethnicity, and Nationalism at the End of the Twentieth Century.* Winston A. Van Horne (ed.). Albany: State University of New York Press, 1997.75-92.

Berry, Faith (ed.). *From Bondage to Liberation: Writings by and about Afro-Americans from 1700 to 1918.* New York: Continuum, 2001.

Boyd, Melba Joyce. "Afro-Centrics, Afro-Elitists, and Afro-Eccentrics: The Polarization of Black Studies Since the Student Struggles." *Race and Reason* 1.1 (Autumn 1994): 25-27.

Boyd, Todd. *Am I Black Enough for You? Popular Culture from the 'Hood and Beyond.* Bloomington, IN: Indiana University Press, 1997.

Chantrell, Glynnis (ed.). *The Oxford Dictionary of Word Histories.*Oxford: Oxford University Press, 2002.

Clarke, John Henrik, ed. *Marcus Garvey and the Vision of Africa.* New York: Vintage, 1974.

Cleaver, Eldrige.*Soul on Ice.* New York: Delta, 1968.

Cross, Brian. *It's Not About a Salary: Rap, Race, and Resistance in Los Angeles.* New York: Verso,

1993.

Crouch, Stanley. *The Artificial White Man.Essays on Authenticity.* New York: Basic Books, 2005.

~. "Straighten Up and Fly Right: An Improvisation on the Podium." *Black Genius: African American Solutions to African American Problems.* Walter Mosley, Manthia Diawara Clyde Taylor, and Regina Austin (eds.). New York: W.W. Norton, 2000. 248-268.

Davis, F. James. *Who Is Black? One Nation's Definition.* University Park: Pennsylvania University Press, 1991.

Dickerson, Debra J. *The End of Blackness: Returning the Souls of Black Folk to their Rightful Owners.* New York: Anchor Books, 2004.

Du Bois, W.E.B."Criteria of Negro Art." *The Norton Anthology of African American Literature.* Henry Louis Gates Jr. and Nellie Y. McKay, eds. New York: Norton, 1997: 752-759.

~. "Two Novels."*The Norton Anthology of African American Literature.* HenryLouis Gates Jr. and Nellie Y. McKay, eds. New York: Norton, 1997: 759-760.

Ellison, Ralph. "Richard Wright's Blues."*The Collected Essays of Ralph Ellison.* John F. Callahan (ed.). New York: Modern Library, 2003. 128-144.

~. "The Art of Fiction: An Interview." *The Collected Essays of Ralph Ellison.* John F. Callahan (ed.). New York: Modern Library, 2003. 210-224.

Ervin, Hazel A. *Ann Petry: A Bio-Bibliography.* New York: Hall, 1993.

Essien-Udom, E.U.*Black Nationalism.A Search for an Identity in America.* New York: Dell, 1964.

Favor, J. Martin.*Authentic Blackness: The Folk in the New Negro Renaissance.* Durham: Duke University Press, 1999.

Fleming, Cynthia Griggs. "Black Women Activists and the Student Nonviolent Coordinating Committee: The Case of Ruby Doris Smith Robinson." *"We Specialize in the Wholly Impossible": A Reader in Black Women's History.* Darlene Clark Hine, Wilma King, and Linda Reed (eds.). New York: Carlson, 1995. 561-577

Franklin, John Hope and Alfred A. Moss, Jr.*From Slavery to Freedom: A History of African Americans.* New York: McGraw-Hill, 1994.

Frazier, E. Franklin.*Black Bourgeoisie.* New York: Free Press, 1997.

Fredrickson, George. *Racism: A Short History.* Princeton: Princeton University Press, 2002.

Gaines, Kevin K. *Uplifting the Race: Black Leadership, Politics, and Culture in the Twentieth Century.* Chapel Hill: University of North Carolina Press, 1996.

Ginwright, Shawn. "Identity for Sale: The Limits of Racial Reform in Urban Schools." *The Urban Review* 32.1 (2000): 87-104.

George, Nelson. *Buppies, B-Boys, Baps & Bohos: Notes on Post-Soul Black Culture.* New York: HarperPerennial, 1994.

Gilroy, Paul. *Against Race: Imagining Political Culture Beyond the Color Line.* Cambridge, MA: Harvard University Press, 2001.

Graham, Adam. "Can 'N-word' Funeral Bury Hatred?" detnews.com. Detroit News, 7 Jul. 2007. 17 Aug. 2009 www.detnews.com.

Hall, Stuart. "New Ethnicities."*Stuart Hall: Critical Dialogues in Cultural Studies.* David Morley and Kuan-Hsing Chen (eds.). New York: Routledge, 1996: 441-449.

~. "What is this 'black' in black popular culture?" *Stuart Hall: Critical Dialogues in Cultural Studies.* David Morley and Kuan-Hsing Chen (eds.). New York: Routledge, 1996.465-475.

~. "Ethnicity: Identity and Difference." *Becoming National: A Reader.*Geoff Eley and Ronald Grigor Suny (eds.). New York: Oxford University Press, 1996. 339-349.

Hammon, Jupiter. "An Address to the Negroes in the State of New York."*From Bondage to Liberation: Writings by and about Afro-Americans from 1700 to 1918.* Faith Berry (ed.). New York: Continuum, 2001. 51-59.

Hare, Nathan. *The Black Anglo-Saxons.*Chicago: Third World Press, 1991.

Heath, Joseph and Andrew Potter.*Nation of Rebels: Why Counterculture Became Consumer Culture.* New York: Collins, 2004.

Hurston, Zora Neale. "What White Publishers Won't Print." *The Prentice Hall Anthology of African American Literature.* Rochelle Smith and Sharon L. Jones (eds.). Upper Saddle River, NJ: Prentice Hall, 2000. 973-976.

Hine, Darlene Clark, William C. Hine, and Stanley Harrold.*The African-American Odyssey.* 3rd ed. Upper Saddle River, NJ: Pearson/Prentice Hall, 2006.

Hughes, Langston."The Negro Artist and the Racial Mountain."*The Norton Anthology of African American Literature.*Genry Louis Gates Jr. and Nellie Y. McKay, eds. New York: Norton, 1997: 1267-1271.

Ice Cube. "The Nigga You Love to Hate," *Amerikkka's Most Wanted.* Priority, 1990.CD.

~. "Horny Lil' Devil."*Death Certificate.*Priority, 1991.CD.

Jackson, Jr., John. *Real Black: Adventures in Racial Sincerity.* Chicago: University of Chicago Press, 2005.

James, Joy. *Transcending the Talented Tenth: Black Leaders and American Intellectuals.* New York: Routledge, 1997.

Johnson, E. Patrick. *Appropriating Blackness: Performance and the Politics of Authenticity.* Durham: Duke University Press, 2003.

Johnson, James Weldon. Preface to *The Book of American Negro Poetry. The Norton Anthology of African American Literature.*Genry Louis Gates Jr. and Nellie Y. McKay, eds. New York: Norton, 1997: 861-884.

Kelley, Robin D. G.."Looking for the "Real" Nigga: Social Scientists Construct the Ghetto." *Walkin' the Talk: An Anthology of African American Studies.* Vernon D. Johnson and Bill Lyne (eds.). Upper Saddle River, NJ: Prentice Hall, 2003. 690-707.

~. "Kickin' Reality, Kickin' Ballistics: "Gangsta Rap" and Postindustrial Los Angeles."*Race Rebels: Culture, Politics, and the Black Working Class.* NewYork: Free Press, 1996, 183-227.

Kennedy, Randall. *Nigger.The Strange Career of a Troublesome Word.* New York: Vintage, 2003.

Kitwana, Bakari. *The Hip Hop Generation: Young Blacks and the Crisis in African American Culture.*New York: BasicCivitas Books, 2002.

Levering Lewis, David.*W.E.B. Du Bois: The Fight for Equality and the AmericanCentury, 1919-1963.*New York: Henry Holt, 2000.

~. *When Harlem Was in Vogue.* New York: Oxford University Press, 1981.

Locke, Alain (ed.). *The New Negro.* 1925. New York: Atheneum, 1992.

Maquet, Jacques. *Africanity.The Cultural Unity of Black Africa.*Joan Rayfield, transl. New York: Oxford University Press, 1972.

Malcolm X. "Malcolm X v. James Farmer: Separation v. Integration Debate." *Negro Protest Thought in the Twentieth Century.* Francis L. Broderick and August Meier (eds.). New York: Bobbs-Merrill, 1965. 357-383.

McWhorter, John. *Authentically Black: Essays for the Black Silent Majority*. New York: Gotham, 2004.

Mills, Charles W. *The Racial Contract*. Ithaca: Cornell University Press, 1997.

Murray, Pauli. "The Liberation of Black Women."*Words of Fire: An Anthology of African-American Feminist Thought*. Beverly Guy-Sheftall (ed.). New York:The New Press, 1995.186-197.

"NAACP delegates 'bury' N-word." MSNBC.com. 9 Jul. 2007. 17 Aug. 2009. www.msnbc.com.

Nero, Charles I.. "Toward a Black Gay Aesthetic: Signifying in Contemporary Black Gay Literature."*African American Literary Theory: A Reader*. Winston Napier (ed.). New York: New York UP, 2000. 399-420.

Norrell, Robert J. *The House I Live In: Race in the American Century*. Oxford: Oxford University Press, 2006.

Patterson, Orlando. *Rituals of Blood: Consequences of Slavery in Two American Centuries*.Washington, D.C.: Civitas Counterpoint, 1998.

Pierson, Eric. "Blaxploitation, Quick and Dirty: Patterns of Distribution." *Screening Noir* 1.1 (Fall/Winter 2005): 126-152.

Public Enemy. "Welcome to the Terrordome." *Fear of a Black Planet*. Def Jam, 1990.

Ramsey, Guthrie P. Jr. *Race Music: Black Cultures from Bebop to Hip-Hop*. Berkeley: University of California Press, 2003.

Reid-Pharr, Robert. "Tearing the Goat's Flesh: Homosexuality, Abjection, and the Production of a Late Twentieth-Century Black Masculinity."*African American Literary Theory: A Reader*. Winston Napier (ed.). New York: New York UP, 2000. 602- 622.

Ross, Marlon B. "Some Glances at the Black Fag: Race, Same-Sex Desire, and Cultural Belonging." *African American Literary Theory: A Reader*. Winston Napier, ed. New York: New York UP, 2000. 399-420.

Shelby, Tommy. *We Who Are Dark: The Philosophical Foundations of Black Solidarity*. Cambridge, MA: Belknap Press, 2005.

Small, Michael. *Break It Down: The Inside Story from the New Leaders*. New York: Citadel Press, 1992.

Smith, Rochelle and Sharon L. Jones (eds.). *The Prentice Hall Anthology of African American Literature*. Upper Saddle River, NJ: Prentice Hall, 2000.

Sollors, Werner. *Beyond Ethnicity: Consent and Descent in American Culture*. NewYork: Oxford University Press, 1986.

Tatum, Beverly Daniel. *"Why Are All the Black Kids Sitting Together in the Cafeteria? And Other Conversations about Race*. New York: Basic Books, 1997.

Terrell, Mary Church. "Please Stop Using The Word 'Negro.'" *Black Women in White America: A Documentary History*. Gerda Lerner (ed.), New York: Vintage, 1992. 547-550.

Thomas, Kendall. "'Ain't Nothin' Like the Real Thing': Black Masculinity, Gay Sexuality, and the Jargon of Authenticity." *The House that Race Built*.Wahneema Lubiano (ed.). New York: Vintage, 1998. 116-135.

Williams, Patricia J. *Seeing a Color-Blind Future.The Paradox of Race*. New York: The Noonday Press, 1997.

Woodson, Carter G. *The Mis-Education of the Negro*. 1933. Trenton: Africa World Press, 1990.

Zinn, Howard. *A People's History of the United States: 1492 to Present*. New York: HarperPerennial, 1995.

The "Defining" Problem of Black Authenticity in Canada: Real Slang and the Grammar of Cultural Hybridity

Dara N. Byrne and Jean-Jacques Rousseau

"Yo instead of your boys

We talkin about 'di man dem'

When talkin about 'your bredrin

Yo we talkin about 'your friend'[...]

When you talkin about a 'thug nigga'

We talkin about a 'shotta'

When you think you got it locked, T dot comin much hotta

You think we all Jamacian, when nuff man are Trini's

Bajans, Grenadians and a whole heap a Haitians

Guyanese and alla di West Indies combined

To make the T dot O dot, one of a kind

~Kardinal Offishall
on "Bakardi Slang"

The lyrics above were taken from the 2001 Canadian and international hit single "Bakardi Slang" by Toronto rapper Kardinal Offishall. The song, which aptly depicts the cultural landscape in Toronto, is situated against the backdrop of black Canadian insider/outsider politics and sets in motion a series of questions about race, space, and place in everyday Canadian life. An interplay of Jamaican Patois, African American Vernacular English, and Standard English, Offishall's lexicon—"the slang"—contextualizes his black Canadian identity, one that is positioned between 'back home' (Jamaica) and home (Toronto), with recognition of the ongoing influences of mainstream and black American cultures. In fact, even with a simple statement such as "instead of your boys we talkin about di man dem," Offishall's you/we juxtaposition first makes clear that his black Canadianness is linguistically un-American. This illustrates Offishall's sense that the power of language is the power of being and that by innovating and codifying language one can more accurately represent the local and national conditions that shape one's identity. Clearly, his lyrical proficiency, one that enables him to speak across three varieties of English, is as much about interpellating his local community as it is about defining cultural authenticity.

A Canadian hip hop anthem, Bakardi Slang inserted the politics of black migrant identity formation into the public sphere. By innovating and inventing, in naming and in defining, fusing and diffusing, this discourse offered black Canadian youth a new kind of consciousness. Interestingly, the song was on constant rotation on mainstream Canadian radio and television, outlets that are often criticized for not supporting the home grown urban scene[i]. In fact, years earlier, "Northern Touch" by Vancouver based Rascalz featuring rappers Choclair, Checkmate, Thrust, and Kardinal Offishall became one of the first widely consumed rap songs boasting about a distinct Canadian urban identity. The song was so popular it eventually won a Juno Award, the Canadian equivalent of a Grammy. However, Rascalz declined to accept the Juno in part because the award show would not televise the rap category and as protest to the Canadian music industry's inadequate support of its urban artists[ii]. But by 2001, when Bakardi Slang reigned the charts, it quickly went platinum and even made it on to American airwaves, making it a benchmark of urban black Canadian identity abroad.

Significantly, Ottawa-based rapper Prosper, who originally hails from Montreal, released the song "Grand Marnier," a 2002 response—better yet counteraction[iii]—to Offishall's Bakardi Slang. Grand Marnier uses the same rhythm and lyrical stylings of Bakardi Slang but lays challenge to Offishall's vision of a black Canadian identity by notifying the rapper of his failure to be inclusive of the black Francophone community. Prosper lets it be known that Offishall's mere 'shout out' to Haitians is not enough. Whereas Offishall's you/we is a black America/black Toronto juxtaposition, Prosper's is a black

Toronto/black Montreal one that cautions about the dangers of essentializing blackness as a purely Anglophone one.

We don't say "what's up bredren"

Mont-real says "sak paser"

We don't sip Bacardi drink

we sip on Grand Manier

If you get one chance and also best rip da show or

We'll ante up your chain give a gat down your throat

You talk 'bout cut 'n hittin' skins, we're talking 'bout kogner fem lan

Mont-real niggas will crash your parties if you don't give 'em l'argent

Translation – You say money but here we say "kob"

Yes we're also on the map so don't quit your day job

For sure – We come correct, and we're, live 'n direct

Think that we're only speak French son, you haven't heard nuttin' yet

So hear the drill you now, Technical Sense is ill you know

You're from the wrong place son you might get killed you know

RDP, P-9, 67 District, NDG Lasalle, West Island, South and North Side

Use me

Show you how the Mont-real roll,

Live and direct from Quebec

Definitely from the cold now

Chorus:

What the...chill [mixed from Kardinal Offishall's song]

My fellas from the streets, throwing real slang each and every single time we meet

What the...chill [mixed from Kardinal Offishall's song]

Ladies with sex appeal

Body shape and dancing skill

representin' the Mont- real

~Prosper on "Grand Marnier"

Instead of a strictly English based lexicon, Prosper offers a mélange of Haitian Creole, Jamaican Patois, African American Vernacular English and Standard English, what he calls "the real slang." Like Offishall, Prosper testifies to the power of language to reflect one's relational positionality, but he eclipses this by noting that a rubric for understanding black Canadian identity utilizing only English based language varieties is simply inadequate. Clearly, Prosper only issues his message in English in order to respond to the language of the original call. But this response is not a translation~a rendering of the original meaning; rather, it signifies his willingness to engage in a dialogue outside of his preferred tongue as he would wish others to be capable of doing with him. The hope then would be for Offishall and others to recognize that a Canadian rap anthem, including the 1998 Rascalz hit Northern Touch, is incomplete without French and Haitian Creole.

The most interesting aspect of this call and response is that it serves as an important resource for constructing a framework for reading black Canadian discourse, well beyond the realm of popular music. Likewise, this dialogue shows the role that language innovation plays in revealing the complexities of cultural hybridity in Canada. That both seek to communicate culture and belonging and to identify what is authentically black Canadian by incorporating a multilingual discourse, exemplifies the difficulty in defining the black experience in this country. Indeed both songs refute the possibility of a singular black identification—a nationalist discourse~which is also consistent with the country's larger preoccupation with the nature of its Canadianness. But both rappers do lay claims to a contextually specific discourse that gives both space and place for the articulation of lived reality, one that accepts and rejects the concreteness of being Canadian. It is important to note that neither song reflects the identities of black communities that have existed in Canada for hundreds of years. When either rapper asserts his notion of Canadian blackness, he does so by normalizing migrant otherness. Nonetheless, this exchange still ushers in the possibility of questioning the very premise of community~whether material, ideological, diasporic, or unified~even in the very sense of contesting the language mode that will be used to best represent The Community.

That this exchange entered into popular discourse is also significant because it confirms that rap can serve as a viable site for struggling over such definitions and that local airwaves can be avenues for making this exchange more widely accessibly on our own soil. Reminding us of why Chuck D once called rap the CNN of black youth[iv], Offishall and Prosper have provided a template for talking about who we are from our own multiple standpoints (epistemological points of reference).   In this manner, Canadian rap is as legitimate a source for understanding social and cultural politics in Canada as Austin Clarke's *The Polished Hoe* or Dionne Brand's *A Land to Light On*. How fitting that an instance of call-and-response, as authentically West African as it gets, is the catalyst for investigating black authenticity in Canada.

A Useful Feud

"Clarke is a remarkably adept chronicler. *Black Like Who?* spoke into a place of theoretical and conceptual absence and therefore its own failure lies in its inattentiveness to cataloguing evidence and anecdotes. Herein lies one source of friction between my position and Clarke's position."[v]

~ Rinaldo Walcott in Intro to second edition of *Black Like Who?*

The Offishall/Prosper clash serves as an instructive entry point into a feud between the two titans of black Canadian cultural studies, a counteraction that has been rippling for several years. Rinaldo Walcott, Canada Research Chair in Social Justice and Cultural Studies and sociology professor at University of Toronto, and George Elliot Clarke, an internationally renowned poet and the E.J. Pratt Professor of Canadian Literature, also at the University of Toronto, have exchanged words on a (perhaps *the*) fundamental problem of codifying blackness in Canada.

Like in so many feuds, the disagreement is not over the fundamental facts of black Canadian history but rather over the significance of that history (capital H!) and how to approach it methodologically. Clarke indulges in micro-histories with offerings that tend to stay close to his Africadian[vi] heritage, while Walcott's writings have a diasporic flavor and call for a unifying 'black grammar'[vii]. The one proposes to archive diverse stories and the other yearns to classify them. These two approaches are complementary, a position the authors of this chapter will later underscore, but neither Clarke nor Walcott is so accommodating.

Pulling at each other are antagonistic sensibilities. Clarke's is the voice of the rural, politically muted, historic black settler that revels in names, dates, and little known stories of more remote and often ignored communities, whereas Walcott's is that of the urban, overtly activist, recent black immigrant that is at home both with titles and black working class politics. Coming from these very different perspectives, these scholars risk speaking past each other.

Consider Walcott's claim that his 1997 collection of essays *Black Like Who?* "spoke into a place of theoretical and conceptual absence"[viii]. But can this be right? To speak of a place of theoretical and conceptual *absence* is to deny the presence of any prerequisite that leads to disagreement in the first place[ix]. (Can there be any speech without grammar?) For one so steeped in post-structuralist thought as Walcott to see Clarke's work as a *mere* cataloguing (as if it were possible to mindlessly pick facts) is suspect. He well knows that facts have intertextual flavors that lend them momentum in one semantic direction or other. So, his bother cannot be the smallness of Clarke's stories, although he does charge them with the crime of "regressive localism,"[x] but Walcott is more put off by Clarke's "impossible need to belong to the nation"[xi]. This explains Walcott's somewhat condescending gesture at Clarke when the latter is moved to ask of Montreal slave Marie-Joseph Angélique who burned Montreal in search of freedom: 'where is her *rue* in the city?'[xii]. According to Walcott, one should not be so concerned about securing the affection of a state, with a publicly designated street no less, when that state cannot even imagine her as part of its formation[xiii].

Yet, it is Clarke who cautions black intellectuals against "the potentially toxic allure of nationalism."[xiv] If Walcott sees Clarke as pathetic for his need to belong, it is partially because he overlooks their differences on the function and aims of nation[xv]. Indeed, by turning his back to the nation in favor of diaspora, Walcott seems to conflate nation and state. On the other hand, Clarke appears to subscribe to Pierre Elliott Trudeau's notion that nation is "retrograde" to the extent that it implies a homogeneous group rather than "ethnic complexity."[xvi] Perhaps Clarke's nation is not as exclusionary as Walcott imagines.

Indeed, Walcott proposes that the problem facing blacks in Canada is in fact a failure of "imagination" on the part of the nation. It is therefore humorous that Walcott himself finds it difficult to imagine certain scenarios. There seems to be some symmetry here. The nation fails to imagine blacks as playing a fundamental role in its formation, some black Canadians fail to imagine themselves as part of the nation, and whole black communities fail to imagine the full range of their history, like Angelique's story in 1734, especially when it may fall outside of the experiences of one's local or more recent community.

Whereas it can be argued that the pillars of black American life include slavery, segregation and the Civil Rights Movement, no equivalent exists for black Canadian life. Indeed, this begs a much bigger question that must be addressed first: not *where* is Angelique's *rue*, but what *should* be Angelique's *rue*, her marked place, in the popular reconnaissance of black Canadian communities? In the absence of common events that serve as rallying points for disparate communities, the outcome has been that collective action is made difficult, to the point where it may have not taken place at all. In comparison, the collective thrust appears to be alive in black America. Consider that the number of attendees at the Million Man March in 1995 surpassed the 250,000 that marched on the Washington Mall in 1963 at the height of civic action in the Civil Rights Movement[xvii].

Contrary to the popular perception that Canada is a racism-free idyll, direct and systemic anti-black racism continues to plague black communities across the country, whether by way of policing and the criminal justice system, employment and equity issues, or tougher immigration policies.[xviii] The spate of shootings of black men in Toronto by the police and the debate about the community "playing the race card" serves as just one recent example[xix]. In fact, the 2003 Statistics Canada Ethnic Diversity Survey shows that nearly one-third of blacks reported having experiences with racial discrimination or unfair treatment within the last five years.[xx] Interestingly, The African Canadian Legal Clinic, a not-for-profit organization that provides legal advocacy in racial discrimination cases in Ontario, attributes this ongoing racial climate (and the actions by the state) to the almost two hundred years of Canadian slavery and its ties to colonialism.[xxi]

Significantly, a 2003 report by Doudou Diène, the United Nations Special Rapporteur on Racism, Racial Discrimination, Xenophobia and Related Intolerance, acknowledged what many blacks already knew: "that racism still exists in Canada."[xxii]After reviewing over two hundred submissions on racism, touring the country, and meeting with representatives from various levels of government, Diène further noted that while a good "legal framework exists for combating racism," there was **no national strategy** in place for profoundly impacting those most vulnerable to its effects[xxiii]. Similarly, the absence of a dialogue between government and those vulnerable communities was evidenced in the "serious lack of knowledge about the impact of laws and policies."[xxiv]

The ongoing presence of direct and systematic racism, coupled with what Diène would see as the absence of community dialogue and a national strategy, has been particularly detrimental for black Canadians who have not even settled on what blackness ought to mean, much less developed a mandate for responding to laws and policies that impact the Community. Whereas shared black conditions in the United States provided for what Toni Morrison calls cultural "rememory,"[xxv] a shared consciousness with a connected citizenry, the disparate experiences of blacks in Canada and a more local and individualized sense of community has not yet provided a unified platform for civic engagement. The result has been an overwhelming failure to hold the state accountable for the persistence of anti-black racism on a large scale to the extent that the authors of this paper cannot site **any** form of sustained or synchronous civic response that would parallel the March on Washington or the Million Man March.

So what is the best way forward from here? Interestingly, the way forward might be to take Prosper's notion of "the real slang" seriously. If synchronous Community action is the end game, then Walcott's notion of diaspora may well be useful for emphasizing our inter-relatedness, distinct from geographic and temporal community spaces. Consider the identity of Haitians in Montreal, a group linked to Haitian communities across North America and beyond, past and present, and to Haiti itself. It exists in a space that former Haitian president Jean Bertrand Aristide called 'le dixieme departement'[xxvi], what he sees as a special place annexed somehow to the nine departments (administrative regions) of the Republic of Haiti. In this way, communities bound by more than the realities of bloodlines, geography, and circumstance have a much larger sense of their Nation. This type of thinking is especially alluring to any group that lives in "a nation that seeks to render [it] not there"[xxvii]. Developing a diasporic sensibility frees one from the unrequited love of the nation, helps us to 'get over it' by reminding us that we are not alone, were not always here, and may never be.

But this pilgrim mentality can only account partially for the reality of black Canadian lives. Like pilgrims, blacks here are aware of a migratory experience; but unlike them, black Canadians have a stake in what happens here in the long term. One is reminded that diasporic spaces do not sustain the institutional conspiracy that builds infrastructure, creates jobs, and promotes human rights; states do that. Some bridge is needed between an abstract diasporic space and the reality of many blacknesses so that blacks can achieve political (normative) projects like equality.

Of course, local stories provide us with useful legacies of survival for which new and old communities alike can draw on for rhetorical, political, and cultural endurance. Clarke's (and others') archival work has indeed provided much needed material for rewriting chronologies and critical analyses on black history, both inside and outside of the country's metropolitan centres. It is due to this archiving of a range of experiences that a community can become better positioned to connect its local experiences with that of the diaspora writ large; as we well know, in every African community stands a griot.

All this is still too tentative. To imagine one's place within the nation means to create a space from which the collective can make demands on the state without necessarily sacrificing migrant or regional uniqueness (yes, like Paul we can be both Christian and Roman). This is where our leading scholars can take notes from our leading rappers. Aside from being a cautionary tale against black Canadians getting caught in the warfare between Quebec and the Rest of Canada, the exchange between Kardinal Offishall and Prosper sheds light on the fruitful outcome of asserting the real slang. Both Offishall and Prosper employ a slang that is the composite of all that influences them, richly infused with Caribbean nonstandard, African American Vernacular English, and Standard English or Standard French, respectively. The rappers work equally hard to make sense, for their community, of what could otherwise just be babel. They demonstrate that real authenticity is polysemous, ever-evolving, and will reflect all the experiences that contribute to it.

In fact, the real slang is the real black Canadian cultural polyglot, the most useful metaphor, for what is clearly a necessary precursor to Walcott's desire to see a grammar of blackness in Canada. The Prosperian way, coming to the table in our own tongues, is a non-essentialist position on black authenticity. What he sees as our responsibility as black Canadians, to be multilingual and open to other ways of testifying, not only creates a platform for sharing similar and divergent experiences, but it allows us to be heard on our own terms. The real slang is not about being able to translate--perform a modest interpretation; rather, it is the effort to retain cultural codes (relevance) and specific meanings. By not submitting to the rules of the dominant, we fight against the monolangue of black absence, one that de-naturalizes, de-politicizes and thus renders black Canadianness inauthentic. The real slang is, as Walcott might say, "what a truly multicultural place might sound like"[xxviii].

Notes

1   For example, a 1999 telephone interview with Juno nominated Toronto rapper Saukrates, once the youngest hip hop artist in Canada to sign with a major label, expressed his frustrations with the music industry and media for being very slow to respond to the growing urban trend. He noted that many artists go to the US, not because they prefer the America, but rather that it seemed to be the somewhat easier of the two avenues at that time.

2   Matthew McKinnon's 2005 article "Misconductin' Thangs: The tortured history of rap at the Junos" chronicles the 14 year history of the award category. He notes how 1998 was probably "rock bottom" in its tumultuous history because of Rascalz public refusal due to the show's penchant for omitting urban music from the televised program. McKinnon quotes member Misfit as saying "[The award] feels like a token gesture towards honouring the real impact of urban music in Canada." The following year, however, when they returned to perform Northern Touch, it was indeed broadcast live.

3   Smitherman (1977) defines call and response as "spontaneous verbal and non-verbal interaction between speaker and listener in which all of the statements ('calls') are punctuated by expressions ('responses') from the listener" (p. 104). It is a basic in the black oral tradition and an example of the West African cultural continuum. Smitherman further indicates that the response functions as an affirmation of the call or completes a particular request. In the case of this essay, we use the term "counteraction" for two reasons. For one, Prosper utters these words before beginning his response. Second, the term that was likely deliberately used because of its meaning, 'to clash with', in Offishall's Jamaican heritage. Unlike the affirmation that Smitherman speaks of, counteraction denotes much more of an antagonistic stance. There are rumors of ill feelings toward Prosper's counteraction though neither rapper has gone on record to verify this.

4   Chuck D & Yusuf, J. *Fight the power: Rap, race, and reality.* New York: Delta., 1997

5   *Black Like Who?*, 15.

6   Africadian is a term that refers to African and Acadian, and denotes black culture in the Maritime region, particularly communities in Nova Scotia

7   Rinaldo Walcott. *Black Like Who?* Toronto: Insomnia Press, 1997:13.

8   *Black Like Who?* 3.

9   Clarke for one disagrees that such an absence exists. He quotes Walcott on the need for a 'black Canadian grammar' and comments: "Yet, he (Walcott) fails to notice that [black Canadian writer André Alexis's] 'Borrowed Blackness' article struggles – despite its explicit Euro-Canadamania – to articulate a 'Canadian grammar for black'" (see "Treason", 5).

10 *Black Like Who?* 13

11 Ibid, 16

12 A Portuguese born slave, Angelique lived in Montreal (then New France) in the 18th century and was tried and hanged for burning her owner's home and "half of Montreal." Afua Cooper's book *The Hanging of Angelique: Canada, Slavery and the Burning of Montreal*

(2006) draws on court records that document Angelique's testimony about her beatings. As Cooper's work shows, Angelique was still convicted of arson, tortured, her legs crushed; she was eventually hanged not before being driven around Montreal tied to a cart with a sign depicting "arsonist;"and shortly after she was taken to a church to beg forgiveness from God and the King of France. Cooper reports that her hand, the one that set the fire, was also amputated. According to custom, after she was hanged her body was burned and her ashes scattered.

[13] Walcott seems a bit harsh on Clarke for wanting this history to be accepted as truly Canadian. After all, Canada is still in denial of its own conspicuous history of slavery, preferring to take up the banner of being "Canaan land" for America's runaway slaves. Is Clarke so wrong for trying to redress this? In 1989 Public Enemy expressed regret over the absence of black faces on US stamps on their hit song "Fight the Power." Likewise, is there not a tinge of sadness in Erykah Badu's resignation on "A.D. 2000," inspired by the 1999 killing of Amadou Diallo in New York: "You won't be naming no buildings after me/ To go down/ Dilapidated ...," knowing that a monument honoring a black life would not be cared for.

[14] "Treason of Black Intellectuals", 2

[15] *Ibid*, 4

[16] Op Cit.

[17] The actual number of attendees at the Million Man March remains controversial. The Nation of Islam estimated that more than 1.5 people attended. However, the National Park Service reported to media officials the size was approximately 400,000. Dr. Farouk El-Baz, professor and Director of the Center for Remote Sensing at Boston University released a figure of about 870,000 people (margin of error of 20%) by enlarging the National Park Service's aerial photographs. As such, the crowd is thought to be anywhere between 670,000 to 1,004,000.

[18] Cheryl Teelucksingh's (Ed.) book *Claiming Space: Racialization in Canadian Cities* (2006, Wilfred Laurier University Press) is perhaps one of the best and most recent collected volumes to examine race in Canada.

[19] Canadian Broadcasting Corporation (CBC radio) reporter Mary Wiens' feature serves as a good backdrop to the ongoing discussion of gun violence in Toronto. The article can be retrieved online at http://www.cbc.ca/toronto/features/marywiens/.

[20] The results of the survey can be found in its entirety on the Statistics Canada website http://www.statcan.ca/english/freepub/89-593-XIE/89-593-XIE2003001.pdf

[21] The African Canadian Legal Clinic keeps an archive of its annual reports online. This report is based on findings from the 2001 United Nations World Conference Against Racism in Durban, South Africa

http://www.aclc.net/un_conference/report8.html#_Toc486830917

[22] Noted in a September 2003 press release and report from The Canadian Race Relations Foundation, a non-profit organization that has consultative status with the Economic and Social Council of the United Nations.

[23] Op cit.

[24] Op cit.

[25] "Rememory" is a term that Morrison uses in her novel *Beloved* to describe a shared consciousness borne out of the common slave experience. It redefines individuality,

citizenship, and freedom by locating the nexus of the consciousness in the continuity of the black community, not in allegiance to the state. "Rememory" conjoins past and present, absence and presence through a montage of traditional African oral narratives which place ex-slaves at the center of their own stories by creating a first person historical account of post-Civil war blacks. Elsa Barkley Brown notes how African-Americans developed their sense of community through the bond of the struggle: "After emancipation African American men, women and children, as part of black communities throughout the South, struggled to define on their own terms the meaning of freedom and in the process to construct communities of struggle" (The Black Public Sphere Collective, ed. 113). Resiliency becomes part of the identity of the community as it develops strategies for survival, surpassing the loss of family, love, culture and the lack of property, safety, and capital. Likewise, citizenry is formed out of a willingness to contribute to the community, opening "channels of charitable exchange" that sanction "alternatives to modern forms of market exchange" (Peterson, ed. 95).

[26]   Aristide writes "...la diaspora, vrai dixième département de la République d'Haïti, est un phénomène qui s'inscrit dans la durée" ("Nouvelle image pour cette diaspora qui nous entretient à coups de millions," in L'année économique 99, LeNouvelliste/Haitian Information Project).

[27]   *Black Like Who?* 20

[28]   *Black Like Who?* 12.

Works Cited

Barkley, Brown, E. "Negotiating and transforming the public sphere: African American political life in the transition from slavery to freedom." The Black Public Sphere Collective (Ed.), *The Black Public Sphere: A Public Culture Book* Chicago: University of Chicago Press, 1995:111-150.

Chuck D & Yusuf, J. *Fight the Power: Rap, race, and Reality.* New York: Delta, 1997.

Clarke, George Elliot.Treason of the Black Intellectuals?Working Paper of the Third Annual Seagram Lecture. Nov. 4, 1998. Retrieved June 4, 2005, from http://www.athabascau.ca/writers/geclarke_essay_treason.html

Cooper, Afua. *The Hanging of Angelique: Canada, Slavery and the Burning of Montreal.* Toronto: Harper Collins Canada, 2006.

El-Baz, Farouk."Million Man March." Center for Remote Sensing at Boston University. 1997. Retrieved June 13, 2006, from

http://www.bu.edu/remotesensing/Research/MMM/MMMnew.html

McKinnon, Matthew. "Misconductin' Thangs: The Tortured History of Rap at the Junos." 2005. Retrieved June 11, 2006, from http://www.cbc.ca/arts/music/misconductin-thangs.html.

Morrison, Toni. *Beloved*. New York: Plume, 1998.

Smitherman, Geneva. *Talkin and Testifyin: The Language of Black America*. Boston: Houghton Mifflin, 1977.

Statistics Canada.Ethnic diversity survey: Portrait of a multicultural society. 2003. Retrieved July 6, 2006, from http://www.statcan.ca/english/freepub/89-593-XIE/89-593-XIE2003001.pdf

Teelucksingh, Cheryl., Ed. *Claiming Space: Racialization in Canadian Cities*.Waterloo, Ontario: Wilfred Laurier University Press, 2006.

Torres, R.F. "Knitting and Knotting the Narrative Thread—*Beloved* asPostmodern Novel." N.J. Peterson, Ed. *Toni Morrison: Critical and Theoretical Approaches*. Baltimore: Johns Hopkins University Press, 1997. 91-110

Walcott, Rinaldo. *Black Like Who?* Toronto: Insomnia Press, 1997.

Privileging the Popular at What Price? A Discussion of Joan Morgan, Hip Hop, Feminism, and Radical Politics

David M. Jones

Can popular culture be of use to cultural activists who want to lead American society towards greater justice, fairness, and sustainability? I pose this question as I take a second look at a 1999 collection of essays by Joan Morgan, *When Chickenheads Come Home to Roost*.Morgan is a former editor of *Essence*, a magazine that you might call the black *Cosmopolitan*, the most popular fashion magazine among African American women. Morgan introduces herself as a hip hop feminist to characterize her standpoint in this collection and to point out that one can support equality and justice for women and still embrace the music, fashion, and activism inspired by hip hop culture.

Morgan's book is still a great read years after its initial publication because it insists that we consider how popular culture can move us toward radical political change. More specifically, at the time *Chickenheads* was published, hip hop culture was favored by many intellectual activists as an authentic site of African American musical and political expression, a site where excluded black voices could gain access to local, regional, and national audiences and find a compelling platform to call for righteous and progressive cultural expression. As we begin the second decade of the 21st century, there is a common suspicion among many activists that hip hop has not proven to be the transformative cultural force that it appeared to be during its emergence in the early 1970s. Instead, musical and cultural expressions of hip hop have in many cases been co-opted by mass corporate culture, its imagery shaped by pervasive misogyny, internalized racism, narcissism, and crass materialism –often serving to reify stereotypes about African Americans. A question, then, emerges for intellectual activists of our time who value vibrant black cultural expression and hope for greater tolerance and economic vitality in all of African America: how should we regard mass-produced black popular culture, including hip hop, which many audiences consider to be *the* authentic black aesthetic expression?

Because I doubt that mass-mediated popular culture as it is currently constituted can nurture the imagination enough to inspire timely and progressive political transformation, it surprises me when an incisive critical thinker such as Morgan relies so much on popular culture as a starting point for observing the world and taking collective action. It is common knowledge at this point that popular culture fills our lives with randomized sounds and spectacles (*Grand Theft Auto*[1] and SnoopDog[2], Ronald Reagan films and *Stark Trek Voyager*[3], Janet Jackson's breast[4], and so much more emerging faster than our cultural memories can keep track of them). Individual pop culture events may appear novel or may be compelling as kitsch, and more sophisticated pop culture may find a niche audience, generate national discussion, or offer a temporary promise for enduring transformation (in popular music history, perhaps British Invasion groups, James Brown, Aretha Franklin, and other soul musicians, and hip hop group Public Enemy possess such sophistication). That being said, once we move decades away from the initial emergence of such compelling pop culture moments, it is fair to ask what enduring changes in American cultural life have resulted--and to ask further what qualities of aesthetic richness, cultural context, and historical timing provide any pop culture text with the power to transgress and transform. It is time to examine hip hop culture with these questions in mind.

Indeed, a burgeoning body of work has sought to assess the role of black popular culture in movements for social change, as Morgan's text does. A couple of my enduring favorites are Nelson George's *Hip Hop America* and Hazel Carby's *Race Men*, both of which use historical context and critical race theory effectively to comment on what popular culture says about the people who produce and consume it.[5] George might fairly be considered an industry source, with his credits as a producer and hip hop journalist coming of age in the region that has produced so many seminal texts of hip hop culture; one can safely assume that he will not repudiate the cultural style he has long been engaged in. Writing from a more traditional black feminist standpoint, Carby is a skeptic due to the misogyny embedded in hip hop which influences both conservative and progressive African American men and movements. For her, the core question of how seriously to regard *mass produced* black popular cultureremains open. Can black popular culture, as it is now imagined in relation to the perceived racial authenticity of hip hop, consistently inspire the public to fight for a fair economy and a racially just social order?

This question is well worth posing in 2011 in view of the fact that three decades after the emergence of hip hop, racial discrimination and achievement gaps have endured in American society on a grand scale. Evidence abounds to illustrate the persistence of racism when one looks at major measures of the state of African America.   Achievement gaps in education, recent discrimination court settlements against Coca-Cola Company, Abercrombie and Fitch, Federal Express, Texaco, and the U.S.D.A.[6], and persistently higher rates of infant mortality, unemployment, and incarceration are a few of the alarming findings one can cite as evidence for how entrenched and institutionalized anti-black racism remains.[7] These problems persist despite four centuries of anti-racist activism, including the landmark legal and political accomplishments of the 1950s and 1960s ranging from Brown vs. Board to the Voting Rights Act, despite all the famous firsts that this nation celebrates during Black History Month (Jackie Robinson, Shirley Chisholm, Art Shell, Colin Powell, and Condoleezza Rice, to name a few[8]), and despite the manifest achievements of African American superstars in the arenas of sport and popular music. If hip hop culture has indeed been a force for furthering racial justice as its strongest supporters claim, it is relevant to ask: whose human interests have been served by hip hop culture? Posing that question in fact demands that we consider where hip hop culture is located within the larger landscape of popular culture, what stories it tells, and how multiple audiences encounter and respond to it.

From my vantage point as a professor of African American literature and culture at a predominantly white university who has a skeptical view of nearly all political nationalisms and claims that any text or phenomenon can be "racially authentic," I find that popular culture is the first place that my students point to when I ask them if the United States has made progress on the racial front (i.e. "Hollywood isn't racist anymore.   Look at Denzel Washington."). As a site within popular culture, hip hop is a powerful source of images and narratives that give meaning to racial identity, providing a place for normalizing racist notions about African American criminality and "thug life." Such racial notions underlie stereotypical explanations for all manner of public controversies, musical or not: Mike Tyson, Ol' Dirty Bastard,[9] Randy Moss's moon and the Vikings' "Love Boat" scandal in the state of Minnesota.[10]   The persistent messages are that black men are criminally minded, oversexed, irresponsible, and hot; other than the overt claim that black men are sexually alluring, these same ideas are consistent with the white supremacist ideology one might find in a Ku Klux Klan publication. One need not travel far for particular examples of hip hop texts that convey these problematic messages. Film documentarians have probably built the case for hip hop's reifying of white supremacist ideology most successfully and accessibly. The Media Education Foundation's film documentaries have been critical in this respect, including bell hooks's *Cultural Criticism and Transformation* (1997), Sut Jhally's *Dreamworlds 2-3* (1995/2007), and Byron Hurt's *Hip Hop: Beyond Beats and Rhymes* (2006). Of course, radical critiques of hip hop's excessive machismo and sexism are also available elsewhere; I favor starting with Barbara Ransby and Tracy Mathews' "Black Popular Culture and the Transcendence of Patriarchal Illusions," but Michael Dyson or Nelson George might serve to start the conversation as well.[11] In any case, extensive critical attention to the problematic ties between hip hop and white supremacy took some time to emerge, but such critiques are now widely available. Nevertheless, an enduring critical conviction that forms of cultural expression can be authentically black still invites and engenders rigorous debate today. At the very least, as we mine popular culture to find the music, literature, and fashion that inspires us to think radically and progressively, we must bear in mind that the most common and enduring racial stereotypes are sometimes reinforced by black popular culture.

Nonetheless, Morgan's text highlights reasons why she considers hip hop culture a vital site of black popular expression. She argues that hip hop culture has produced for her a deeper consciousness of the tensions between men and women in black communities, allowing her to consider generational differences between her peers and her parents' traditions and to celebrate black cultural achievement. It is worth noting that this collection was published when Morgan was in her early thirties, meaning that the emergence of hip hop culture and the fading of the 1960s/1970s activist consciousness both occurred as she was coming of age. However, in her introduction, Morgan observes that she is not attempting to speak for the entire cohort of African Americans who also came to consciousness during the 1980s and 1990s. Instead, she seeks to "tell my truth as best I could from my vantage point on the spectrum" (26). I appreciate Morgan's recognition of the varied personal histories among African Americans of this cohort, including differences in economic class, region, gender, and sexual orientation. Though many African Americans are nostalgic for the time when we could speak of a singular black consciousness, the fact is that we have always been a more diverse community than the history of American racial discourse would suggest.

Given the absence of a singular black consciousness, it is critical to recognize that at its most incisive, popular culture relies not on a narrow rhetoric of authenticity but uses multiple "racial" and ideological standpoints to inspire its audiences, challenging and expanding their understandings of racial identity. The possibility that popular culture can energize and inspire audiences in this way helps to keep critical intellectuals interested in popular culture as a potential site of transformation. I suspect that nearly all of us who were raised in post-World War II America can recall moments when higher-level thinking about race and ideology was inspired by pop culture texts. For instance, I can recall hearing reggae and ska for the first time in 1980, music that made me consider the international dimensions of anti-racist struggle. The music made me aware of Black Britain, as I noted that major ska bands such as the Specials and the English Beat were multiracial. One might argue cynically that college students like to pretend they're political radicals or can tap into the Jamaican *zeitgeist* while listening to Bob Marley's *Legend* or other recordings by international artists, but the fact remains that for some of those listeners, these recordings are their first encounter with the international political perspectives of the African Diaspora.

I could name several additional creators of black popular music that also help us imagine black identity politics in radical ways--Jimi Hendrix, Sly Stone, Tracy Chapman, Lauryn Hill[12]--but I have to add that these are exceptional examples of artists with uncommon vision and a remarkable ability to resist the influences of white supremacist and patriarchal ideology in their expression. Even texts that aim for a progressive politics struggle to resist these influences. I'll use a feature film to illustrate this point. In courses I teach to university freshmen, I have sometimes paired Kimberly Price's 1999 feature film *Boys Don't Cry* and the related documentary *The Teena Brandon Story* to introduce the topic of homophobia to literate but naive college freshmen. Despite the film's dramatic effectiveness as an accusatory depiction of a triple murder in 1990s Nebraska, certain suspect qualities of the film's ideology give reason to interrogate its factual accuracy and ideological soundness. The life and death of Teena Brandon, a transgendered youth, is treated centrally and thoughtfully, while the murder of disabled African American Philip DeVine in the same incident is not even mentioned in the film. Carol Siegel notes a quality that *Boys Don't Cry* shares even with romantic comedies produced in Hollywood under the ideological framework of compulsory heterosexuality: "The film sidesteps issues of hierarchy within masculinity when it virtually ignores the murder of Philip DeVine. Instead it implicitly asserts that the only meaningful hierarchy in America is the gender binary" (Siegel).

The film documentary released shortly before the feature film, *The Brandon Teena Story* (Susan Muska and Gréta Olafsdóttir, directors)at least acknowledges the murder of Phillip DeVine as a factual part of this episode and offers viewers the chance to consider how themes of disability and interracial sexuality challenge Price's presentation of gay bashing as the "real" story in *Boys Don't Cry*. Disappointed as I was to discover (several years after my first viewing of *Boys Don't Cry*) that the film treated the death of a disabled black man as less significant than the other deaths, my discovery was a useful reminder of how deeply white supremacist ideology can be entrenched even in progressive and potentially transformative texts of popular culture. Thus, I choose to view corporately produced and distributed hip hop using a similarly skeptical lens. Claims that a text is either politically progressive or racially authentic are always suspect; as critics, we must account for the ubiquitous influences of white supremacy and patriarchy as we examine black popular culture.

As we reflect on the possibilities and limitations of popular culture as a tool for inspiring critical thought and action, it is instructive to recall Joan Morgan's conviction that authentic perspectives on African American life and culture may in fact be initiated, recycled, and reified through hip hop music. The first full-length essay in Morgan's text is "Dress Up," which starts with comments on fashion trends as they influenced the author's personal and racial identity. Given that the author worked as an editor for *Essence* magazine, it seems fitting to begin with a focus on fashion. In her description of a dress she owned, she discusses the shaping of her fashion sensibilities by the impressions of black identity she acquired from images in popular culture:

> It started with a dress. A hot little thing. A spaghetti-strapped Armani number, with a skintight bodice and a long flowing skirt, in that shade of orange that black girls do the most justice. I bought it in La-La Land precisely because it reminded me of New York in the seventies, with its sexy sistas (girls with names like Pokie, Nay-Nay, Angela, and Robin) and those leotard and dance skirt sets they used to rock back in the day. (17)

Following a common strategy in cultural criticism applied also in work by Greg Tate and bell hooks, among others, the passage uses phrases from African American English (AAE) to illustrate the author's close relationship to contemporary black culture, and this rhetorical strategy reinforces the claims made about recent trends in black fashion on both U.S. coasts. Using AAE in this context is widely understood as a strategy that not only expands the audience for cultural criticism but also challenges the primacy of so-called "standard" English as a tool for unpacking African American experience, given the class, race, and regional biases that are structurally connected to "standard" English. I must say here that I well understand and support the legitimacy of using AAE as a tool for expression within cultural criticism, but I also doubt that AAE is a more legitimate tool than other varieties of American English for describing the varied and diverse experiences of African Americans even in discussions of popular culture. When AAE is deployed as a sign of black authenticity within the wide context of corporately produced hip hop expression, audiences are encouraged to understand black identity narrowly –

in terms of the urban "cool" and "hipness" that are associated with everyday African American life. Such a signaling of authenticity, one might say, stands also in a somewhat tense relationship with the European high-fashion Armani dress that, ironically, is connected here with phrases signaling a 1970s big-city, street-wise blackness.

The essay moves on to discuss Ntozake Shange's famous 1975 play *for colored girls who have attempted suicide when the rainbow is enuf*. Shange's text provided Morgan with an understanding of black femininity and black feminist discourse among women of her mother's generation. Morgan writes that generations of black women born after her mother's time cannot and should not try to jump on the "old school" bandwagon—as Morgan herself could not do after seeing *for colored girls* produced for the first time in 1995. Instead, she argues, changes in circumstances following the periods of civil rights, black power, and soul mean that younger African Americans must re-establish their commitments to social change by reflecting on more recent collective experiences and social issues of their time.

To illustrate this need for self-examination and action, Morgan describes advice she gave to a 16-year old aspiring actress she was working with at a high school. Revealing the influence of Shange's characterizations of black women, the young actress was attempting to convey a black female voice on stage by imitating the "eye-rollin', smart-talkin', finger-snappin' Miss Thang, but she wasn't believable" (25):

> In a society of ever-shifting identity politics, I was asking this sixteen-year-old to sift through so many conflicting interpretations of femaleness and blackness and free her voice. In order to do this she was going to have to liberate it from the stranglehold of media stereotypes – the pathetic SheNayNay impersonations of black male comedians, the talk-to-the-hand Superwomen, the video-hos, crackheads, and lazy welfare queens – that obscure so much of who we are. And she was going to have to push her foremothers' voices far enough away to discover her own. (26)

Morgan details how the young actress was hindered by notions of black female authenticity from Shange's era and by more recent pop culture stereotypes which she internalized as a part of her racial identity. In this way, Morgan names and criticizes stereotypical images of African American women that have persisted into the 21st century despite any claims one might make about progress in race relations – ranging from black male impersonations of black women (Flip Wilson, Eddie Murphy, Tyler Perry, et al) to dramatic portrayals of drug addicted women widespread in 1990s ghettocentric cinema (*Boys in the Hood* and *Menace II Society* are two examples). At this point in her text, Morgan recognizes that these images are widely internalized by African Americans themselves because they are the prevailing media images available to most observers of popular culture.   Clearly, these images are common in the style of recent African American comedians such as Martin Lawrence, the Wayans Brothers, Cedric the Entertainer, Dave Chapelle, and Bernie Mac[13], who in the era of hip hop culture lay claim to the kind of racial authenticity in comedy once associated with Red Foxx and Richard Pryor – the idea that with these comedians, a viewer gets politically incorrect but culturally authentic black humor.[14]

Whether or not one accepts the standard defenses that these comedians either undermine stereotypes through satire or reproduce authentic personalities of African American women, it is undeniable that such comedians make stereotypes more visible in the public setting of popular culture--and as much as Morgan expresses her admiration of hip hop culture in Chickenheads, she also recognizes that African American women pay a personal cost due to these stereotypical images, not the least of which is the constricting effect on the artistic imagination.   However, Morgan hesitates to take the next critical step that I would suggest--to assert that popular culture has far too much influence over the socialization of all American youth, African American youth included, and despite problematic stereotypes, audiences tend to read popular culture as if it were a fair representation of lived experience.   As I have argued throughout this essay, a vigilant observer must bear in mind that much of popular culture is mass produced in the context of global capitalism, with a process of production that has little to do with the day-to-day experience of African Americans.

Beyond a hesitation to account for the deep structure of culture industries or to challenge consistently the assumptions of racial authenticity that influence how audiences read hip hop, Morgan's essays are full of keen insights.   An essay titled "From Fly-girls to Bitches and Hos" lays out Morgan's case for a legitimate feminist standpoint on hip hop culture. The essay acknowledges that sexism and misogyny figure prominently in the ideology of hip hop as a whole.   Despite the sexism, Morgan believes that it is important and necessary to listen to the voices emerging from a music form that, despite its connection to patriarchy, is

> not only the dominion of the young, black, and male, it is also the world   in which young black women live and survive. A functional game plan for us, one that is going to be as helpful to Shequanna on 142nd as it is to Samantha at Sara Lawrence, has to recognize hip-hop's ability to articulate the pain our *community* is in and use that knowledge to create a redemptive, healing space. (76)

Being a fan myself of musically adventurous and politically savvy mid-school hip hop expression by Sister Carol, Public Enemy, KRS-One, and Digable Planets, I agree that the music can serve as a consciousness-raising tool across lines of class, race, and nationality, as long as artists with distinctive stylistics and visions can find a place at the mass media table.

The compelling aesthetics of Morgan's essay help to make a case for the continuing vitality and future potential for cultural dialogue represented by hip hop, beginning with a letter to "Boo," a metaphor for men within hip hop communities. The letter speaks of love and trouble in relationships between African American men and women in urban communities. Morgan is dismayed by the substitution of the negative terms "bitches and hos" in new and mid-school hip hop music instead of the complimentary term "fly-girl" for women in old school recordings. Morgan writes that, "here I am, Boo, lovin' you, myself, my sistas, my brothers with loyalties that are as fierce as they are divided" (69). Morgan adds that even when hip hop music contains misogynist lyrics, it still reports the condition of African Americans who have suffered most from racism in this society, as expressed by one chilling line: "When brothers can talk so cavalierly about killing each other and then reveal that they have no expectation to see their twenty-first birthday, that is straight-up depression *masquerading* as machismo" (73). Elsewhere in the essay, Morgan provides sociological evidence for the damaging effects of violence and other consequences of excessive machismo expressed by African Americans against each other, and I agree that hip hop music provides some insight into these issues. However, it should be clear to careful observers that hip hop music is far from the only source of such insights. The limits of an understanding of black cultural life based on hip hop stem in part from its genre—the musical form is largely, though not entirely, produced for entertainment and not for critical observation. Its insights are also limited by the narrow range of artists that receive mass exposure and by the genre's overdetermined thematic and stylistic practices. As obvious as it may seem—rather than expecting compelling insights from hip hop music, a critically vigilant observer seeking a better understanding of contemporary African American culture and life would be better served using established methods of knowledge acquisition: reading published fiction and memoir, making personal observations through conversation, experiencing volunteer work, traveling, and becoming familiar with current sociological literature, including texts written from the standpoint of critical and constructionist race studies. As cultural critics, we must *consistently* recognize not only the potential for black popular music to make thoughtful observations about race and culture but also its limited utility for expanding knowledge and consciousness as well as its propensity for reinforcing stereotypes.

Thus, the next logical step for Morgan and all of us is to consider the larger problems that result from relying excessively on black popular culture as a site of cultural analysis and a site of anti-racist resistance. As Ransby and Mathews, Cornel West, and Morgan herself have observed, even in the wide field of hip hop (a cultural style that, as I have noted earlier, is often taken to be the most authentic reflection available of the lived reality of African American youth), lyrics and imagery commonly reinforce racist notions about black criminality, sexual prowess, and cultural primitivism. I do believe that music, film, and fashion can be starting points for observing American culture, but the mass produced images we select represent experience only anecdotally, often without unpacking racial notions that are embedded in American cultural expression. For instance, even in Morgan's aforementioned call for a new "game plan," i.e. a strategy for social change for younger African Americans, she refers to African American women stereotypically as "Shequanna on 142nd" and "Samantha at Sara Lawrence." Morgan means to illustrate the diversity of experience among African American women, but the passage taps into assumptions about racial identity and naming that helped reproduce the "SheNeyNey" stereotype that Morgan rightly criticizes in her intro.Further, not all "Shequannas" or "Samanthas" think the same way about hip hop music's accuracy in describing African American life and culture. No single musical style--no matter how carefully crafted--can represent the diverse range of human experience among African Americans. This may seem to be an obvious point to make, but since popular culture continues to rely on a narrow range of images to convey truth about large populations, radical intellectuals should challenge this practice explicitly.

I am equally suspicious that any single "game plan," or ideology, can be fashioned that will result in meaningful and positive social change for large numbers of African American simultaneously, given differences in class, ideology, and the like. This call for singularly focused collective change is familiar within black activist traditions, based in part on justice-seeking movements that have successfully sought remedial action to counter legal racism. There remains an enduring longing in black popular culture for charismatic leadership and messianic public figures: Harriet Tubman, Booker T. Washington, Martin Luther King, Malcolm X, or Jesse Jackson, for example, have come to stand for entire historical periods and positions within African American cultural history. While the work of such individuals has been instrumental for achieving legal and political landmarks as well as transforming the everyday lives of African Americans, no single "game plan" will provide the silver bullet solution to persistent problems of racial stereotyping in black popular culture as well as achievement gaps across our society. Persistent, progressive, yet incremental social change requires clear vision and considerable patience and purposeful action among critical activists--including a clearer understanding of what hip hop cultural expression can deliver, and what it cannot.

I'd like to end by widening this discussion, commenting on a few key economic and cultural practices under global capitalism, and connecting a wider critique of the global political economy to Joan Morgan's standpoint as a hip hop feminist. The work of neo-Marxist cultural critic Frederic Jameson is helpful for this argument. In *Postmodernism: the Cultural Logic of Late Capitalism*, Jameson identifies a recurring problem in the way that many radical intellectuals write about art and popular culture, which is a tendency to focus on individual texts and trends, rather than on the industries and power structures that oversee the mass production of popular culture. To characterize the ways that popular culture is produced by industries such as television networks, film studios, and media conglomerates, Jameson writes as follows:

> ...aesthetic production today has become integrated into commodity production generally: the frantic economic urgency of producing fresh waves of ever more novel-seeming goods (from clothing to airplanes), at ever greater rates of turnover, now assigns an increasingly essential structural function and position to aesthetic innovation and experimentation. (4-5)

Jameson asserts that under postmodern corporate capitalism, the quest for artistic innovation is conflated with the need to produce new commodities on a short-term business cycle. To read hip hop in this way, as a commodity embedded within the structural processes of global capitalism, is a significant challenge to the once-common assumption that hip hop represents authentic African American culture. As I have noted throughout this essay, while there is precedent in cultural criticism for recognizing the commodification of blackness[15], a temptation remains to revere the "novel-seeming goods" of hip hop rather than to recognize the negative effects of corporate control and failures of the aesthetic imagination to move past familiar and crude stereotypes of African Americans.

It follows further that since mass and corporate production of cultural expression utilizes the logic of profit maximization, with the goal of profitability--producing and selling as many units as possible, shaping public taste through marketing and advertising strategies--dominating other creative influences, the racial identity of the artist or producer has increasingly less bearing on the racially-specific "truths" expressed in the texts. This phenomenon is not new in popular music; Motown Company, for instance, has often been admired and sometimes criticized for its historically successful production of African American soul music for a mass audience. But while cultural observers often criticize the integrationist, pop music sensibility of

Motown recordings (Gerald Early describes Motown's work as "middlebrow" (Early 5), and Nelson George distinguishes Motown ,"the sound of Young America," from the culturally authentic James Brown, who "was clearly the king of black America" (George 99)), the influence of late capitalist logic on all major music distributors since the 1980s is not nearly as well noted. A range of contemporary music critics continue to distinguish between "commercial" black music and "authentic" black music, as if Def Jam or Death Row Records are driven any less by commercial impulses than classic Motown or Flyte Time Productions.[16]

There are cases in which African American artists have had effective control over the performance, production, and distribution of their material at a number of points in the history of hip hop, and there remains a thriving underground marketplace where visionary musicians and entrepreneurs retain their creative independence. However, as bell hooks suggests in her film *Cultural Criticism and Transformation*, the logic of capitalism suggests that monetary success resulting from the emergence of a compelling artist or style needs to be repeated until the market for that product is saturated. Any of my readers could name examples where the radical texts of a given era are repackaged as advertising jingles, as a nostalgic soundtrack for a film production, or as decoration for a new clothing line. Vigilant observers of global capitalism should expect these practices and recognize that texts of popular culture may, in one respect, point audiences toward radical insights, but simultaneously enable entertainment conglomerates such as AOL/Time Warner, Sony, and Disney to market a narrow range of images and ideas to a global audience.

Jameson is more willing than Morgan or even hooks to suggest that popular culture as a whole is an agent through which forces hostile to the ideals of human justice exert control over the production of culture:

> ...I must remind the reader of the obvious; namely, that this whole global, yet American, postmodern culture is the internal and superstructural expression of a whole new wave of American military and economic domination throughout the world: in this sense, as throughout class history, the underside of culture is blood, torture, death, and terror. (5)

American capitalism has used the appeal of popular culture to concentrate power and wealth in fewer and fewer hands, and the production of hip hop music and the assumption that its texts are racially authentic has enabled mass distribution of damaging racial stereotypes, making it more difficult for Americans of all races to identify their cultural similarities and common political interests.

As a final response to Morgan's text, I would argue that in relation to hip hop, we have reached a point similar to the waning of the Black Power and "soul" movements of the 1960s and 1970s. Those movements faded as the movement's symbols were co-opted and commercialized (ranging from the mass marketing of Africanesque clothing to the de-politicizing and mass production of soul music through disco). Also, by the time those movements ended, many observers had called into question the movements' usefulness for inspiring positive change in the future, in part because the movements favored simplified notions about authentic African American identity as predominantly urban, predominantly Muslim, or "down" with the language and style of then-current popular culture. I hope, then, that the lesson we have learned since then is that periodically, activists should re-imagine and re-articulate a set of goals and aims, based on the multiple perspectives on race, ideology, and divisions of power that exist in society at a given moment.

In later writing, Morgan herself has re-imagined and re-articulated some of her positions regarding hip hop culture. In her columns in *Essence* and elsewhere in the 2000s, Morgan has expressed more explicit concerns about the misogyny and commercialization of hip hop music than she did in *Chickenheads*. Her strongest statement of her change in perspective is her 2002 column in *Essence*, "Sex, Lies, and Videos," in which she notes the growing disillusionment of young black college women with the imagery used to market hip hop and raises some questions herself about her loyalty to the style. Early in the article Morgan outlines her reaction to hip hop videos in critically vigilant, feminist terms:

> Remaining a hip-hop loyalist these days is a formidable task with a questionable payoff. Rap music has journeyed from the South Bronx underground to Corporate America, as 70 percent of hip-hop consumers are now White. For many artists, the shift in the market has meant adopting mainstream values, resulting in the proliferation of thin, White and light images of women. When you couple that with a visual aesthetic that relies heavily on T&A and crotch shots, suffice it to say the average rap video taps into just about every insecurity and erroneous belief about sensuality related to Black women. Especially troubling is the unavoidable message that shaking our half-naked asses in front of a man is the only way we have to secure male affection. ("Sex, Lies, and Videos" 120)

This strongly condemnatory language is largely missing from Morgan's assessment of hip hop in *Chickenheads*. Later in this same essay, she describes the responsibility that African American mothers have toward their children in relation to hip hop video, suggesting that they do not accept the industry's "most clichéd disclaimer--that rap's content is intended for mature audiences" ("Sex, Lies, and Videos" 120). Her advocacy for black consumers voting with their dollars and resisting the industry's appeals to a manufactured racial authenticity is a significant shift from the positions expressed in her earlier essays, such as "from fly-girls to bitches and hos."

In a 2006 interview in *Callaloo*, Morgan was asked if she thinks hip hop aesthetics will ever move away from its current immersion in sexualized, violent, and imitatively commercial images in favor of more righteous and politically incisive content. Her reply highlights a new awareness of how centrally the ideology of profit maximization influences the art (and the artists) of hip hop:

> There is a lot of money and willingness to keep things just the way they are, not just in terms of the corporate structure, but by the artists themselves. I don't think that there is going to be this moment of consciousness where hip-hop is going to revert back to something else. Hip-hop never really had a moment where it was all consciousness. What happened is that there has just been a real narrowing of the kind of hip-hop we get to hear. There were all these different kinds of music to sort of balance out what these images are. I have always said, much to people's regret, that I'm really not that pressed about hip-hop dying out. I think it's part of the sort of arrogance and naiveté of youth who assume that hip-hop will always be around in this form, with this kind of cultural force and presence, forever. The reason I say that is no other music has really done that. (Carpenter 768)

Morgan provides historical perspective by recognizing that jazz, blues, and other black-identified musical styles have all had their moments where they were considered cutting-age forms of musical expression. In each case, however, the impact of historical and cultural change was to alter not only the aesthetic qualities of the music but also the size of the audience and the appeal of the music to a mass market. Morgan tacitly acknowledges the naïve idealism that she and many others held about hip hop culture at points when the music and meaning appeared equally compelling and righteous. Now, Morgan seems to recognize that the moment when critical intellectuals could singularly speak of hip hop as a liberating cultural force has passed. However, despite the changes in cultural politics and Morgan's own stances since the publication of *When Chickenheads Come Home To Roost*, the collection remains a source of incisive and relevant thinking about hip hop culture and the future of racial politics. It continues to reward readers who wonder--or who doubt--if popular culture texts can or will ever deliver the careful critical analysis that is needed to inspire progressive social change.

Notes

[1] *Grand Theft Auto* is a *video game* series developed by the company Rockstar in 1998. The game provides players with a fantasy experience in a criminal underworld, with roles as pimps, hit men, and fugitives available as a part of the game player's adventure. The games series has inspired many imitators in the marketplace for "mature"-rated video games and has also been criticized for its violent, sexist, and often racist qualities.

[2] Snoop Doggy Dogg is one of the best known rappers of the West Coast gangsta style. His work on *The Chronic* (1992) by Dr. Dre and *Doggy Style* (1993), his debut solo recording, launched a remarkable successful career that has transitioned from an edgy oppositional performer to product spots in a corporate mainstream context.

[3] *Star Trek Voyager* ran for seven years as a show that created a backstory for some of the previously produced *Star Trek* series, including the original series. Notably, the show starred Kate Mulgrew as Captain Kathryn Janeway, the first time a female lead was cast for the long-running *Star Trek* saga.

[4] The "accidental" exposure of Janet Jackson's breast at the halftime show of Super Bowl XXXVIII has generated a lively conversation about media and cultural values that has yet to subside. For the record, the FCC fined the broadcasting network, CBS, "a maximum $27,500 for airing Jackson's fleeting display of nudity during the 6 a.m to 10 p.m. window when federal rules ban indecent programming" (Hearn 14). The short term effect of the ban was to inspire FOX network, the next broadcaster of the Super Bowl, to feature ex-Beatle Paul McCartney for the halftime spectacle, and indeed, no wardrobe malfunction occurred during his performance.

[5] Hazel Carby's text examines masculinity in the context of both popular culture and politics, with fascinating pieces on Miles Davis, the Danny Glover film *Grand Canyon*, and black male subjectivity as read by multiple audiences. Nelson George's text is similarly focused on reading text and historical context to consider how hip hop has emerged as a primary cultural sign for African Americans in mass media during the last three decades.

[6] The amount of damages and range of companies involved in high-profile racial discrimination suits illustrates the enduring assumptions about African American inferiority that persist despite continuing social action to bring about a change. In 2000, Coca-Cola settled a discrimination suit for $192.5 million brought by employees of the company. Texaco paid out $176.1 million to settle a similar suit, with taped conversations of executives denigrating African Americans providing an important piece of evidence. The suit against Abercrombie and Fitch, settled in 2004, received a great deal of publicity since its clothing line had been marketed to upscale consumers, with discrimination alleged in both the choice of models and the hiring and promotion of employees; the company settled for $50 million. Federal Express was ordered by the EEOC to pay a smaller amount, $1.57 million, at the conclusion of a bias suit, but the USDA is still in court after admitting it had discriminated against black farmers, and a 1997 settlement of

$400 million was challenged by plaintiffs as being inadequate. A $20 billion lawsuit was field in 2005 on behalf of the Black Farmers and Agriculturalist Association (Holmes 36).

[7]   The Urban League's annual report *The State of Black America* provides a sound overview of achievement gaps in education, health, and income. The 2005 report notes, for instance, that African Americans have a life expectancy six years shorter than whites, are 2.3 times more likely to be unemployed, and that African Americans are three times more likely to become prisoners once arrested. See the executive summary and full text of the 2005 report for more information; citation is listed in the works cited.

[8]   Jackie Robinson is undoubtedly the best known of these figures who were "famous firsts," with his breaking into major league baseball in 1947. Among the others, Shirley Chisholm was the first African American woman to embark on a major-party campaign for president, running for the Democratic Party nomination in 1972 (she finished fourth at that year's national convention). In 1989, Art Shell became the first African American head coach in the modern history of the National Football League. Colin Powell and Condeleeza Rice become the first and second African Americans to serve as secretary of state, albeit in an administration that has never had much support among African American voters. In 2002, Halle Berry became the first African American to win an Oscar for best actress, for her seamy and sensational role in *Monster's Ball*.

[9]   Iron Mike Tyson remains well-known as one of the most spectacular and controversial heavyweight boxing champtions in sports history. Ol' Dirty Bastard became a star rapper in 1993 when his group, the Wu-Tang Clan, released their first record. After a successful career as a solo artist and making the news often due to legal troubles, ODB died of a drug overdose in 2004.

[10]   In recent years, the Minnesota Vikings have been the press-favored example of choice for media voices that decry the moral degeneracy of professional athletes. Former Minnesota Vikings player Randy Moss probably drew the biggest headlines in a playoff game against Green Bay on January 9, 2005, when he pretended to "moon" Green Bay Packers fans after scoring a touchdown. The next year, after the blockbuster trade of Randy Moss, several Minnesota Vikings players made headlines when a team party was hosted on a Lake Minnetonka cruise boat by Viking Fred Smoot during an-off week, on October 6, 2005. According to the staff of the boat and police reports, several Vikings player engaged in lewd behavior and public sex, and at least two misdemeanor convictions were handed down as a result of the event.

[11]   From among many cultural critics who have examined sexism, misogyny, and racial stereotyping in hip hop expression, I will mention two essays here that I have found especially helpful. An essay by Barbara Ransby and Tracy Mathews, "Black Popular Culture and the Transcendence of Patriarchal Illusions" (in *Words of Fire: an Anthology of African-American Feminist Thought*, Ed. Beverly Guy-Sheftall, 1995) assesses the connection between the reifying of aggressive masculinity in 1960s black nationalist thought and images of abusive and self-destructive behavior in hip hop music and video. Cornel West's "Nihilism in Black America" (in *Race Matters*, 1994) is also an indispensable essay on the cultural politics that have generated hip hop music and culture, even if the musical form is not the primary focus. The essay remains incisive more than 12 years after its original publication. Reading these two texts and Joan Morgan's "from fly-girls to bitches and hos" provides both historical and recent perspectives on sexism, misogyny, and racial stereotyping in hip hop. Michael Dyson's *Holler If You Hear Me: Searching for Tupak Shakur*

(Basic: 2001) and Nelson George's *Hip Hop America* (Penguin: 1999) are well worth the read, though not as incisive in their responses to the pernicious effects of celebrity culture.

[12] Jimi Hendrix and Sly Stone are both West Coast musicians that embodied an integrationist spirit for much of their musical careers in the 1960s and early 1970s, but they were also influenced by Black Aesthetics and Black Power movements during their later years, in recordings such as Hendrix's *Band of Gypsies* (1970) and Stone's *There's a Riot Going On* (1971). Tracy Chapman and Lauryn Hill emerged in the 1980s and 1990s with an alternative view of pervasive homophobia and misogyny in musical movements of their eras, particularly with Chapman's self-titled debut release from 1988 and Hill's dynamic work with the Fugees (*The Score*, 1996) and as a solo artist (*The Miseducation of Lauryn Hill*, 1998).

[13] Television and film star Martin Lawrence actually introduced the She-ney-ney character in 1992 on his sitcom, *Martin*, and other situation and film comedies by Bernie Mac (*The Bernie Mac Show*), the Wayans Brothers (*In Living Color*)Cedric the Entertainer (*Barbershop*), and Dave Chappelle (*The Dave Chappelle* Show) arguably are revivals of "comic darky" images that date back to the era of minstrel comedy, complete with eye-rollin', shuffling, and mock dialect.

[14] Redd Foxx (1922-1991) is most famous for his lead part in the television comedy *Sanford and Son*, but his standup career included extensive experiences in black nightclubs, and thus a claim to a status as an originator of contemporary black comedic style. Richard Pryor (1940-2005) has an even stronger reputation as a comic of conscience for the post-civil rights generation, based on film, television, and standup performances.

[15] My preferred classic piece on this theme is published in bell hooks' *Black Looks: Race and Representation* (New York: Routledge, 1992): "Selling Hot Pussy."

[16] It is a commonplace now in music criticism to refer to the music of Motown as white-identified. In her comparison of business models for Chess and Motown Records, even blues and soul superstar Etta James in *Rage to Survive* notes that "Berry Gordy, like Chuck Berry before him, went after the white teenager because the white teenager had the money" (James 159). I find that music and racial identify have a more complex relationship, given the importance, for instance, of white performers such as Jerry Wexler in shaping the "black" sound of Atlantic and Stax Records, and given even the role of white audience support in shaping the aesthetics of hardcore rap. These issues remain in need of more detailed and thoughtful treatment in cultural and music criticism.

Works Cited

"Abercrombie OKs $50M To Settle Bias Lawsuit." *Brandweek.com*. November 22, 2004.

"Black Fed Ex Workers File Discrimination Lawsuit." *Jet*, January 6, 2003: 15.

Carby, Hazel. *Race Men*. Cambridge: Harvard University Press, 1998.

Carpenter, F. Chatard. "An Interview with Joan Morgan." *Callaloo* 29.3 (2006): 764-772.

Daniels, Lee and Rose Jefferson-Frazier. Corporate Author: National Urban League. *The State of Black America, 2005*. New York: National Urban League, 2005.

George, Nelson. *Hip Hop America*. New York: Viking, 1998.

Hearn, Ted. "FCC Fines CBS $550K; O&Os Penalized for Halftime Fiasco; Affiliates Spared." *Multichannel News*, September 14, 2004: 14.

Holmes, Tamara. "Black Farmers Sue USDA for $20.5 Billion." *Black Enterprise*, December 2004: 36.

hooks, bell. *Black Looks: Race and Representation*. New York: Routledge, 1992.

hooks, bell. *Cultural Criticism and Transformation*. Videorecording. Dir. Sut Jhally. Northampton, MA: Media Education Foundation, 1997.

James, Etta and David Ritz. *Rage to Survive*. New York: De Capo Press, 1998.

Jameson, Frederic. *Postmodernism, or the Cultural Logic of Late Capitalism*. Durham: Duke University Press, 1991.

Morgan, Joan. "My Extreme Stress Makeover." *Essence* 35.6 (October 2004): 204-210.

—. "Sex, Lies, and Videos." *Essence* 33.2 (June 2002): 120.

—. *When Chickenheads Come Home to Roost*. New York: Simon and Schuster, 1999.

Morgan, Marcyliena. "Hip-Hop Women Shredding the Veil: Race and Class in Popular Feminist Identity." *South Atlantic Quarterly* 104 (2005): 425-444.

"Multi-Million Dollar Discrimination Cases." *Workforce Management*, April 1, 2003: 38.

Muska, Susan and Greta Olafsdottir, Directors. *The Brandon Teena Story*. Documentary – DVD Recording. Pro. Bless Bless Productions. Distributed by Zeitgeist Films, 1998.

Pearlman, Cindy. "It's One Small Step for Women – One Giant Leap for Hollywood." *Chicago Sun-Times*, November 30, 1997: Show Section, 1.

Price, Kimberly, Director. *Boys Don't Cry*. Feature Film -Videorecording. ProHart-Sharp Entertainment. Distrubuted by Fox-Searchlight Pictures, 1999.

Ransby, Barbara and Tracy Mathews. "Black Popular Culture and the Transcendence of Patriarchal Illusions." *Words of Fire: an Anthology of African American Feminist Thought*. Ed. Beverly Guy-Sheftall. New York: New Press, 1995: 526-535.

Schiesel, Seth. "Gangs of New York." *New York Times*, October 16, 2005: Arts and Leisure Section, p. 1.

Siegel, Carol. "Curing Boys Don't Cry: Brandon Teena's Stories." *GendersOnline Journal* 37 (2003). Accessed December 5, 2006. http://www.genders.org/g37/g37_siegel.html

Springer, Kimberly. "Third Wave Black Feminism?." *Signs: Journal of Women in Culture and Society* 27(2002): 1065-1069.

West, Cornel. *Race Matters*. Boston: Beacon Press, 1993.

Claiming Hip Hop:
Authenticity Debates, Filipino DJs, and Contemporary U.S. Racial Formations

Antonio T. Tiongson Jr.

Even during its humble beginnings hip hop was never strictly a black thing. It has always been multiracial, multicultural, and multilingual. Those qualities formed a movement that has defied all attempts to impose the strict racial definitions and caricatures that endeavor to limit its potential reach and influence. By insisting on borrowing from various cultural, musical, aesthetic, and political traditions, hip hop became an incredibly rich fountainhead of youth creativity and expression. While black youth play a central role in hip hop, white, Latino, and Asian youths continue to make their mark on the movement, too.

S. Craig Watkins, Hip Hop Matters: Politics, Pop Culture, and the Struggle for the Soul of the Movement (2004)

Yes, it's become en vogue to imagine hip-hop as belonging to everyone. Sure, there have been other cultural influences. But influences are just that, influences. Black American cultural attitudes, style, verbal and body language, as well as insider Black cultural perspective, not only were prevalent at hip-hop's origin but remain at its core today.

Bakari Kitwana, Why White Kids Love Hip Hop; Wankstas, Wiggers, Wannabes, and the New Reality of Race in America (2005)

In recent years, scholarly and popular discourse addressing hip hop and its various articulations has grown to the point where there is now a fairly substantial body of writing that can be categorized under the rubric of "hip hop studies." This body of writing includes hip hop magazines such *as The Source*, Tony Mitchell's edited volume *Global Noise: Rap and Hip Hop Outside the U.S.*, Tricia Rose's *Black Noise: Rap Music and Black Culture in Contemporary America*, Raquel Z. Rivera's *New York Ricans from the Hip Hop Zone* and more recently, Jeff Chang's *Can't Stop Won't Stop: A History of the Hip-Hop Generation*. The growth of this literature, however, has not proven to be seamless. Instead, it has come to be characterized by contentious debates and discussions revolving around a particular set of issues, what I consider fault lines within the literature. There has been a good deal of debate and discussion, for example, regarding the commercialization of hip hop and its impact on the culture's dynamism, politics, and integrity or authenticity. There has also been a good deal of debate and discussion regarding the gender and sexual politics of hip hop and in particular, the pervasiveness of sexism, misogyny, and homophobia in the culture.[1] No one issue, however, has generated more heated debate and discussion than the issue of cultural origins, entitlement, and authenticity particularly as they revolve around hip hop's apparent "blackness." An emergent theme in the literature is that it can no longer be assumed that hip hop is an exclusively African American expressive form or that it is simply a signifier of blackness given the formative role that other racialized groups and their attendant cultural practices and traditions have played in its evolution and in hip hop's popularity on a global scale. In many ways, the S. Craig Watkins epigraph that opens up this chapter is symptomatic of the "multiracial, multicultural, and multilingual"[2] turn in hip hop historiography. Nonetheless, cultural critics like Bakari Kitwana make the assertion that hip hop is undeniably an African American form even as these critics acknowledge the multiple origins and influences of hip hop. Hip hop, in other words, has proven to be a key site over which competing claims of cultural ownership, race, and authenticity are made.[3]

In what follows, I attempt to make sense of the broader implications—both theoretical and political—of this recent turn in hip hop literature through a consideration of the ways in which knowledge of hip hop culture is constructed, framed, and conveyed around questions of cultural origins, belonging, and authenticity and the ways a group of non-black youth go about carving out a niche in a cultural form historically associated with African Americans. I'm interested in the questions raised by the assertion that hip hop can no longer be considered an African American phenomenon: What does this do to hip hop's status as a "black thing"? Does hip hop cease being a "black thing"? Does it mean that any group can claim hip hop as their own? Or do African Americans have a particular claim to hip hop because of their historical relationship to it? How are the contrasting and competing claims of different groups to be adjudicated? At the same time, I'm interested in the way a group of young people—in this case Filipino DJs—go about claiming cultural legitimacy given their location outside the foundational narrative of hip hop. What kinds of authenticating claims do they make and what authenticating strategies do they rely on? How do Filipino youth position themselves in relation to hip hop's hierarchy of authenticity that places a premium on exhibiting signifiers of blackness? What does it mean for Filipino

DJs to make the claim that hip hop is as much a "Filipino thing" as it is a "black thing" even as they acknowledge its origins in black culture?

I argue that underexplored in this emergent body of work is what is at stake when blackness is invoked either as a way to claim or problematize claims of cultural ownership (typically through charges of essentialism). More broadly, I look to these debates and discussions revolving around issues of cultural ownership, origins, and authenticity as a potentially rich site for illuminating the contours and trajectory of contemporary U.S. racial formations and discourses and, in particular, racial formations and discourses in the post-Civil Rights era. I argue that in many ways, the terms by which this debate has taken place is symptomatic of contemporary racial discourse—the tendency to conceive of race and cultural ownership either in narrow, exclusive terms in which there seems to be no room to account for variegated origins and influences, or in liberal, pluralist terms in which "difference" seems to no longer matter or make a difference.

Contemporary Scholarship: Interrogating Hip Hop, Interrogating Blackness

Although hip hop literature is marked by diverse theoretical approaches, perspectives, and subject matter, one can identify particular themes that are rearticulated and recapitulated in both popular and scholarly accounts to the extent that they have become transparent and seemingly self-evident. According to standard historical accounts of hip hop, for example, the South Bronx constitutes the birthplace of hip hop, the place where the constituent elements of hip hop—DJing, MCing, writing, and b-boying—first coalesced in the 1970s. Another central tenet is the notion of hip hop as an African American phenomenon, an expressive form rooted in African American cultural practices and traditions. It's not a surprise, therefore, that what passes for authentic in hip hop is still largely predicated on exhibiting signifiers of blackness or adopting a distinct cultural style associated with black masculinity.

According to Rivera, a key moment in the African Americanization of hip hop is the mid-1980s, a period marked by the commercial ascendancy of rap and the concomitant commercial decline of breaking and writing. She makes the point that the mass commodification of rap and subsequent entry into the mainstream not only meant the conflation of hip hop with rap but also the intensification of the association between blackness and MCing and DJing.

Another contributing factor is the perceived roots and origins of these two elements of hip hop. In Rivera's view:

> Rhyming and DJing were from the beginning more ethnic-racially identified with African Americans and closed to perceived outsiders by virtue of their reliance on dexterity in the English language. Thus, they were most easily traceable to the African American oral tradition and primarily employed music considered to be African American. Hip hop's musical dimension seems to have been premised on an Afro-diasporic urbanity, where, although the participation of young people of Caribbean ancestry was pivotal, this music was often narrowly identified solely with African Americans.[4]

More specifically, Rivera asserts that notwithstanding hip hop's incorporation of various kinds of music, funk is considered its musical core. This is significant because funk is widely regarded as an African American musical form.

More recently, however, cultural critics have reconsidered, complicated, and questioned what previously have been considered foundational themes of hip hop historiography. To illustrate, the South Bronx may be hip hop's birthplace, but it is no longer assumed that youth in surrounding areas did not engage in similar practices or that the different expressive forms constitutive of hip hop just suddenly came together in the South Bronx, what one writer has aptly called the "romanticized Big Bang theory" of hip hop. Instead, recent works have begun to map out the differential racialization history and trajectory of each constituent element of hip hop.[5] Accordingly, this re-envisioning of hip hop has paved the way for the publication of scholarly works that aim to complicate and disrupt the links between hip hop and blackness.

Hip Hop as a Diasporic Expressive Form

While acknowledging hip hop's black antecedents, a growing number of cultural critics point to the eclectic and wide ranging formative influences of hip hop that exceed the bounds of African American culture and complicate claims of hip hop as a strictly African American phenomenon. Accordingly, these critics call for a more nuanced narration of hip hop history that does not underplay or underestimate the degree to which the cultural histories of various groups overlap. Cultural critic Paul Gilroy, for instance, takes issue with the African Americanization of hip hop or the racialization of hip hop as an African American phenomenon. Conceptualizing hip hop this way, Gilroy argues, effectively erases its origins in the black diaspora and the formative role of black diasporic cultural practices in its emergence. Notwithstanding its multiple origins and influences, however, considerations of hip hop continue to be informed by African American exceptionalism as evidenced by the use of the term "rap" or the deployment of accounts that conceive of hip hop as a direct descendant of jazz, soul, and the blues which Gilroy argues is more evocative of African American influences and genealogies. Instead, he calls for an alternative understanding of hip hop and other black cultural productions that is not rooted in discourses of nationalism and ethnic exceptionalism but one that is predicated on a recognition of the syncretic character of black cultural formations.[6]

Gilroy also takes issue with how music has become an important medium to make authenticating claims and, in the case of hip hop, a potent signifier of racial authenticity and, in particular, blackness. He finds especially troubling the valorization of African American-based hip hop by African American scholars as authentic and the concomitant devaluation of hip hop rooted in other locations in the black diaspora as inauthentic, a function of its purported distance from a specific (and identifiable) point of origin. What potentially can serve as a vehicle for unsettling the notion of authenticity (because of its syncretic character), therefore, has been deployed as signifier of authenticity. Gilroy goes on to assert that the issue of authenticity has not only persisted but assumed greater significance among practitioners, consumers, and fans alike, even with the proliferation of hip hop related styles and genres on a global scale. Authenticity has actually enhanced the appeal of black cultural forms and has become an integral part of the ways these forms are marketed, packaged, and sold.[7]

Hip Hop and the Formative Role of Puerto Ricans

From a different vantage point, Juan Flores and Raquel Rivera aim to complicate the genealogy of hip hop through a consideration of the formative role of Puerto Rican youth in the emergence and development of hip hop. These Puerto Rican Studies scholars argue that the construction of hip hop as an exclusively African American phenomenon is problematic in light of the distinctive relationship of Puerto Rican youth to hip hop. Alongside black youth (as well as West Indian youth), Puerto Rican youth were there from the very beginning, making their mark as co-creators and innovators in all the constituent elements of hip hop including rap years before hip hop became a mass commercial form.   Flores and Rivera suggest that the narrow identification of hip hop with African Americans has compromised Puerto

Ricans' perceived cultural entitlement to hip hop and obscured the pivotal role that Puerto Rican youth played in the development of hip hop. Instead, the Puerto Rican presence in hip hop has been commonly seen either as an intrusion into a black realm (at least until recently) and/or a betrayal of Puerto Ricanness, as if Puerto Ricanness and blackness were mutually exclusive categories. This kind of formulation has served to perpetuate the construction of Puerto Ricanness as distinct from blackness and to elide efforts by Puerto Rican youth to forge their own distinct identity and culture in ways that cannot be accommodated by models of cultural assimilation and loss.[8]

For Flores and Rivera, then, hip hop constitutes yet another moment in the long history of African American-Puerto Rican mutual collaborations and exchanges, a function of the similar social location that both groups occupy in New York City. Accordingly, the emergence and subsequent evolution of hip hop only makes sense within the broader context of shared African American and Puerto Rican cultural traditions and practices. They raise the point that accounting for the formative role of Puerto Rican youth would mean expanding the boundaries of Puerto Ricanness in order to account for the shared history between African Americans and Puerto Ricans, but it would also mean expanding the boundaries of blackness to account for the fact that Puerto Ricans are also part of the African diaspora in the Americas.

Hip Hop as a Global Phenomenon

Attention has also been given to what it means for hip hop to be diffused on a global scale and taken up in settings and contexts far removed from its South Bronx origins. A number of cultural critics assert that hip hop cannot be viewed merely as an African American expressive form imported from the U.S.; instead, it has become a global youth form adapted to local circumstances for local purposes. In other words, the diffusion of hip hop on a global scale has given rise to new forms and identities that belie the status of hip hop as a "black thing." In the introduction to the volume entitled *Global Noise, Rap and Hip-Hop Outside the U.S.A.*, for example, Tony Mitchell asserts that the roots of hip hop are not simply African American but "culturally, eclectically, and syncretically wide-ranging as they are deep."[9]

A focal point in the volume is how youth in different parts of the globe establish their cultural legitimacy given the lack of historical, cultural, and racial continuities between the originators of hip hop and themselves. To illustrate, Australian youth consider hip hop as much their thing as it is a black thing. In making such a claim, this group of youth relies on a number of authenticating strategies, strategies which range from fidelity to the core values or principles of hip hop to fidelity to one's true self. For them, authenticity is not a matter of geographic, racial, or class specificity or affiliation. Instead, it is more a matter of being true to what they consider the "essence" of hip hop, which encompasses a commitment to upholding the various elements of hip hop including the use of two turntables and a microphone (purportedly hip hop's "original" instruments) in their music.[10]

Collectively, this body of work has served to expand and complicate the racial grounds on which to consider hip hop historiography and authenticity. It has served to problematize authenticating claims based on hip hop's apparent "blackness." At the same time, hip hop criticism has raised a number of fundamental questions that has both political and theoretical implications and yet, these implications remain uninterrogated. What remains underspecified in this emergent literature, in other words, are the complications and complexities of cultural imbrications, appropriations, and crossings.

Hip Hop, Cultural Ownership, and Authenticity: The Case of Filipino of DJs

In my own work, I not only provide a reconsideration of hip hop literature but I also rely on personal accounts of Filipino DJs in an effort to shed light on the way a group of young people go about claiming cultural legitimacy given their location outside the foundational narrative of hip hop. In the case of Filipino youth, one has a group of young people who are not in a position to make originary and historical claims as the basis of their cultural entitlement and authenticity. Unlike Puerto Rican youth, for example, Filipino youth were not among the first MCs, DJs, writers, and b-boys/b-girls, a position which could have buttressed their claims of cultural belongingness. In addition, Filipino youth and black youth do not have a sense of shared history and culture, at least not to the same extent as that which exists between Puerto Ricans and African Americans in a place like New York, where the two groups have overlapping experiences of racialization, marginalization, and labor exploitation. Also, some Puerto Ricans claim an African/diasporic racial identity. So while hip hop constitutes an important realm of interaction, collaboration, but also conflict between Puerto Rican youth and black youth, it does not constitute the same kind of space for Filipino youth and black youth.[11]

The incommensurability of the Filipino presence in hip hop with the Puerto Rican presence—what one author describes in another context as "the absence of a cultural, ethnic, geographical, or historical continuity with the origins of hip-hop"[12]—means that Filipino youth cannot rely on the same set of legitimizing discourses and claims, and thus they have to advance a very different set of discourses and claims and deploy other strategies to bolster these claims. The question then becomes how Filipino youth go about framing their engagement with hip hop and establishing cultural legitimacy given their location outside the foundational narrative of hip hop.

One of the ways my respondents attempt to establish and enhance their cultural legitimacy is by foregrounding lived experience as the basis of their cultural entitlement. In other words, they authenticate their involvement by narrativizing their experiences of growing up with and embracing hip hop at an early age. With regards to the question of whether hip hop is part of Filipino culture, for instance, several of my interviewees responded affirmatively.

> Deendroid: Yeah, I think it's part of Filipino culture because it's what the generation, that's what we're doing here and we're Filipinos. And you know, hip hop is part of growing up. And so yeah, it's definitely part of being in the Filipino culture because it's there. It's around you.[13]

> Cellski: And plus, I mean I know where it came from and who put it out but then growing up in Vallejo, Filipinos were doing it and that's what I grew up with. So I was not feeling like we're doing a black thing. It is a Filipino thing and even my uncles when I was four who just came from the Philippines, they were breakdancing in the garage. And I remember that, I remember that from long time ago, seeing it around my neighborhood and in my family.[14]

> Rygar:...That's what mostly Filipinos are into. That's just the way, it's just part of us now cause I mean generations and generations will come, it's just going to go bigger to the point where...I don't even know; it's just part of us already. No one can deny it...I would have to say that DJing cause yeah, whenever people look at Filipinos I'm pretty sure they think of DJing, DJs you know.[15]

They may not have been there from the start, but for my respondents, hip hop is as much a part of their lives as forms and practices commonly identified as Filipino, a widespread practice among relatives and peers within the Filipino community. Within this context, then, authenticity is grounded in the specific historical and social experiences of Filipinos and intimately bound up with forms of local knowledge and experience.

Another way my respondents attempt to stake out their cultural legitimacy is by emphasizing that Filipino youth have been true to the principles or values of hip hop. Several of the DJs I interviewed, for example, emphasize their "love" and "respect" for the culture and commitment to what they perceive as the true essence of hip hop.

> Soup-a-Crunk:I think it does matter. I think it's a good thing mainly because it's a part of hip hop and we have a firm hold on it. But really, Filipinos represent in all aspects. It's a matter of recognition. I mean, it's not like we're looking for recognition cause we're gonna be in it whether or not we do. It's just that we're in it because we love it. I think it's important because it shows how diverse it is, how hip hop is, and it represents how it is for the people.[16]

In Soup-a-Crunk's view, it is this emotional attachment to and investment in hip hop that not only legitimizes Filipino participation in hip hop but also makes it possible to transcend racial difference. In other words, assertions of belonging are made on the basis of affective claims which allow anyone to establish cultural legitimacy and become part of a broader community that transcends history, geography, culture and race.

Another way my respondents attempt to stake out their cultural legitimacy is by pointing to hip hop's transcendent appeal even as they acknowledge its black antecedents. Soup-a-Crunk, for example, refers to hip hop as a "human thing" while Onetyme refers to it as a "worldwide thing."

> Soup-a-Crunk: Definitely. I mean it originated from them folks. I mean originally it was a way to keep people out of violence with Afrika Bambaataa. It was a way to speak to the fellows and bring them up and keep them from violence. But then really, it's more of like, it's not just a racial thing; it's kind of like a human thing that spoke to the people rather than just a specific race you know. That's why so many people feel it—it's because it comes down to human qualities.[17]

> Onetyme: I think television, it's all the media cause that's all they show. They don't go to these underground shows where it's total diverse groups, like you see a lot of Latin Americans or Filipino Americans or African Americans, white Americans. They're just like all there peacefully watching a concert. But I think the media plays a big role. They just show like the money and like the fights and everything bad that goes down. But they don't see all these different ethnicities coming together at a party just having fun. So I think hip hop, turntablism is worldwide thing which a lot of people don't know. Like they've it in Germany, it's really big in Japan and like the UK and people don't know that. They need to be more aware of that.[18]

For both Soup-a-Crunk and Onetyme, no one group has a sole proprietary claim on hip hop as they question the notion that ethnic and racial affiliation has a direct bearing on questions of cultural belonging and entitlement. For Soup-a-Crunk and Onetyme, then, hip hop signifies a utopic space of togetherness and inclusion, a kind of populism that has been associated with other expressive forms such as dance culture.

Hip Hop, Blackness, and Contemporary Racial Formations

The DJs I interviewed are very much aware of the racialized discourses that have come to define the contours of hip hop, acknowledging hip hop's black antecedents and subscribing to the notion that it began as an African American mode of cultural expression. Yet there is also recognition that the boundaries of hip hop based on its perceived blackness have been in constant flux. In other words, hip hop may have started out as a black phenomenon, but it has now evolved into something encompassing the participation and contributions of multiple groups. On the one hand, Filipino youth participation in hip hop could be read as one of intense cultural negotiation with its perceived ethno-racial scope and authenticating claims based on its purported blackness that has implications for the way Filipino youth define their position and presence in U.S. society. In staking out their cultural legitimacy, my respondents are deploying their own signifiers of hip hop authenticity and, in the process, broadening the underlying basis of cultural entitlement within hip hop and making it a more inclusive space. A case could be made, therefore, that Filipino youth involvement in DJ culture is symptomatic of the broadening ethno-racial scope of hip hop and the need to come to terms with hip hop's complex genealogies and trajectories.

At the same time, a case could be made that in considering DJing as much a Filipino thing as cultural forms and practices considered Filipino, my respondents are subscribing to a view of cultural identity not predicated on conventional cultural markers such as language, food, and religion to construct their sense of Filipinoness. Instead, the turn to DJing as a source of Filipinones can be understood as symptomatic of the need to expand the frame within which the contours of Filipinoness have historically been defined. It is symptomatic of the need to consider how Filipinoness is transformed and reconstructed in the diaspora referencing not only formations "back home" but also formations in a variety of diasporic contexts. Rather than signifying a "loss of culture" or a "loss of tradition," then, the turn to DJing could be seen as signifying a reworking of culture and tradition by Filipino youth in an attempt to redefine for themselves what it means to be Filipino at this contemporary moment as well as make culture relevant and meaningful.

On the other hand, however, one could easily argue that my respondents are providing a deracialized account of hip hop, and if so, this is problematic because of the way it obscures how different groups of youth are racialized in different ways which, in turn, conditions the manner in which they negotiate the racialized discourses and authenticating claims circulating within hip hop.

This kind of account is problematic because its fails to illuminate the field of racial positions within hip hop and the power asymmetries that underwrite these positions. To borrow from Anita Mannur in another context, this sort of reading divests expressive forms (in this case hip hop) "of any racialized or classed implications."[19] Likewise, this kind of reading overlooks how culture is differently or differentially experienced and contested within and between groups of youth.[20] In other words, a level of equivalence is assumed in which difference is acknowledged only to be reconfigured as part of a colorful mosaic that is hip hop.

The reading of hip hop as a transcendent space is also problematic because of the way it obscures the complex, contradictory and vexed relationship between Filipinoness and African Americanness. Given the overdetermination of hip hop as a site of cross-racial identification and solidarity, it is especially crucial not to lose sight of the intricate nature of this relationship. To do so risks engaging in the kind of reading marked by what Helen Jun has described in another context as "a teleological investment in 'interracial solidarity'—a notion that relies heavily on the premise of identification"[21] that serves to flatten the complications that mark the terrain of black/brown interconnections. Rather, what needs to take place is the elucidation and elaboration of the contours of this identification. In other words, it cannot be assumed that hip hop serves as a point of identification between Filipinos and African Americans. Though beyond the scope of my study, I believe one has to take into account the contingent and contextual nature of particular modes of cultural engagement.[22]

To conceive of hip hop as a transcendent space is symptomatic of the ways the discourse of race works in the U.S. as well as the ways this understanding of race informs contemporary articulations of Filipinoness. It can be seen as an instance of a broader discourse about race, culture, and difference that overlooks the ways racialization has played out differently for various groups. The tendency is to shy away from overt identity claims (particularly along the lines of race) and instead resort to claims of liberal pluralism in which "difference" is rendered benign and safe for consumption in the marketplace and elaborated in nonracial or cultural terms, what Virginia R. Dominguez has called in another context as the "culturalization of difference."[23] According to this formulation, then, Filipinoness becomes just another marker of difference, "a kind of difference that does not make a difference of any kind" overlooking the social, economic, and historical contexts surrounding the racialization of Filipinos in the U.S.[24]

This is not to argue that hip hop is the absolute or specific cultural property of African Americans because they created it, or to argue that the participation of nonblack practitioners and participants have brought about a "dilution" of hip hop as a function of their purported distance from hip hop's point of origin. Rather, it is to argue for a much more complex understanding of culture, one that probes the limits of different modes of cultural engagement. It is to argue that the kinds of exchanges that take place within hip hop cannot be simply conceived simply as a matter of drawing inspiration from or being influenced by black culture, for to do so makes it seem as if the traversing of cultural boundaries is a seamless and straightforward process rather than one fraught with tensions and ambiguities.[25]

While it is indeed the case that hip hop has not only become multicultural but also global in terms of its scope and appeal and therefore cannot be simply viewed as an expression of African Americanness, it does not follow that hip hop has also become, in Juan Flores' words, "an all-purpose-thing, of equal utility and relevance to anyone, anywhere, as long as you're 'with it.'"[26] To conceive of hip hop as such fails to do justice to the complexities of power relations among racialized groups. Instead, questions of power and structure are collapsed into questions of cross-cultural appeal and understanding. To borrow from Jacqueline Urla, "appropriations and border crossings are always inflected by histories of power that shape when cultural, ethnic, or linguistic boundaries are asserted, when they are transgressed, and they are misunderstood."[27] It is precisely these "histories of power" that are overlooked in recent scholarship on hip hop and glossed over in the personal accounts of Filipino DJs. It is precisely these "histories of power" that are overlooked in critiques of authenticating claims based on hip hop's apparent "blackness." And yet, it is precisely these histories of power which condition and shape the participation of different groups of youth in hip hop, histories of power which need to be interrogated and centered in the analysis of the contemporary trajectory and contours of hip hop.

Notes

[1]   See, for example, Byron Hurt's film, *Hip-Hop: Beyond Beats and Rhymes*, that provides a critical examination of the gender and sexual politics of hip hop and in particular, the way

it has served as a vehicle for the perpetuation of hypermasculinist images of black men. Byron Hurt, dir. *Hip Hop: Beyond Beats and Rhymes*, Sundance Film Festival, 2006.

[2] S. Craig Watkins, *Hip Hop Matters: Politics, Pop Culture, and the Struggle for the Soul of the Movement* (Boston, MA: Beacon Press, 2004), 150.

[3] See also Imani Perry, Prophets of the Hood: Politics and Poetics in Hip Hop (Durham: Duke University Press, 2005); John Szwed, "The Real Old School," *The Vibe History of Hip Hop* (1999).

[4] See, for example, Rivera, *New York Ricans*; Ivor L. Miller, *Aerosol Kingdom: Subway Painters of New York City* (Jackson, Miss.: University Press of Mississippi), 2002.

[5] Paul Gilroy, *The Black Atlantic: Modernity and Double Consciousness*(Cambridge, MA: Harvard UP), 1992.

[6] Gilroy, *The Black Atlantic.*

[7] Gilroy, *The Black Atlantic*

[8] Rivera, *New York Ricans.*

[9] Tony Mitchell (ed.), *Global Noise: Rap and Hip-Hop Outside the U.S.A.* (Middletown, Conn.: Wesleyan University Press, 2001), 4.

[10] Ian Maxwell, "Sydney Stylee: Hip-Hop Down under Comin' Up," in Mitchell (ed.), *Global Noise.*

[11] This is not to deny that at times, Puerto Ricans have challenged their racialization as black in the U.S. or instances when hip hop does serve as an important realm of cross-racial interaction between Filipino youth and black youth (or between Filipino youth and other youth for that matter) but more to account for the specificities of Filipino youth and Puerto Rican youth and to recognize that Filipino involvement in hip hop is not easily mapped onto the critical frames that hip hop scholars like Rose, Flores, and Rivera deploy for black and Puerto Rican youth respectively. Tricia Rose, *Black Noise: Rap Music and Black Culture in Contemporary America* (Hanover and London: Wesleyan University Press, 1994); Juan Flores, *From Bomba to Hip-Hop: Puerto Rican Culture and Latino Identity* (New York: Columbia University Press, 2000); Rivera, *New York Ricans.* See also Frances Negron-Muntaner, *Boricua Pop: Puerto Ricans and the Latinization of American Culture* (New York and London: New York University Press, 2004); London: New York University Press, 2004); Roberto P. Rodriguez-Morazzani, "Beyond the Rainbow: Mapping the Discourse on Puerto Ricans and 'Race,'" in Antonia Darder and Rodolfo D. Torres (eds.), *The Latino Studies Reader: Culture, Economy, and Society* (Walden, Mass.: Blackwell Publishers, 1998); Juan Flores, "Puerto Rican and Proud, Boyee! Rap, Roots and Amnesia," in Andrew Ross and Tricia Rose (eds.), *Microphone Fiends: Youth Music and Youth Culture* (New York: Routledge, 1994).

[12] Ian Maxwell, "Sydney Stylee: Hip-Hop Down Under Comin' Up," in Tony Mitchell (ed.), *Global Noise: rap and Hip-Hop Outside the U.S.A.* (Middletown, Connecticut: Wesleyan University Press, 2001), 264.

[13] Deeandroid interview with the author, 19 November 2002.

[14] Cellski interview with the author, 06 November 2002.

[15] Rygar interview with the author, 03 February 2003.

[16] Soup-a-Crunk interview with the author, 18 January 2003.

[17] Soup-a-Crunk interview with the author, 18 January 2003.

[18] Onetyme interview with the author, 14 November 2002.

[19]   Anita Mannur, "Model Minorities Can Cook: Fusion Cuisine in Asian America," in Shilpa Dave, LeiLani Nishime, and Tasha G. Oren (eds.), *East Main Street: Asian American Popular Culture* (New York and London; New York University Press, 2005).

[20]   Leti Volpp makes a similar point in relation to her nuanced discussion of the depoliticizing effects of cultural discourse.   See Leti Volpp, "Blaming Culture for Bad Behavior," *Yale Journal of Law & the Humanities* 12:89 (2000): 89-116.   See also Leti Volpp, "(Mis)Identifying Culture: Asian Women and the 'Cultural Defense,'" in Jean Yu-wen Shen Wu and Min Song (eds.), *Asian American Studies: A Reader* (New Brunswick, New Jersey: Rutgers University Press, 2000).

[21]   Helen H. Jun's focus is nineteenth century black press engagement with Orientalist discourse as a means to grapple with the complications attached to African American citizenship. See Jun, "Black Orientalism: Nineteenth-Century Narratives of Race and U.S. Citizenship," *American Quarterly*, 58.4 (2006), 1051.

[22]   To illustrate, there is a body of writing that looks to U.S. occupation of the Philippines at the turn of the 20th century as a lens through which to examine the convergences between African Americans and Filipinos. Rene G. Ontal, for example, looks to African American involvement in the Philippine-American war as a critical locus for examining affinities forged between the two groups and characterizes the identifications forged in the war as an important "moment of anti-imperial alliance" between African Americans and Filipinos even as he acknowledges complications posed by the presence of blacks in the Philippines. More specifically, Ontal notes how Filipinos themselves subscribed to a color hierarchy and embraced anti-blackness as evidenced by the way the children of black soldiers and Filipinas were marginalized. See Ontal, "Fagen and Other Ghosts: African-Americans and the Philippine-American War," in Angel Velasco Shaw and Luis H. Francia (eds.), *Vestiges of War: The Philippine-American War and the Aftermath of an Imperial Dream 1899-1999* (New York: New York University Press, 2002).

[23]   Virginia R. Dominguez, "Invoking Culture: The Messy Side of 'Cultural Politics," *South Atlantic Quarterly* 91:1 (Winter 1992), 32.

[24]   Stuart Hall, What is This "Black" in Black Popular Culture?," in Gina Dent (ed.), *Black Popular Culture* (Seattle: Bay Press, 1992), 23.

[25]   In my view, the more pertinent questions include the following: What sort of power relations are embedded, reproduced, and/or contested in the kinds of intercultural exchanges that take place within hip hop? How should cultural boundaries be constituted and on what terms? What does it mean to deploy the signifier "black" in relation to hip hop today given its diffusion on a global scale? How does one make sense of the global diffusion of hip hop without losing sight of its "black" origins and continued "black" influence? How do we hold these two in a productive tension? What does the appeal to "roots" and "origins" mean in this context and to what effect? Does an appeal to roots and origins invalidate forms and practices that do not emerge from the original context of hip hop? Or, to pose the question in slightly different terms, what is obscured by positing the impossibility or irrelevance of origins? What are the politics at stake? This has become a fairly standard move among contemporary cultural critics who, in an effort to provide a more complex understanding of culture, posit the plurality or impossibility of identifying a specific point of origin, a move deemed as essentialist. These same critics point to the syncretic character of cultural forces yet undertheorized are the politics at stake, how this kind of claim is easily recuperated by liberal pluralist discourse. The tendency particularly with regard to black expressive forms and practices is to conceive of the kinds of

intercultural exchanges that take place as one simply of appropriation or a cultural "free-for-all." In other words, black culture is conceived simply as something to be plundered or a level of equivalence is assumed among the different groups of youth participating. In either case, black culture is located outside history and disentangled from politics. Overlooked are the specificities of the groups in question—their status and positionality—as well as the ways culture remains linked to race despite efforts to obscure this connection.

[26] Juan Flores, "Puerto Rican and Proud, Boyee! Rap, Roots and Amnesia," in Andrew Ross and Tricia Rose (eds.), *Microphone Fiends: Youth Music and Youth Culture* (New York: Routledge, 1994), 95.

[2] [7]Jacqueline Urla, "'We Are All Malcolm X!': Negu Gorriak, Hip-Hop, and the Basque Political Imaginary," in Tony Mitchell (ed.), *Global Noise: Rap and Hip-Hop Outside the U.S.A* (Middletown, Conn.: Wesleyan University Press

"Faking the Funk": A Journey Towards Authentic Blackness

Wendy Alexia Rountree

I loved watching *The Cosby Show* (1984-1992) when I was a kid. Thursday nights at eight o'clock were sacred times in my household. Normally, I was not allowed to watch television on school nights, but Thursdays were exceptions. We sat and watched the Huxtables solve humorous family dilemmas in thirty minute episodes. My parents were pleased to see a "positive" African-American show on a major U.S. television network. They praised the show for exhibiting and valuing aspects of black culture such as jazz and paintings by African Americans. Personally, I just wanted to be a Cosby kid; I would have loved to have been a famous child actor on the show, but even more, I could identify with the characters, their lives. Unlike characters on previous predominantly African-American television shows like *Good Times* (I didn't grow up in a Chicago housing project), or *The Jeffersons* (I didn't grow up on the east side of Manhattan either), I could identify with the Cosby kids.

Their parents were highly-educated, black professionals (a doctor and a lawyer); my parents were highly-educated black professionals (a college counselor and a public school teacher). Both of my parents were children of southern sharecroppers; they valued education for themselves, me, and other African-Americans. The Cosby kids' parents expected them to excel academically as well. They grew up knowing both sets of grandparents, and so did I. I remember spending two weeks during several summers with each pair of grands. The Cosby parents exposed their children to world culture through the arts; my parents did the same. I specifically remember my mother making me sit through Georges Bizet's *Carmen* on PBS one Christmas holiday. I resisted, but by the end of the production, I loved it. Later, I was pleased to watch Dorothy Dandridge and Harry Belafonte in the film *Carmen Jones*, an African-American adaptation of the opera.

As I grew older, I learned that many critics thought that some of the show's characteristics, the same ones I found identifiable and could relate to, were actually not depicting the reality of the majority of African Americans. They suggested that the show was creating the false impression that most

African Americans had achieved "the dream" and had entered mainstream, middle-class America. The show supposedly promoted the idea that African Americans had "overcome" racism and discrimination (as exhibited by the ethnically diverse friendships and working relationships on the show) in the "Don't Worry, Be Happy" 1980s while in actuality, the African-American community, especially the urban underclass, continued to suffer from poverty, high unemployment, increased teen pregnancy, gang violence, and the rise of AIDS and crack cocaine addiction.

I could then, even as a child, and still now understand and acknowledge those critics' points. *The Cosby Show* could have been used by neo-conservatives and others who wanted to eliminate the then current welfare system and Affirmative Action policies for their own socio-political agendas. However, I felt that their criticism of the show was also a criticism or a denial of my own experience as an African-American. I knew African-Americans of all socio-economic backgrounds who loved and watched the show. Granted, it was one of the few times a US television network aired "black folks" on TV, but I also think that there was a sense of pride throughout the general African-American community that a black family sitcom was rated number one in the country.

Still, I wondered whether shows that depicted African-Americans in poverty were the only ones that could be deemed "authentic" representations? And if so, why did intellectuals and scholars criticize *Good Times* for its portrayals of African Americans, too? While the show was praised for depicting a nuclear family with a present and strong black father, it was criticized for promoting the character JJ, arguably a stereotypical buffoon. Perhaps, the old adage "You can't please everyone" fittingly applies here, especially when discussing depictions of African-Americans in the U.S. and, arguably, world-wide media. Portrayals of blacks in U.S. media outlets (advertisements, film, newspapers, and television) have been less than sympathetic or flattering in the past and, to a lesser degree, the present. Over the years, African Americans have been depicted as primates and ignorant savages, as humble, self-sacrificing, uneducated mammies and uncles, and as dangerous criminals and oversexed jezebels. It is no wonder that African-Americans are sensitive, even hypersensitive at times, about stereotypes and seek to control the group's image. Stereotypical and denigrating images were used by racists and hate groups to dehumanize blacks and to justify the lynching of black men and the general subjugation of black people.

Or, perhaps, *The Cosby Show* simply wasn't "authentic" enough, *black enough*. This issue of black authenticity was indirectly addressed in an episode called "Vanessa's Rich." In the episode, Vanessa tries to join the school pep squad. After inviting two of the members to her home, she tells them that one of the paintings in the home is worth a great deal of money. Soon, other members of the squad begin to call her "stuck up" and "rich girl." Vanessa's peers see her as "inauthentic" because her parents are financially able to buy expensive artwork. I personally identified with this particular situation. I experienced similar bullying as a child for some of the same reasons and have fictionalized the experience in a young adult novel called *Lost Soul* (2003). So, why is the under and working-class considered the only "authentic" representation of African-Americans? Do middle-class African-Americans have to go without validation of their own experiences because the advancement of blacks as a whole is more important than that of any one subgroup? Can or do groups ever advance as a whole, all at the same time?

When W.E.B. Du Bois aptly stated in his seminal work *The Souls of Black Folk* (1903) that "the problem of the twentieth century is the color line" (xxxi), he described the psychological condition of blacks in America, which he named double consciousness, as "this sense of always looking at one's self through the eyes of others, of measuring one's souls by the tape of a world that looks on in amused contempt and pity. One ever feels his twoness, - an American, a Negro; two souls, two thoughts, two unrecognized strivings" (3). He accurately expressed the difficulties that African-Americans had and have defining themselves and blackness. This complex condition was caused by the fact that African-Americans were initially not able to define themselves; they were labeled slaves by white slave owners. Once African-Americans began defining themselves, the questions, "Who is *really* a black person?", "What is blackness?" and "What is 'authentic' blackness?" became crucial questions that had to be answered; otherwise, the definitions given by white oppressors would continue to dominate. Even Ralph Ellison grappled with the ambiguity of blackness in the Prologue of *Invisible Man* (1952). African-Americans have fought hard against white supremacist notions and even at times with each other to define what characteristics entitle a person to be considered "authentically" black.

The more personal question for me, however, was "Why was *I* not perceived as being "authentically" black by my peers?"

Martin Favor, in *Authentic Blackness* (1999), states that "the definition of blackness is constantly being invented, policed, transgressed, and contested" (2), and that "the perceived necessity to delineate ideologically and aesthetically that which is most 'real' about African American experiences has been a driving force behind social and artistic movements" (3); 20th century examples are The Harlem Renaissance, The Civil Rights Movement, and The Black (Power) Arts Movement. But these movements gave differing answers to the questions surrounding definitions of blackness, each responding to different sets of circumstances.

So, is "authentic" blackness defined by socio-economic class? I do believe that African Americans of higher socio-economic class gain access to the American mainstream more readily, living, as not a few of them tend to, in predominantly white suburbs and attending predominantly white educational institutions. Because of these circumstances, they are more exposed to and thereby more influenced by lifestyles and values that are associated with being "white," though they may be regarded as being influenced by class more than by ethnicity. Be that as it may, as a result of living middle class lives, economically better-off African Americans are seen as moving away from lifestyles and values that are considered characteristically "black," and, therefore, they are classified as less "authentically" black. Even so, it has been well documented in recent years that African American children, regardless of socio-economic class, continue to struggle with standardized tests. It seems that money cannot solve some problems that still hinder African-American advancement, not the least of them being the "double-consciousness" defined by W.E.B. Du Bois, the sense of always being looked at by white America.

Or, is authenticity defined by physical traits like skin color and hair texture? In the past, the "one-drop rule," rooted in U.S. slavery legislation, meant that anyone who had any African-American relative (usually the mother) was considered black, whether he or she had a fair or ebony complexion. There was no such thing as bi- or multi-racial; there was just black or white. However, more categories do exist today, enabling bi- and multi-racial persons like Tiger Woods to claim all of their ethnic ancestries and identities and not a black identity exclusively. (However, one must note the derisive reaction Tiger Woods received for claiming to be a "Cablinasian," especially from some African American commentators.) Yet there are other bi- and multi-racial persons such as Halle Berry who embrace a black-only identity because they feel more "culturally" connected to the black community . It seems that defining blackness is becoming more, not less, complicated in the 21st century.

For most African-American academics, intellectuals, and activists, "authentic" blackness is a self-identification, a commitment to the advancement of black people, and an acknowledgement of a shared history with other African Americans. One of the reasons I was asked to write this essay on black authenticity is because I do self-identify as an African-American. My grandparents were sharecroppers in eastern North Carolina during the early part of the twentieth century, and my parents grew up in the segregated south during the 1930s-1950s. My mother was the first in her family of 10 to graduate from college. My father, an only child, was also the first in his family to become a college graduate. Although I grew up in the post-Civil Rights South and may have never lived the "authentic" black experience, I am only one generation away from segregation. I was raised in a Southern, Christian, black, middle-class household. Those are quite a few adjectives, but each shaped my individual identity and to a certain extent complicated my ethnic group identity.

My personal struggle with "authentic" blackness began in the fifth grade when I was cornered by four "authentically" black girls after a gym class. They pushed me around and goaded me to fight because I "talked white" and tried to "act white." That moment changed my adolescent life, and not for the better. Only a year before, I was not attacked for my speech or behavior. Why fifth grade? I believe it is a time when kids begin learning to associate certain behaviors and characteristics with certain groups; this is a way for kids to find a social place to belong. We start to see the preppies, the jocks, the nerds, and other cliques or social groupings on the school playgrounds.

Why were the girls chastising me, trying to bring me in line with the official ethnic aesthetics? One way to think about it, the easy way, the one I only half-way believed, was that they were jealous of my perceived higher socio-economic status. For example, while most of the girls wore generic-brand clothes, I wore name brand clothing such as a *Members Only* jacket, *Jordace* jeans, and *Treton* sneakers. These articles of clothing were worn primarily by white kids in our school; they wore brands that were highly advertised on television. I was following the mainstream popular trends, but it became obvious that I was hooking on to the wrong ones.

I also spoke standard English–all the time. I did not use code-switching, a method of survival used by many African-Americans to navigate social interactions with whites or other African Americans. Standard English was what we spoke in my home. Although I was well aware of black English and heard it used at church and by some family members, it was generally not spoken in my family and social circles unless someone wanted to emphasize a particular sentiment. My lack of code-switching caused me a great deal of torment. I was made fun of when I raised my hand and answered a question from the teacher. This caused me to become quiet and less assertive in the classroom. It seemed to me that I was seen as being "white" because I wanted to make good grades. However, some of the kids taunting me made good grades, too, particularly in math. The problem was that I was open about my desire to please the teacher and to succeed academically. In any case, apparently I was not acting like an "authentic" black person.

Additionally, my family lived in a predominantly white neighborhood. Most of my close friends were white until we reached puberty, the age when people start dating. My mother warned me about this period of time and prepared me for it. I began to make more black friends and eventually lessened my contact with the white ones. Nonetheless, something had to be wrong with me. I had thought I had an automatic pass since my complexion identified me with blackness. I soon realized that, at least in the eyes of my black peers, this was not the case. Ultimately, I became unsure of myself, my thoughts and opinions. The perceptions of others dominated my perception of myself. What was worst for me was that, unlike with Du Boisian double-consciousness, in which the frustration derives from black-white interactions, my experience with my peers caused an intra-racial alienation. Inter-racial double-consciousness was a general part of black life that I had learned to expect and to counter. This intra-racial alienation actually wounded me more deeply because I did indeed feel rejected by my peers.

In a phrase, my peers thought I was "faking the funk." My skin was black, but my behavior was not, or at least not black enough. I am playing off the term "funkiness" in Toni Morrison's *The Bluest Eye* (1970), in which the term can be considered a synonym for "authentic" blackness. The character Geraldine, an educated, middle-class black woman, from the South, no less, is taught in white-subsidized, black institutions of higher education to embrace Western cultural and social aesthetics. Morrison writes,

> they [Geraldine and other women like her] learn ... how to behave. The careful development of thrift, patience, high morals, and good manners.In short, how to get rid of the funkiness.The dreadful funkiness of passion, the funkiness of nature, the funkiness of the wide range of human emotions. (83)

In fact, Geraldine does not fake funkiness/blackness; she hates it and seeks to eliminate it from her surroundings (her home and son, Junior, Pecola) and in herself (she displays a lack of passion for life and lack of compassion for others.) She is portrayed as sexually repressed, emotionally detached (except from her cat), and cold. When I read the novel for the first time, it was clear to me from Morrison's depiction that Geraldine was not "authentically" black and was a villain.

I have to acknowledge that a little Geraldine was present in my own psyche. As the novel does with regard to Geraldine, I blamed white racism for creating this dichotomy within me. Though my parents instilled in me a strong sense of self and pride in my ethnic background, I also lived in a world dominated by a white supremacy mentality that perpetuates its aesthetics thought media, celebrating white attributes and traits while vilifying or marginalizing black ones. I did indeed desire to have hair that blew in the wind. I had been manipulated, but I wasn't alone. Whoopie Goldberg poignantly satirized the issue in her "Little Girl with Blonde Hair" monologue in her critically-acclaimed Broadway show *The Spook Show* (1982). Though I definitely didn't think that "white is right," I did desire to possess attributes that were associated with whiteness.

As I grow older, however, I began to think that the definition of "authentic" blackness is, in the end, based not on self-perception but on the perception of others. The dictionary definition of "authentic" is that something "is in fact as represented; genuine; real," which suggests a subjective judgment call by some, or any, "Other." For example, after attending an academic conference at Oxford University in September of 2006, I had an experience at Heathrow International Airport that illuminates this aspect of "authentic" blackness. Because of a recent terrorist threat, there was a high security alert. During the conference, I learned from another African American presenter that all African passengers were being overtly and more thoroughly screened by British immigration officers; in fact, a fellow panelist from Nigeria never arrived at the conference, having been detained at the airport and not allowed into the country.

After presenting my paper, I had to rush to the airport in order to make my evening flight and did not have an opportunity to change into more informal clothing. I later discovered that my formal attire also identified me as a possible threat. As I walked through the security line, I could tell that one of the security men had identified me as a person who would need additional screening. Sure enough, I was physically patted down after walking through a metal detector. After clearing another line of security and after another immigration officer checked my passport, I sat to wait for my flight. Immediately, the same immigration officer sat next to me and struck up a "casual" conversation because he was on his break.

It soon became clear that our "casual" conversation was a way to determine my ethnic/national background (He wanted more of an explanation when I identified myself as an *African*-American) and to ascertain my political allegiances and my knowledge of and attitudes towards current British and American foreign policies in the Islamic world. As we talked, I noticed that he was obviously analyzing the texture of my hair. At the end of the conversation, we shook hands and parted; I had passed the test and would not be detained. Needless to say, I was thrilled when I set foot on American soil, but it was a truly enlightening encounter: British security officers not only perceived me as black but as so "authentically" black that they thought I was from the motherland, Africa. Their perceptions of me, of my blackness,

directed their behavior towards me.   They didn't care about my socio-
economic status.   They didn't care whether I spoke Standard English or
Ebonics.   I was identified as a dark foreigner and a possible threat to their
national security primarily because of my physical appearance; my American
passport was not enough to allay their suspicions.   I am grateful for this
experience because I have learned from my brief travels that we can analyze
and theorize "authentic blackness" in academic circles, but in actuality, what
many black people know and experience is that globally, black is undoubtedly
black.

Even so, African-Americans have fought long and hard for the right to
self-determination as a group, to counter experiences such as the one I had at
Heathrow, experiences that remind one that the meaning of blackness is still
often decided by people who are not black--and the collective black struggle for
self-definition must be commended and continued.   However, I do believe
that African-Americans are also entitled to develop individual identities that
are not considered in conflict with their ethnic group identity but as a
legitimate part of it.   I know that I acknowledge a shared history with other
African Americans.   I know that I desire and work for the advancement of
black people.   In the end, I'm "authentic" enough for some and probably still
not "authentic" enough for others.   But I now know that I'm black enough for
me.

Works Cited

Du Bois, W.E.B. *The Souls of Black Folk.* 1903. New York: Bantam Books, 1989.

Favor, J. Martin.*Authentic Blackness: The Folk in the New Negro Renaissance.* Durham, NC: Duke
    UP, 1999.

Morrison, Toni. *The Bluest Eye.* 1970. New York: Plume, 1994.

Rountree, Wendy Alexia. *Lost Soul.* Baltimore: PublishAmerica, 2003.

Brown Boy Blues...inna Jamaica

Gregory Stephens

"No one screams about Babylon more than a brown boy."

(Participant in an on-line discussion about Damian Marley, Bob Marley, and

the "brown boy" phenomenon of Jamaican culture and politricks).

Intro

My father used to say: "I wrote all my books about child-rearing before having children." I wrote all of my books and essays about Jamaican music and culture before living in Jamaica. Since moving to Jamaica in the wake of Ivan the Terrible in 2004, I have mostly maintained a public silence about Jamaican culture. I knew before accepting a three-year position at the University of West Indies-Mona that I could not pretend to "teach" Jamaicans anything about their culture, nor challenge their often blinkered preconceptions about "race" and gender. My experience in Jamaica has strengthened my impression that rational discussions about race and gender in Jamaica are at best difficult for Jamaicans, much less for outsiders.

There was a disjuncture between Jamaicans and myself from the moment of my arrival. Many of them were intent on getting into the U.S., literally or figuratively. I had for a couple of decades been distancing myself from my homeland, at first culturally, then physically. So it sometimes felt like we were hailing each other from two ships sailing in opposite directions. Still, we share many references. It is easy for me to feel a sense of cultural kinship with Jamaicans, although few yardies, seeing me as a "white man," can imagine why I would claim to have anything in common with them. Both perspectives are true. We share a Biblical heritage, and a great love for the whole sweep of "black" popular music. But we have little common understanding about what America is, because: 1) Jamaicans suffer from a delusion that they don't live in the Americas, and 2) Jamaicans see the world not only in black and white, but black-vs.-white. This produces collective myopia. Much of what is "authentic" about Jamaican culture is disappearing with astounding speed, which sometimes produces a reactionary affirmation of racial community—the supposedly authentic touchstone from which to resist "the white man's country."[1]

When I was asked for a *polemical* essay for a book about "black authenticity," the timing was right: with my departure from Jamaica nearing, I felt my tongue loosen. But hear me now: I must stress that my critique of Jamaican racialism, however ferocious it may sometimes seem to be, emerges from a genuine affection for Jamaican people, and a love for their heritage. But it also is driven by a disenchantment with the consumerist direction that contemporary Jamaica has taken, and by a dismay with a particularly virulent form of Jamaican binary racialism.

For most of my sojourn here, rather than trying to challenge Jamaican materialism or racialism directly, I have approached these subjects through the back door. By directing my critique towards the U.S, I was able to get my students nodding, and beginning to recognize just how much they really had in common with U.S. commercial culture. And by focusing my discussions of "race" and ethnicity primarily on Latin American models, and throwing some African American dissidents such as Ralph Ellison into the mix, I was able to take my Jamaican students into places they freely confessed they had never faintly imagined before.

So approaching these hot-button issues via Latin American cultures and multi-ethnic American literature, I have mostly been able to say what I please, *in the classroom*. This includes telling my Jamaican students that their country is now an offshore colony of the U.S.–which they admit is true. I also tell them that their "mental slavery" nowadays has everything to do with their uncritical, full-time consumption of United States commercial culture, mostly via cable TV.

After exploring concepts of "multicentric" identity in *nuestra América* and elsewhere,[2] they are able to think about diversity in their own families (personal, national, regional, and outernational), in a way that would be impossible if we only used Jamaica or the U.S. as a point of reference, which Jamaicans will almost inevitably reduce to a black-white binary. Jamaicans tend to feel morally superior to the United States, and in an instant can launch condemnations of United States racism or imperialism. But I have found that it is relatively easy to steer debate towards the implications of the U.S.-model consumer culture that Jamaicans are enthusiastically embracing. Half of Kingston residents seem to drive an S.U.V.[3] Hence, U.S. military occupations of oil-rich countries serves to protect the interests of most Jamaicans as well.

But dialogue with some colleagues was a different matter. UWI-Mona is an authoritarian ex-plantation. In his essay "Why I Love and Leave Jamaica" Roger Mais famously called UWI "a moated tower of mediocrity [that] has acquired such a body of mediocre opinion about itself that *it is useless to try to make a dent in its smugness.*" In an oft-cited report, Garth Baker painted UWI as a parasitic "suffocating bureaucracy" which is "defensive and *immune from criticism.*"[4] In the early 21st century, a culture of criticism hardly exists in this institution. I learned early on not to take defensiveness and ignorance personally: stories abounded about foreigners who had been savaged for daring to question conventional wisdom. Still, I found it instructive that when some colleagues publicly tried to push me towards the exit, they focused obsessively on my use of materials from Latin America. For those accustomed to seeing the world in black-vs.-white, the kinds of voices being heard by a majority in the Americas—45 million Latinos in the U.S. and another 400 million or so Spanish-speaking Latin Americans—were a grave threat because they so consistently challenge a black-white binary. In particular, Latin Americans in nearby places like Venezuela, Panama, and Puerto Rico often seemed to contradict, by the way they lived, many of the tenets of Jamaica's theology of black victimization.

So as I began to plan for life after Jamaica, I began to think about publicly voicing certain "unspeakable truths" which, however, have been the subject of frequent private conversations between friends and colleagues here. I knew that the time had come to break my silence and attempt a summing up of what I have learned about Jamaica, and its relation to the U.S., to Latin America, and to broader currents of Afro-diasporic thought.

Jamaica is an island in transition: it is still deeply shaped by its former colonial relation to Great Britain, but moving towards almost complete identification with the U.S.—and a profound isolation from the mostly Spanish-speaking countries that surround it. As a symbol of this reorientation, construction of the U.S. Embassy in Liguanea aroused some resentment. When this complex finally opened in late 2006, throngs of Jamaicans crowded outside, seeking emigration papers. As I passed on the bus, riders observed this scene and kissed their teeth disdainfully. Clearly this is not how Jamaicans would like to see themselves, and be seen. But it's a lot closer to reality than the "One Love" myth that has become Jamaica's best-known mask abroad.[5]

Browns as "Others" and as Culture Heroes

I want to discuss an obsession with the "white other" in Jamaican culture in relation to two broader phenomena: primarily Jamaica's theology of *black victimization* (as I call their "black authenticity" discourse), but also in reference to *mestizaje* (mixed-ethnicity culture). (A related idea in a somewhat different register, the discourse on Creole cultures, appears in the Franco- and Anglo-Caribbean).[6]The notion of *mestizaje* as the norm in Latin America has generated its own sometimes over-heated polemic, but I present *mestizaje* (though not uncritically) as an alternative to Jamaica's black-white binary.

Two aspects of Jamaica's obsession with a non-"black" other are my primary concern: A) A compulsive othering of "brownness" in Jamaica, which is really a blues about the absence of the often proclaimed but seldom experienced racial authenticity; B) a fixation on "white appropriation of black culture," resulting in a rejection of ideas crucial to the "second emancipation,"[7] including the notion of "One Love," or "One Blood," variants of which are celebrated throughout "nuestra América" as an essential component of mestizaje.

The othering of "brown peoples" is a widespread phenomenon in Jamaican culture. Note the evolution of the Rasta saying, "Death to white oppressors," to "Death to white and brown oppressors." Those who were visibly mixed or brown, historically a small slice of Jamaica society, were often viewed as a sort of "middle-man" between the white-man-as-oppressor, and the black-man-as-victim. Yet there is also a lengthy history of brown people who fought for "black liberation," a legacy so pronounced in Jamaica politics and popular culture that one can speak of an archetypal "brown redeemer."[8]

One could start with George William Gordon, a mulatto who coauthored the 1865 Morant Bay Rebellion, as Paul Bogle's sponsor. He paid for his support of black liberation with his life, as did Bogle. Gordon and Bogle are among seven "Jamaican National Heroes" who "dared to challenge the institution of colonialism."[9] But while Bogle is ritually celebrated, Gordon is all but forgotten. It is not comfortable for Jamaicans to think about the pervasive role that "white" and "brown" people have played not only in their enslavement, but in their liberation, and in the translation, transmission and international consumption of their remarkable culture. One could point to other brown men who were portrayed as political "redeemers," among them Alexander Bustamante, who used anti-white rhetoric to mobilize his black followers in the 1930s, and Prime Minister Michael Manley, who was successful for a time in using the symbols of black nationalism and Rastafari to mobilize disenfranchised Jamaicans (from 1972-1980).[10]

There is an ongoing, often acrimonious debate about the role that skin color had in the success of Bob Marley, Jamaica's best-known "brown culture hero." There is considerable resentment about "one love" being held up by foreigners (which Jamaicans mostly style as "the white man") as emblematic of Jamaica's "black" culture of resistance. Some of this resentment gets transferred to Bob's son Damian, even more fair-skinned than his dad, and to other "brown" stars such as Sean Paul, who are accused of co-opting the "authentic" Jamaican music of the black masses. Never mind that the spirit of resistance in Jamaica today is almost non-existent. That too is surely something for which Europeans and "white" Americans can be blamed: if they hadn't embraced songs like "One Love" as the "song of the millennium," then radical songs like "War" would presumably be getting attention, and Jamaicans would be following its liberatory message, rather than donning the "One Love/ No Problem Mon" mask which they employ to rake in so many tourist dollars.

The memory of racial conflict is an "echo in the bone" which cannot be wiped away so easily.[11] My students tell me that they learn to hate white people at UWI. I cross paths with colleagues who teach the theology of black victimization, often paired with a belief in black supremacy, based in a view of people of European descent that has evolved little from Malcom X's "white man is the devil" phase. I hear their opinions coming out of the mouths of my students. Although most Jamaicans treat me with respect as family man, there are still plenty of indications of just what "whiteness" represents in Jamaica. This ranges from the general refusal of Jamaicans to buy white eggs, to the homeless Rasta I pass on my bicycle on Mona Road, who curses me: "Die white man!"

At least this dread says what is on his mind. His attitude is not so far from some grassroots attitudes in either the U.S. or Jamaica, as evidenced by Kamau Kambon's 2005 call on C-SPAN "to exterminate White people off the face of the planet."[12] More typically, Jamaicans who conserve milder variations of this hostility exhibit a semi-conscious impulse to engage in guerrilla warfare against "the white man." The resulting groupthink leads to attacks against those guilty of sins of commission (criticizing the "black masses"; too friendly to whites), or omission (insufficiently enthusiastic in the defense of black people, i.e., Garvey's "racial empire"). Much of this residual hostility gets displaced onto browns.

The opening quote of this essay comes from Wayne Marshall's blog. One of his Jamaican students at Brown University wrote a screed on the supposed threat of "brown boys." She looks at Damian Marley and sees "the image of every brown boy who went to Hillel."[13] One gets the sense that this supposed "brown boy domain" is seen as offensive, or a threat, precisely because it has achieved a certain critical mass. So Marshall's Brown student (the university, not the color) talks about Damian "being backed by...a whole slew of supportive brown boys." And she tries to place this in a broader, historical context, with brown boys all over Jamaica claiming that Bob Marley is their father. Her conclusion is polemical, but with an undeniable kernel of truth: "Bob was a brown boy. The way he spoke, the frass weede look on his face, the constant righteous terminology, the anger towards the government, all typical of a brown boy."[14]

Did Bob Marley "scream" about Babylon because he was a brown boy? That would be too reductive. But still, "experience teaches wisdom." I've seen far too many brown youths loudly proclaiming their solidarity with black people to discount this student's typology. My colleague Matty Dread (a lecturer at UWI) and I have discussed this often, and are in agreement that brown or "biracial" people indeed often try to be the most radical. They seem to share a passion to prove their creds re: the perennial question, "Are you black enough?" I've seen that in the U.S. for decades now; Matty confirms the depth of the same phenomenon in Jamaica.

The commercial success of Damian Marley and Sean Paul (they chart in R&B and Rap, not just dancehall) brought a lot of tensions into the open. Take, for example, a discussion about the "white-pot head appropriation of Bob Marley" on *Breath of Life*, a website run by Kalamu ya Salaam and his son Mtume ya Salaam, and advertised as "a conversation about black music": "I grew up thinking of Bob Marley as a black revolutionary," writes Mtume. But after going to a predominantly Anglo high school in New Orleans, and working four years at Tower Records in the French Quarter, Mtume "learned that Bob Marley wasn't a black revolutionary after all. In actuality, Bob was part of an (un)holy trinity [along with Che Guevara and Jimi Hendrix] of wild-eyed, long-haired, brown-skinned, pot-smoking dudes whose chief function seemed to be giving white hippie wanna-be's something to put on the front of their T-shirts."[15] Never mind that Che smoked cigars rather than spliffs and was fair-skinned. The point was that these "black revolutionaries" had been devalued because they had been embraced by too many ignorant white people. "Why is it that a white embrace of a non-white other so often ends up being an appropriation?" Kalamu asked after a heated exchange with a reader.

A dismissal of Bob Marley had become reflexive for many in his generation, Mtume noted. For one friend, "the dominant image of Marley is holding a spliff looking down from a white pothead's dormroom." Thus, the revolutionary power of the icon has been defused for many in the African diaspora. "We don't want to be associated with the masses of silly white people who listen to them," as a reader Rosalind observed. But like many Afrocentrists in this domain, she believed that "We have the power to take them back and place them in their rightful positions within Black culture."

Reclaiming "Black Culture"

In his book *Against Race*, Paul Gilroy suggests that the "militaristic, and essentialist theories of racial difference that are currently so popular [are] symptoms of *a loss of certainty around 'race'*." Many racial romantics, or "squeamish insiderist" critics, in Gilroy's words, "do not want to face the extent to which, in a global market for these seductive products, white consumers currently support this black culture."[16] Gilroy is following scientific consensus that "race has no biological justification."[17]

Rather than trying to come to terms with the implications of the world's remarkable embrace of Jamaican music, most of the people in positions of authority whom I have heard here in Kingston are busy trying to launch a crusade to "take back" Jamaica music from foreigners, especially "white people," whom they feel have co-opted it. A proposal for a "Global Reggae" conference circulated at UWI by Carolyn Cooper, director of the International Reggae Studies Center, observes with dismay that "Most of the books on reggae have been written by non-Jamaicans." It warns of the danger of "giv[ing] away the intellectual property that is our heritage." It criticizes foreigners who are writing "a lot of nonsense," and proposes to take back scholarship about reggae from those who have "appropriated" reggae in order to "fashion it in their own image."[18]

This follows a broader stream of thinking in diasporic thought, mostly in the United States and the Anglo-Caribbean. Expressing a thoroughly mainstream take on culture as a racial property, Pulitzer Prize-winning playwright August Wilson once wrote that black culture is "the property and possession of black people." He was lobbying for a black director for his play *Fences* and argued that "White directors are not qualified for the job." This rhetorical gesture lived on as a statement of the theological nature of many African American and Afro-Caribbean attitudes about "race."[19] But the film was never made. Wilson himself is, in Jamaican terms, a brown man, or biracial: the son of a German father and an African American mother. He grew up in Anglo-dominant suburbs. So his search for "authentic" black culture fits within the typology outlined above: the more uncertainty there is about racial boundaries, the shriller the calls for racial solidarity. Brown boys (and men) are both indexes of this uncertainty, and often the most determined advocates of racial authenticity.

In Jamaica, there can be no more powerful symbol of supposedly authentic "blackness" than Marcus Garvey. His perceived racial authenticity is linked to his valorization of (largely fictional) African cultures, to his ferocious opposition to race-mixing, and to his descriptions of all "white" peoples as the enemy of "the African race." In Jamaica, Garvey's legacy has been mostly obscured by a militant sort of hagiography. The unwillingness to examine who Garvey actually was, what he really said, and how he lived, was depressingly evident at the Kingston premiere of the PBS documentary "Marcus Garvey: Look For Me in the Whirlwind" in February, 2001.[20] During a panel discussion, Garvey's son Julian Garvey accused the director Stanley Nelson of "character lynching." The word lynching describes the mood of the Kingston audience in relation to the (African American) writers and producers who were on hand that night. They audience shouted down Nelson when he argued (accurately, in my opinion) that "the reality of Garvey is much more important than the myth." The audience heckled Marcia Smith, who wrote the script for the documentary, when she argued that "African people [should] be prepared to say what is true about our heroes." And the audience seems to have been particularly vicious in its treatment of Robert Hill, a Jamaican-born Garvey scholar at UCLA who was a consultant for the film.[21] A colleague of mine who witnessed this told me that Hill was so distraught that he cried afterwards. Hill seems to have been singled out for spite because he is a brown man. But a column about the film by Cecil Gutzmore, a black victimologist at UWI-Mona, made clear that nationality was a bigger issue than skin color for the film. Their worst sin was that they were citizens of the United States, and that they had centered on an effort to understand Garvey's experience in the U.S. "Any attempt" to discuss Garvey "in terms of the U.S. experience" was "dangerously partial," Gutzmore wrote.[22]

Gutzmore made disparaging comments about the participation of a "white female scholar," and sneered at the "multi-racial funders/audience" of the film. But the biggest problem was really that hagiography was incompatible with standards of scholarship and documentary film-making in the United States. Gutzmore speaks from the perspective of faith, rather than critical objectivity, when he describes Garvey as "the greatest global African philosopher-activist...of all time." Because that is in fact a blind faith, it leads not only to public condemnations, but as Garvey had advocated, "whispering campaigns" against those who question some facets of the faith, or who espouse its dogma with insufficient fervour.

I was already well aware of the explosive nature of this terrain long before I wrote a book chapter on Bob Marley that began with a critical re-examination of Garvey's attitudes about race, following the trail blazed by scholars like Robert Hill. I had already had confrontations with black nationalists and white-haters in Austin, Texas in the late 1980s and Berkeley, California in the early 1990s. These included both physical and rhetorical assaults against me. So I was prepared for the reception I received when I went on book tour for *On Racial Frontiers* in 1999 and encountered a small but vocal minority in my audience who were angry that I had said anything critical about Garvey, or that I had focused on Bob Marley's biraciality.

After giving a talk about Garvey's concept of a "second emancipation" to a conference of Pan-Africanists in 2001, I experienced a more or less terminal case of "race fatigue" and shifted into a primary concentration on Latin American studies.[23] Still, when I was hired to teach at UWI-Mona in 2004, it was partly on the strength of my various works about race and gender in Jamaican music, and my scholarship about Bob Marley in particular.[24] So when I was asked to give a public lecture during my first year, and this lecture fell during observations of Marley's 60th earthday, I had a dilemma on my hands. I knew that if African Americans could not say anything to Jamaicans about Garvey, then for me as an Anglo to attempt it would be something akin to a suicidal impulse. But on reflection, I decided that if I did not have the courage to present my research to Jamaicans while in Jamaica, then I would not be able to face myself in the mirror. So against my better judgement, I gave a lecture titled "A 'Second Emancipation' Transfigured? Reflections on Bob Marley at 60." A version of this talk, in essay form, was published on *Jahworks*.[25]

The core of my message was that Garvey's "second emancipation" from mental slavery was a timely, and timeless idea, but that Garvey's own pronounced racialism had been a stumbling block. It was Bob Marley and the Rastas who had actually pointed the way past or around this stumbling block, the mental slavery of racialism—"the insidious confusion of race with culture," as Ralph Ellison wrote.[26]They charted this emancipatory path via a concept of transracialism rooted in a Biblical philosophy of One Blood.

To make visible the permeable boundaries of this international community that listens to, has been influenced by, and often now are co-creators of Jamaican-inspired music, I made two main points. The first is that most Jamaican-inspired music (among which I would include reggae, dancehall, and dub) is not made in Jamaica. The vast majority is made abroad—in Miami, Los Angeles, New York, Toronto, London, Paris, Germany, and Japan, just to name a few thriving centers of both production and consumption.[27] This is common knowledge to anyone with a rudimentary knowledge of international reggae music, but seemed counter-intuitive, or even heretical, to some of my Jamaican colleagues (although not to their children).

My second argument was to assert my own place in this culture—not to center on myself, but to emphasize that Europeans and other non-Jamaicans had a long stake in this culture. I did this by focusing on Bob Marley's decentering of race, in his comments about his own brownness ("I'm not on the black man or the white man's side"), his references to Biblical notions of non-racial community ("One Blood" / "we are neither Jew nor Gentile, male nor female, slave nor free, for we are all one..."),[28] and above all, by stressing how Bob Marley grounded his fusion of African pride and trans- (if not post-) racialism in Haile Selassie's own words: "Until the color of a man's skin is of no more importance than the color of his eyes, and until equal rights are guaranteed to all without regard to race, there will always be war."

To further the point about the illogic of making "race"/skin color the primary criterion of authenticity--or of admissibility to Jamaican-inspired culture--I pointed out that my own children were the same skin color as Bob Marley. I made this point advisedly: I knew through experience that many in my audience of African diasporians would be unable to separate the messenger from the message. Rather than bury my head in the sand and pretend that my Jamaican audience did not see me first, foremost, and always as a "white man," and therefore as an outsider, and indeed to some degree as an enemy, I decided this time around to confront the issue head-on.

By calling attention to the biraciality of my own children, I infuriated many Jamaicans in the audience, including several colleagues in my own department, who never forgave me. How dare I insinuate some commonality between my family and Bob Marley? The strength of their reactions proved to me the root psycho-social issue: kinship. If they were to concede that there was no "racial" difference between my children and Bob Marley, then that meant, on some level, that they would also have to recognize some form of kinship with these children's father. And that is of course impossible for people who are so heavily invested in a definition of themselves as a people who have been victimized by, and permanently scarred by, "the white man."

The blind spots into which such racialized definitions of community can lead people were made clear in my colleague Carolyn Cooper's comments to the audience, following my speech. "I've always had problems with that part of Selassie's speech in 'War'," Cooper said. Many Jamaicans had been citing "War" as an example of the radical Bob that the global community had supposedly whitewashed. But when it became clear that "War" itself lead to a sort of non-racialism that Bob Marley himself had endorsed, well then, Selassie's words themselves had to be repudiated. Which of course means that when it comes to the study of Marley, or Rasta, or Selassie, or Garvey, or the Bible, there is a whole lot of cherry picking going on.

Warring Against "One Love"

Leading up to, during, and following celebrations of the 60th anniversary of Bob Marley's birth in 2005, I noticed a particularly virulent mood in the Jamaican public sphere. This centered on a blind opposition to the version of Bob Marley that the global public endorsed, and a re-assertion of a xenophobic definition of racial community. Melville Cooke, a race-baiting columnist for the *Jamaica Gleaner*, set the tone when he declared that he "despised" Marley's song "One Love." "This idea of loving everyone on an equal footing," wrote Cook, "may be all right for other races," but "it is a dangerous fantasy for black people."[29] And what Marley classic did Cooke propose as an anthem of black unity, of Jamaican resistance to the international white-washing of Marley? Why, "War," of course...

Examples of such blind resistance, filtered through a binary racialism, have been easy to find. Dancehall artist Bounty Killer went on a rant on JTV (Jamaican Television) about why black artists were not made into icons. Marley was made an icon "beca' him the white man son," Bounty Killer claimed, buut not the people's choice, like someone like Bogle, "beca' Bogle don come from uptown" (i.e., he's a downtown black artist, not one of those uptown brown artists that the mass media supposedly favors).[30] Another *Gleaner* columnist, Kevin O'Brien Chang, jumped on the bandwagon, declaring that he was so sick of "One Love" that he switched stations whenever it came on the radio. And even as a Chinese Jamaican, he felt obligated to endorse the notion that "Marley's racial mixture [has] a lot to do with his popularity [and] makes him an ideal global icon."[31]

There is some truth to Chang's question, which I've heard posed by numerous Jamaicans: "Is it merely coincidence that the three biggest selling Jamaican artists ever—Bob Marley, Shaggy, and Sean Paul—are all noticeably part white?" There is also a willful forgetfulness of darker vocalists like Shabba Ranks or Buju Banton who blew up globally. And there is a myopia resulting from the notion that anything favored by white people must be corrupted, and bad for black people ("white democracy," for example, according to Cooke). If you take this line of thinking to its logical conclusion, it means that Marley can no longer be an icon for people of the African diaspora precisely because of his European genes. Which leads us back to the sort of belief in racial purity once espoused by white supremacists.

Neither is this line of thinking a passing phenomenon. A year later Cooke was still proclaiming how much he despised "One Blood" and still focusing on white people in his supposed efforts to put black people first. Elites in Jamaica had only jumped on board Marley's Zion Train "because foreigners...[and especially] (gasp!) white people see him as important."[32] I have seen this blind opposition to everything embraced by "white people" in many different contexts. At the Annual Bob Marley Lecture at UWI in February 2006, I heard Federick Hickling describe the whole of Jamaican popular culture as a negation of "the European Delusion."[33] Indeed, Professor Hickling's generalizations about "the heart of the delusion," i.e., "All that I see is mine," were the most popular part of his lecture, and had students and professors alike rolling in the aisles. The racial myopia at the heart of this particular subculture became disturbingly apparent for me when I saw Dr. Hickling repeat this line of his Power Point presentation nine different times:

"White European

vs.

Black rest of the world."

No leader in this subculture is challenging the notion that everyone who is not European is black, that all Europeans are "white" or still suffer from delusions of racial superiority. Few are wrestling with the reality that this centering of Europeans is a perpetuation of mental slavery rather than a true emancipation. The Europeans are, after all, "only a tiny fraction of humanity, living mainly on that thickly populated peninsula of Asia which juts out into the Atlantic, and calling themselves 'cultured'," Swiss psychologist C.G. Jung once remarked.[34]

However, if one listens closely, there are still a few crazies around from the old days who gleefully poke holes in this over-inflated balloon of racial and national essentialism. In November 2005, Lee "Scratch" Perry, now legitimated by a Reggae Grammy, was asked on TVJ what he thought about Rita Marley's announced plan to rebury Bob in Ethiopia.

Perry—I think Rita Marley should first dig up her family and bury them in Cuba.

Q–But what about Bob being buried close to his father?

A—If he want to be buried close to his father them should bury him in

England.[35]

Still, whatever the apparent irrationality of this opposition to the celebration of Marley as the icon of One Love, there is a context that makes me somewhat sympathetic. And that is the "invasion" of Jamaica in the 2004-2005 period by Robert Roskind, a resident of Blowing Rock, North Carolina, who in 2001 had self-published a book called *Rasta Heart: A Journey Into One Love*. Books about the "discovery" by North Americans and Europeans of Rastafarianism and of Bob Marley's music are a sizeable genre. A few texts about Americans becoming involved with Rastas, or Maroons, even have a pronounced literary quality, as with *Book of Jamaica* by Russell Banks, or Michael Kuelker's ethno-biography, *Book of Memory: A Rastafari Testimony*.[36]

But I found Roskind's testimony, however well-intentioned, to be excruciatingly naïve, and indeed, often embarrassing. Having known plenty of people who idealized Rastafarians, I understand some of the psycho-social dynamics in play when someone like Roskind falls in love with Rastas, envisions them as saviors of the human race, and begins to undertake a sort of "reverse missionary" work. But the heights of Roskin's naiveté were symbolized for me in the scene where he takes a jambox onto a Negril Beach, puts on *Legend*, and begins testifying to Jamaicans about the gospel of "One Love." Beware of the recent convert!

Imagine my surprise, then, when I began seeing Roskind's name everywhere in Jamaica. Penning a letter or editorial for the *Gleaner*, still in full reverse-missionary mode.Putting on concerts all over the island. Sure enough, Roskind soon found co-sponsors for this missionary work in the Marley family and the Jamaican government, who together put on a 60th earthday tribute to Bob in New Kingston, which I attended. There was the portly Roskind on-stage, along with his wife and daughter, kind of a latter-day Ram Dass.

It had been hard for me to take seriously Roskind's reports about his various missions, like carrying One Love to the Havasupi Indians in Arizona's Grand Canyon. But Roskind's interests intersected with those of the Marley family and the Jamaican Tourist Board. The kind of idealized version of Jamaica they were marketing, I reflected, was not so different from the all-inclusive tourist resorts, from which tourists seldom ventured forth to see the "real Jamaica." Surely Roskind's "imagined community" was preferable to the hedonistic (or simply mindless) cultural tourism one can see in films like *Life and Debt* and *Rent a Rasta*. But I'm not convinced that it has anything more to do with the "real Jamaica" that I see every day in Kingston.[37]

So I could understand the resistance some Jamaicans felt towards do-gooders like Roskind coming to Jamaica and preaching to yardies about their moral obligation to live up the ideals of their world-famous, but seldom-practiced-at-home, native philosophy. It was a scenario, I suppose, something like a newly converted Christian Jew who begins reciting the Sermon on the Mount on a portable loudspeaker at the Western Wall in Jerusalem. Which is to say, the natives might view this as a provocation, an offensive sort of moral condescension. Still, the reaction of Jamaican elites reminded me of similar action-reaction cycles I had witnessed in the U.S. Well-meaning do-the-right-thing liberals came out so strongly against any support for post- racial thinking (the movement for multi-racial or "mixed" identity, for instance) that they ended up supporting a reified, essentialized black-white binary. But it is an article of faith for me that it is not enough to criticize what one believes is wrong or misguided: one must also present a more attractive alternative.

Repositioning "Brownness" within the Mestizo Mainstream

The Jamaican discourse about race in general, and brown-ness in particular, is over-determined. I came to the conclusion in the 1990s, and my experience in Jamaica has confirmed, that it is impossible to have a rational dialogue within the binary logic of a black-and-white, victim vs. oppressor worldview. It is necessary to open a middle ground, a third space, which, above all, means putting this Jamaican (and Afro-American) discourse on race into dialogue with the world that surrounds it, which is a predominantly Spanish-speaking world. This means beginning to grapple with the discourse on mestizaje, and multi-centered identity—or what is called, in broadest terms, mestizo (mixed) identity—which is the dominant, if not necessarily the normative, condition of Latin America. Hence it is the predominant condition of the Americas, in the inclusive sense. For the purposes of this essay, I will cite members of the African diaspora who themselves insist on decentering blackness, which is to say, understanding the African heritage as one of several components of identity and community.

In an interview on *Democracy Now*, Venezuelan President Hugo Chávez was asked to comment on being "the first Latin American president we know of who identifies as black and indigenous, [thus breaking] a long tradition of racism in the Americas." Chávez responded:

> When we were children, we were told that we have a motherland, and that motherland was Spain. However, we have discovered later, in our lives, that as a matter of fact, *we have several motherlands*. And one of the greatest motherlands of all is no doubt, Africa. We love Africa. And every day we are much more aware of the roots we have in Africa. Also, America is our motherland. Africa, America - and *Bolívar used to say that we are a new human race in Latin America, that we are not Europeans, or Africans, or North Americans. That we are a mixture of all of those races, and there is no doubt that Africa resounds with a pulse like a thousand drums and happiness and joy.*[38]

The worldview Chávez expresses is not that far, in some ways, from the ideology of One Blood, as sung by Junior Reid—a member of the Rasta sect the Bobo Shanti, who advocate black supremacy. But there is a certain totalizing tendency to the way in which most Christians, and Rastas, articulate a belief in One Blood. The Christian says, I am first and foremost a Christian, which I proclaim as the true path, but within that faith I recognize that there can be no racial prejudice, because all humans are children of the same God. The Rasta says, I am an African, and as such first among equals, but I recognize that all peoples came out of Africa, and hence by blood we come from the same root.

The worldview expressed by Chávez, which is quite mainstream in Latin America, is distinct. It does not react against Eurocentrism by embracing Afrocentrism-- it recognizes several motherlands. So Chávez claims four facets of his multi-centered identity: he is European, by way of Spain, but also African; these two motherlands meet in New World identities, as Venezuelan (the specific nationalism), and American, in the inclusive sense of nuestra América. To call oneself Venezuelan (which is both Caribbean and South American) or American is to claim at a minimum three ethnic heritages: African, European, and indigenous, or Native American.

When I show my Jamaican students a picture of Chávez, they don't see him as black, yet they also have a hard time calling him white. Some describe him as Spanish, in the sense of one of those borderline groups of Europeans who have clearly intermixed with Africans. But when I read them his hymn-like tribute to Africa as having "a pulse like a thousand drums and happiness and joy," then they recognize a certain kinship. This is a rhetorical tradition to which they have been exposed in several strands, including Negritude, black nationalism, and Rasta. The notion of being a "new human race," however, tends to trouble them: they want him to prioritize Africa, not put it on equal footing with European and American facets of the Afro-Caribbean world. This is similar to the disappointment often voiced at Marley's expressions of non-racialism. So I think it would be useful to begin linking Marley and other advocates of trans-racialism to their ideological kin in Latin America. Chávez and the Venezuelans, after all, are just a short boat ride from Trinidad, and hence very visibly linked to the Anglo-Caribbean world, which tends to be the only regional identity to which Jamaicans will admit.

The degree to which Africa is centered varies widely in Afro-Latino cultures. But in general, Latin Americans who embrace blackness or African-ness as a part of their identity and heritage do so within a multi-centered context. For instance, in her book *Getting Home Alive*, the Puerto Rican writer Aurora Levins Morales declares that "I am not African." But on the same page she qualifies this by affirming that "Africa is in me." This distinction is characteristic of *mestizaje*. In her poem "Child of Americas," Levins Morales "shows how the Africa in her is part of her American identity, not merely adding an element of Africa to America but redefining America, itself, to include Africa as much as it includes Europe," writes Suzanne Bost.[39]

The exploration of multi-centered definitions of identity and community has begun to make inroads among African American scholars in places like south Florida, where one is challenged to think about diasporic Africans in ways similar to long-standing Latin American models. Carol Boyce Davies sometimes expresses reservations about mestizo identity excluding those who self-identify as "'Afro-' or 'Black'."[40] But she has integrated several key concepts of contemporary writing on mestizaje and border cultures, notably a critique of the imperialistic implications of Afrocentric as well as Eurocentric versions of what she calls "unicentrism":

> I define Unicentricity as One-Centeredness, a logic which demands a single center ...from which all emanates... Unicentric approaches to culture, such as Afrocentrism and Eurocentrism, create oppressive systems ... Afrocentrism is limiting because it is defined by Eurocentrism. A multicultural approach must recognize diverse cultural currents within the African community and establish ties with all other ethnic communities.

Boyce Davies applies her critique of "the logic of core and periphery" specifically to the imperialistic presumptions which Afrocentrism and Eurocentrism share. "Unicentricity thus cannot imagine multiple and equal centers but instead has to operate with one constantly expanding center. Unicentricity...thus *inevitably can become a colonialist project.* The single center logic, then, is the basis of dominance and control, for it functions with other communities in terms of competition, hierarchy, and subordination."[41]

In the Afro-Caribbean one finds alternatives to racial unicentrism (racialism) above all in popular music. Take, for example, the song "Somos Cubanos" by Los Van Van, which starts with the days of slavery, but focuses on the process of inter-mixture, and its contemporary results. In this song bandleader Samuel Formel celebrates the Cuban version of brown-ness in which Africa is always in the mix:

> Llegó la raza Africana
>
> Y la mezclaron con la Española
>
> Nació la mulata criolla, La Cubana...
>
> Es una mezcla diferente con mucho sabor...
>
> Somos Cubanos, Español y Africanos...
>
> Somos la mezcla mas fina

La combinación mas dura.[42]

[The African race arrived and mixed with the Spaniards.

From this was born the Creole mulatto, the Cuban.

It's a different mixture with a rich flavor.

We are Cubans, Spanish and African...

We are the best mixture, the most kick-ass combination.]

This celebration of *mestizaje* is a counter-myth to binary racial mythologies, such as the myth of the tragic mulatto, or the marginalization of browns. One can scarcely over-emphasize how widespread this counter-discourse is in Latin America. Without endorsing such celebrations of *mestizaje*, one can note that they point to one way out of a dilemma. There are two forms of subservience, David Hackett Fischer wrote: "slavish imitation and obsessive refutation."[43] Either extreme is a form of mental slavery. Many Jamaicans are still enslaved by their simultaneous imitation of the worst of the North Americans, and their obsessive refutation of all things European. The incorporation of African-ness within a multi-centered identity does seem like a more flexible alternative to the black-white binary, to the pathologizing of browns, and to the myopia of an anti-"white" worldview. But this is still a "utopian horizon" which at present is having little influence on the particular sort of racial theology being critiqued in this essay.

Black Victimization as a Theology

In a critique of a "profit while they prophet...black cultural criticism," Norman Kelley has decried "the martyrdom hagiology that...defines African-American political culture." I am well aware that these, and my view of the faith in black victimization as having a theological status, are fighting words. But they accurately describe a history of black theology, in the works of James Cone, Albert Cleage, and others. A binary opposition between white oppression and black victimization is the cornerstone on which the whole superstructure of black theology is erected. A similar strain of thought is also entrenched in a long history of black nationalist and later Afrocentric thought. The tenor of outrage, denial, and accusation that words like "black victimization" often provoke have convinced many to let sleeping dogs lie. But they also indicate how unconscious and largely unexamined these presuppositions are.[44]

Real or presumed victims of violence or racism in diasporic African cultures are often converted into a species of martyrs, which inspire myths-to-live-by in the form of hagiographies, or the lives of saints. An obvious example is a rap star like Tupac, whose violent death seemed a self-fulfilling prophecy, and whose life came to be described in heroic dimensions, like political leaders who died violent deaths, such as Malcolm X or Martin Luther King Jr. This has become a very big business, both for those posing as victims and those who profit from the promotion of African American and Afro-Caribbean cultures along the lines of a victim-based identity. But in contemporary capitalist societies, one does not need to suffer or die for a moral code, or even to adhere to any belief other than self-glorification, or the accumulation of wealth, in order to qualify for martyrdom. One only needs a certain amount of melanin, and an inclination to present oneself as a black victim in a white man's world. "Who the cap fits, let them wear it."

Nowadays, it doesn't matter much if subjects of such "hagiologies" are wet dreams for black capitalism, selling their clothing lines in *Vibe* magazine, or in suburban malls; or if the authors of works on black victimhood are tenured Ivy League professors who are feted in the national media and in some cases even winning prestigious literary prizes while they go on proclaiming their own marginalization to the "white mainstream." Ralph Ellison saw this scheme in full effect back in the early 1960s: "what an easy con-game for ambitious, publicity-hungry Negroes this stance of 'militancy' has become!"[45]

It matters little because the belief in racial victimization is a religious faith, and indeed, a theology with its own highly developed dogma. Like any theology, it can survive all sorts of collisions with reality. The true believers in black victimization have been able to discount all sorts of counter-intuitive phenomena, such as Oprah Winfrey's shilling for American self-help commercialism; Condi Rice's career as George Dubya Bush's brain, and, yes, Bob Marley's ascent to immortality. The easiest way to deal with the seeming contradictions of the material, cultural, and political successes of so many Afro-diasporians is to reflexively proclaim that any diasporian who makes it is not really black. Which I can hear my students at UWI mouth any day of the week as an article of faith, re: Colin Powell, among other examples. So if it is true that Jamaicans copy the worst of the North Americans, then they have certainly taken the theology of black victimization to new, irrational heights.

I do not want my readers to misunderstand me. The history of slavery, as an institution, and the fight against slavery as an international movement, are topics I have studied in depth, have written about, and are themes that I continue to revisit in my classes, over and over again. I am always willing and eager to foreground a discussion of the history and legacy of slavery. A thorough study of the history leading up to the "first emancipation," of course, forms a necessary backdrop to any meaningful discussion of what a "second emancipation" would involve.

But what aspect of the slave experience is being memorialized? And for what purposes? A particular sort of evocation of the middle passage is a cornerstone of what is said, taught, and memorialized in Jamaica. Take for example a lecture by Clinton Hutton, Lecturer of political philosophy and culture at UWI-Mona, as he introduced Kamau Braithwaite, who had returned to Jamaica November 23, 2005 to read from his book of poetry, *Born to Slow Horses*. Hutton went to great length to describe what he clearly saw as a defining moment: slaves lying in their own shit on a slave ship. I heard nothing about who had sold them into slavery, or what happened to those slaves who survived when they reached the New World. It was rather the most degrading moment which drew Hutton's attention, and which he dwelt on in great detail, and with a fervor that I can only describe as religious.

Listening to Hutton, and observing his audience's rapt response, it seemed that his obsessive dwelling upon the moment of slaves-in-shit served a dual purpose. One, that the depths of this degradation was a means of measuring the heights to which the African diaspora had arisen. And two, that this was an original sin which could not be washed clean, and that clearly marked, for all time, an impassable moral boundary between African and European peoples.

The other defining feature in the public memory of slavery that I have noted is that the whole history of abolitionism has been virtually erased. It is not just that abolitionism, as a subject, has been repressed, or elided. I have also been struck by the degree to which the subject of abolitionism fails to arouse curiosity. Even more, the suggestion that abolitionism is one aspect of the experience of the African diaspora which should be taught is often met with incomprehension, or arouses opposition. I have discussed the topic with numerous colleagues, and I have begun to understand some of the reasons for this blind spot. Some reasons I have heard include: Abolitionism was a movement of Europeans, or white people, and hence fails to interest me. Abolitionism was something taught by the British to cover up the depths of their own involvement in the slave trade, whereas we as West Indians teach the true nature of slavery. Abolitionism was a very small movement that really never had an impact on the Caribbean.

I reasoned about these perspectives one day with a neighbor whose son attends the same elementary school as my son Samuel. When I described the tremendous popularity of Frederick Douglass in Europe, and argued that Afro-diasporic spokespersons in fact played a pivotal role in transforming this from a fringe subculture of radical Europeans, to an influential international movement, this colleague expressed a suspicious curiosity. His perspective was that the overthrow of slavery had been accomplished almost entirely by slave revolts. I argued that these were in fact two closely related phenomena. Slave revolts empowered the spokespersons who laid out moral, economic, and political reasons to mass publics in the U.S. and Europe as to why slavery could not be sustained, and must be opposed by all means necessary.

But efforts to argue that people of European and African descent were actually allies at various points in history almost inevitably meet with incomprehension, in my experience. "We often are able to see the schema triumphing over the experience of the individual," Freud once wrote.[46]The schema of blacks and whites as eternal enemies blinds many Afrotopians to "the true inter-relatedness of blackness and whiteness," as Ellison said. Colonial anti-miscegenation laws, for instance, were often passed and enforced with draconian measures precisely because race-mixing was so widely practiced.[47]

But I understand that the Jamaican experience, with the absentee Anglo slaveholder of huge plantations on an overwhelmingly "black" island, is very different from U.S. history, where most Europeans were not slave-holders, and where many "poor whites" and indentured servants lived side-by-side with African slaves, stealing together, sleeping together, and engaging in revolts together, very early in colonial days.[48] This threat of inter-racial cooperation was a specter that played an important role in the development of a philosophy of white supremacy.

In the Anglo-Caribbean, this history of international and interracial collaboration is seldom visible. What is most dominant in the public memory of resistance is the image of the heroic slave, rising up in isolation. One sees this image in statues, and hears it musically in songs throughout classic reggae. The heroic slave is a lonely slave, fighting against the system, with no help from anybody, and often indeed betrayed by his own black brother—especially by brown men—or by his black woman who has been sleeping with the white man. In this racial mythology, browns are the "weak link," making "the black race" susceptible to the corrupting influence of the white world. The purpose of this ahistorical collective memory, to the degree to which it is conscious, seems to be to instill a sense of race pride and solidarity, and to indoctrinate each generation of youths into the irredeemable nature of the white man and his domain—and by extension, to place brown peoples under suspicion, when it does not in fact elide brown-ness or style it white.

I hear variants of this perspective repeated with numbing regularity. My office window faces the Reggae Studies Center, and I often overhear the reasonings going on there. One day I heard a dread tell his companions with great conviction: "you mus know that the white man will always prevail!" I found that profoundly sad, not for what it said about the mythical construct of "the white man," but for what it revealed about the worldview of true believers in racial victimization. Moreover, it demonstrated a severe myopia in regards to a world in which self-defined "white men" and "black people" constitute a small minority of the human race.

I see that some features of this worldview are deeply ingrained in many of my students. When my Jamaican students speak of the United States, almost inevitably, the first thing that comes out of their mouth is the deeply rooted impression that America is, first and foremost, a deeply racist country where they will never be welcome. They may believe that, on some level, the streets are paved with gold, and feel assured that emigrating to the U.S. will let them make a fortune, or at least live in the lap of luxury to a degree to which would not be possible in the Caribbean. But they have no hopes of encountering any sort of community that transcends race. They imagine economic success as occurring in a social and political vacuum.

The irony is that some of these students go to the U.S. with affirmative action funding precisely because they are black. They tell me about their surprise as universities court them as a "prize catch." I watch the female Anglo exchange students throwing themselves at the Jamaican men, especially those with dreads. And I watch the young dreads playing this game with great skill. I know that they will be able to profit from their "victimization" (or their perceived exoticism) in the United States for many years. They will be able to "breed" many women, and if they choose, like most Jamaican men, not to be present for the rearing of their children, then they can always blame racism, or slavery, for their behavior.

These are not the sorts of stories that you will hear Jamaicans tell publicly about their experiences in "the white world." On October 18, 2005, I heard Garvey scholar Rupert Lewis "launch" Noel Erskine's *From Garvey to Marley*. He told a story about seeing European men who would approach Caribbean women and ask them their price (for sexual services). The audience shook their head and kissed their teeth knowingly—the message being, I presume, how little things had changed from the days of Garvey, and how little influence even Marley has had on how European peoples think about and treat black people. I have no doubt that there are some European men who still behave in such a manner. But this again struck me as another example of collective myopia, when I think about the multitude of long-term relationships between European men and Caribbean or African women, and indeed, the profound love affair for Caribbean cultures that one encounters across

Europe. But I know from experience that there is virtually no cure for this myopia, as long as one sees the world in black and white. People will find what they look for. And of course it's not hard to find historical justifications for reducing all relations between Europeans and Africans to a variant of rape, or sexual exploitation.

There are many instances in Caribbean literature of visitors being told, as the Englishman Robert Rutherford learns in *White Witch of Rosehall*, that morals are more lax in the Caribbean than in England.[49] And these lax morals are very much centered, in popular myth, as well as in the practice of the contemporary tourist trade, on interracial sexuality. Power relations may be uneven, but each side in the consensual relation offers and gains something from the interchange. Jamaicans are now selling that myth to the world. They have built an enormous industry catering to tourists who come seeking that looser morality. African Americans of course come seeking more or less the same thing (*How Stella Got Her Groove Back*). But this does little to change the binary opposition, in the Jamaican imagination, between the immoral whites, and the blacks who occupy a moral center. They achieve this moral center precisely through what Martin Luther King Jr. once called "the redemptive power of suffering." And so it is natural that, although this suffering has very real historical roots, it has also developed a mytho-poetical contemporary superstructure. Interraciality has become tainted, as Garvey so ardently desired, in a way that is reified and transmitted in a binary racial code across generations. The proof of black moral superiority is indivisible from a belief in inherent white racism, or inferiority. One cannot thrive without the other; hence, once sees variations of the "cave boy oppressor" myth that inspired much black nationalist rap in the early 1990s.[50] This Manichean schema is then projected onto the world, regardless of the real world's location in intermediary "third spaces" between the theoretical extremes of "black" and "white," which are of course ideological constructs which do not exist in phenotypical reality.

Theologian James Cone once wrote that if Jesus were to return to the U.S., he would have to come as a black man. In the 1980s, it seemed to me that, as with the revisioning of the Creator "through the spectacles of Ethiopia" in the 1930s, this was "psychologically correct."[51] Today, I know that the re-imagining of God as "black" by the Rastas was a historically necessary corrective. It was a step in an evolution away from the doctrine of white supremacy, which projected the false image of a blond-haired, blue-eyed Jesus. But as a final destination, it is "just another illusion" which does not further the quest for a "second emancipation."

I have come to believe that racial categories themselves, and the quest for messianic figures, are both cornerstones of our collective mental slavery.[52] Jamaicans, like any people, have the right to define themselves as they see fit. But because their self-definition is so centered on efforts to oppose, or exclude, a non-black other, then I and my children are indeed involved, and affected, for better or worse. My daughter Sela spent a month at an all-black girl's school near Half-Way Tree, Merl Grove High. She was the only brown girl there, but they styled her as white. One day a student cut in front of her in line, saying "black before white." That incident took on symbolic weight: for me part of the daily proof that "Marcus Garvey's words come to pass"—that the "racial hierarchy and catechism" Garvey advocated has acquired an "eternal life" as a racial theology: an unquestionable encoding of belief that has burrowed into the deepest levels of Jamaican culture and collective (un)consciousness.

If I were to accept, for the sake of argument, the metaphor of a returning Jesus who changed his skin color, or his language, to better blend in with (and speak to) contemporary realities, then in the 21st century, I believe she would have to return as a mestiza. Someone who looked not unlike Bob Marley's children. Or mine.

Conclusion

I often have my Jamaican students look at a Che Guevara poster and ask what "race" he is. They cannot see race in this icon: they see a revolutionary, a look of fierce determination, and since the vast majority of my students are female, often they see a very handsome man. When I tell them that if you take off the beret and shave off the beard, you get a white man, they experience genuine cognitive dissonance. But this opens space for a comparative perspective about what, if anything, is the link between skin color and the "true revolutionary."

When Bob Marley articulated a liberatory non-racialism, he used a Biblical model, but he was still really sticking his neck out in a Jamaican context. When Che self-consciously declared himself in opposition to the injustices suffered by indigenous peoples and other marginalized groups in Latin America, he was following in the footsteps of a history of Latin American freedom fighters, from Simón Bolívar to José Martí.[53] For the young Guevara, an inclusive mestizo identity was the only collective identity capable of correcting such social inequalities.

In a scene from *Motorcycle Diaries*, after drinking a large quantity of *pisco* during a farewell party thrown his honor at a Peruvian leper colony, Che improvised what he described to his mother as "a quintessentially Pan-American speech":

"the division of [Latin] America into unstable and illusory nations is completely fictional. We constitute a single mestizo race, which from Mexico to the Magellan Straits bears notable ethnographical similarities."[54]

In the film version, this possibly apocryphal speech takes on a hagiographic flavor, preceding young Che's fictional swim across the river, heading to the symbolic south, of course, into the arms of the people, in this case, the lepers as the symbol for the marginalized other. But even if it is a fiction, and an ideological gesture, this speech is still culturally and "psychologically true." Some of the most famous advocates of this position have been fair-skinned men of European ancestry who used mestizo unity as a way of declaring solidarity with the darker-skinned majority of the Americas. But that darker-skinned "nuestra América" has over time increasingly rebaptized the theory and practice of *mestizaje* in its own image.

One can note certain similarities that Bob Marley had with Che: both made a determined effort to transcend a rigidly-defined identity ascribed to them because of skin color. Marley's embrace of Rastafari was also an ideological gesture, motivated in part by the anti-brown prejudice he felt as a youth from the "black majority" amongst whom he lived, and with whom he most strongly identified. As *mestizaje* allowed Che to bridge his European biological heritage to the indigenous heart and later to the African cornerstone of *nuestra América*, so Rasta enabled Marley to unite the African and European streams of his own heritage. But whereas Che Guevara could follow in the footsteps of a long history of transracial thinking in the Spanish-speaking world, Bob Marley and the Rastas had little visible precedent to follow in the Anglo-Caribbean.

As I was finishing this essay, I went to the 10th Annual Bob Marley Lecture at UWI-Mona.[55]The speaker, Dr. Leahcim Semaj, was a self-proclaimed Afrocentrist. As expected in Jamaica, I heard no attempt to examine Marley's articulation of a trans-racial philosophy, nor any real effort to come to understand why the Europeans had embraced Marley long before he could get airplay in Jamaica, or before he entered the cultural radar screen of African Americans.

But one thing Dr. Semaj said did ring true for me: much of the revolution of Bob Marley and the Rastas failed to take root in Jamaica, and essentially evaporated in the 1980s, because it had only been embraced on a "cosmetic level." Them*follow fashion*. This would include "One Love" or "One Blood" as a move towards trans-racialism. No amount of exposure to the European world seems capable of moving Jamaicans from their rootedness in Garvey's, rather than Marley's, definition of a second emancipation--a concept that is not only by, for, and about black people, but that requires an ongoing opposition to the non-black world.   In this sense, I don't think that most Jamaicans to this day have even begun to understand the trans-racial implications of the life and music of their most famous Brown Boy Prophet. This was indeed part of the blues that one hears in Bob's voice—"a good man [a prophet] is never honored in his own country. Nothing change," as he sang.

But I do see some signs of hope, especially because of the increasing interchange that Jamaicans are having with the Spanish-speaking majority around them. This includes a growing awareness of sizeable numbers of people of Jamaican ancestry in countries like Panama, who are producing their literature and their own music which bridges Jamaica with nuestra América.[56] Perhaps as Jamaicans begin to discover their place in the Americas, and develop a more critical view of the U.S. version of "America," they will recognize "One Love" not just as "a discourse of social control," but as a sister ideology to the "resistant *mestizaje*" which Florencia Mallon sees as a "liberating force."[57]

Notes

Respect due to Dr. Matthew Smith, Lecturer in History at UWI-Mona, who called my attention to many of the on-line discussions and commentaries in the Jamaican mass media which I have cited here. He, of course, bears no responsibility for the uses to which I have put this material, or the conclusions I have drawn.

Since this is by design a polemical essay, I have not tried to be comprehensive in my references to scholarship about Jamaican history and cultural, critical race theory, etc. Readers who want to know more about my readings in this area can consult the extensive footnotes and bibliography to my first book *On Racial Frontiers: The New Culture of Frederick Douglass, Ralph Ellison, and Bob Marley* (Cambridge UP, 1999), especially the longest chapter: "Bob Marley's Zion: A Transracial 'Blackman Redemption'."

[1] " white man's country"—the title of a song from Mutabaruka's first album, with the refrain: 'It nuh good fi stay inna white man country too long. *Check It!* (RAS 1983).

[2]   nuestra América—see Gregory Stephens, "Monolingualism and Racialism as 'Curable Diseases': *Nuestra América* in the Transnational South," *Globalization with a Southern Face*, ed. James Peacock & Harry Watson (UNC Press, 2005). My sources include Jeffrey Belknap and Raul Fernandez, ed., *José Martí's "Our America": From National to Hemispheric Studies* (Durham: Duke UP, 1998); Christopher Abel and Nissa Torrents, *José Martí: Revolutionary Democrat* (Durham: Duke UP, 1986); Centro de Estudios Martianos, *Siete enfoques marxistas sobre José Martí* (La Habana: Editora Política, 1978).

[3]   Gregory Stephens, "The View from Kingston: Running away on Election Day," November 17, 2004;

     http://www.geocities.com.onelovemcg/political.html

[4]   Roger Mais and the report by Garth Baker are both discussed by Mark Wignall in "UWI Mona and Math Department Mired in Backwardness," *Jamaica Observer* (April 15, 2007).

[5]   One love mask and mythology: for a particularly naïve outsider's view of this, see Robert Roskind, *Rasta Heart: A Journey Into One Love* (Blowing Rock, NC: One Love Press, 2001).

[6]   Verene A. Shepherd and Glen L. Richards, eds., *Questioning Creole: Creolisation in Discourses in Caribbean Culture* (Oxford: James Currey, and Kingston: Ian Randle, 2002).

[7]   Gregory Stephens, "A 'Second Emancipation': The Transfiguration of Garvey's 'Racial Empire' in Rastafarian Thought," *Reevaluating the Pan-africanism of W.E.B. Dubois and Marcus Garvey: Escapist Fantasy or Relevant Reality*, ed. James Conyers (Edwin Mellen, 2006).

[8]   brown redeemer, see Richard D.E. Burton, *Afro-Creole: Power, Opposition, and Play in the Caribbean* (Ithaca, NY: Cornell UP, 1997), 114, 147.

[9]   "challenge the institution," Donna Lewis Essix, "Jamaica's National Heroes," http://www.jamaicans.com.

[10] Anita M. Waters, *Race, Class, and Political Symbols: Rastafari and Reggae in Jamaican Politics* (Transaction, 1985).

[11] Scott Dennis, "Echo in the Bone," *Plays for Today*, ed. Errol Hill (Longman, 1985). "wiped way"—taken from Bob Marley's song "Zion Train."

[12] Cash Michaels, "Activist Explains his 'Exterminate Whites' Comment," http://www.blackpressusa.com/news/Article.asp?SID=3&Title=National+News&NewsID=5412

[13] Hillel, an elite private school in the hills above Kingston, is widely perceived as a "Jewish School," and indeed a producer of upper-class, usually fair-skinned snobs.

[14] "Wayne&wax" blog, titled "Welcome to Jamrock, Indeed," May 1, 2005; http://wayneandwax.blogspot.com/2005/05/welcome-to-jamrock-indeed_01.html. Wayne Marshall had published "Rude boys inna da hood: Rap meets reggae with Sean Paul and Damian "Jr. Gong" Marley," in the *Boston Phoenix* (Oct. 28-Nov. 3, 2005);

     http://bostonphoenix.com/boston/music/top/documents/05050768.asp

[15] Mtume ya Salaam, Kalamu ya Salaam, Paul Roberts, et al., "The white-pothead appropriation of Bob Marley," October 9, 2005; http://www.kalamu.com.

[16] Paul Gilroy, *Against Race: Imagining Political Culture beyond the Color Line* (Belknap Press of Harvard UP, 2000), pp. 8; 374, my emphasis. This is a phenomenon I've been writing about since the 1980s. For a discussion of the "cave-boy oppressor" discourse in 1990s black nationalist rap, see my "Interracial Dialogue in Rap Music: Call-and-Response in a Multicultural Style," *New Formations* 16 (Spring 1992). The gist of the challenge—which has still not been met in writings about hip hop, or Jamaican culture, was noted bluntly by

Professor Griff (Public Enemy's Minister of Information) in 1990: "We didn't attract black people; we had all-white audiences. Black people didn't want to hear what we had to say." *Daily Texan*, June 23, 1990.

[17] "Race has no biological justification." This was the official position of the Association for the Advancement of Science, voiced by Loring Brace of the University of Michigan at the AAS conference, February 20, 1995; quoted in *Los Angeles Times* editorial, Feb. 22, 1995.

[18] "Gobal Reggae: The Transnationalization of Jamaican Popular Culture. An International Conference on Popular Culture to be Convened at the University of West Indies-Mona, Jamaica [during] Janaury 2007." A flyer circulated by Carolyn Cooper and in this author's possession.

[19] white directors, August Wilson, "I Want a Black Director," *New York Times*, August 26, 1990; *Spin* (October 1990). George E. Curry, "August Wilson Glorified Black America in his Plays," National Newspaper Publisher's Association, October 6, 2005; http://www.blackpressusa.com.

[20] Stanley Nelson, director, *Marcus Garvey: Look for Me in the Whirlwind* (PBS "The American Experience," 2001; DVD release 2002).

[21] Basil Walters, "Uproar over Garvey film," *Jamaica Observer*, Feb. 22, 2001.

[22] Cecil Gutzmore, "That Marcus Garvey Film," *Jamaica Gleaner*, May 15, 2001.

[23] "A 'Second Emancipation': The Transfiguration of Marcus Garvey's 'Racial Empire' in Rastafarian Thought," Conference on Africanism, Marcus Garvey, & W.E.B. DuBois at the University of Nebraska-Omaha, May 7-8, 2001. Under the same title, this speech was published in *Reevaluating the Pan-africanism of W.E.B. Dubois and Marcus Garvey: Escapist Fantasy or Relevant Reality*, ed. James Conyers (Edwin Mellen, 2006). Race fatigue: a term employed by Shelby Steele in *The Content of Our Character*.

[24] My on-line writing on Jamaican and gender includes Gregory Stephens, "A Culture of Intolerance: Insights on the Chi Chi Man Craze and Jamaican Gender Relations with Julius Powell of JFLAG" (Spring 2002);

http://www.jahworks.org/music/interview/jflag_interview.html; "The FIYA BURN Controversy: On the Uses of Fire in a Culture of Love and Rebellion" (Spring 2001); http://www.jahworks.org/music/features/fire_burn.html

[25] Gregory Stephens, "A 'Second Emancipation' Transfigured? Reflections on Bob Marley at 60," Jahworks.org, February 2, 2005;

http://www.jahworks.org/music/features/bob_at_sixty.htm

[26] "insidious confusion," Ralph Ellison, "Going to the Territory," in *Collected Essays*, 606.

[27] An example of my writing on the "dub revolution" and Jamaica's international influence: Gregory Stephens, "Finding a Musical Home: Through the German-UK Looking Glass," *Reggae Vibes* (May 2004); http://www.reggae-vibes.com/concert/dubrevol/dubrevol.htm. I purposely did not mention African as one of the important sites of outernational reggae, not because reggae in not important there (it is, with major touring artists such as Lucky Dube from South Africa), but because discussion of African reggae artists is not racialized in the same way as non-Jamaican artists from other continents.

[28] "all one": Galations 3:28; One Blood, Acts 17:26.

[29] Melville Cooke, "Who made 'One Love' Marley's signature song?" *Jamaica Gleaner*, February 10, 2005.

[30] Bounty Killer on "Entertainment Report," JTV February 18, 2005.

[31]   Kevin O'Brien Chang, "Oh, for a Jamaica music day!" *Jamaica Gleaner*, February 13, 2005.

[32]   Melville Cooke, "(Dis)re(membering) Bob Marley," *Jamaica Gleaner*, February 9, 2006.

[33]   Frederick Hickling, "We Neva Now We Wudda Reach Dis Far: The Psychology of Stardom in Jamaican Popular Culture," The Annual Bob Marley Lecture, sponsored by The Reggae Studies Unit, University of West Indies-Mona, Febuary 17, 2006.

[34]   C.G. Jung, *Two Essays on Analytical Psychology*, Collected Works V7 (Princeton UP, 1953/1970), 204.

[35]   Lee Scratch Perry, interview with Anthony Miller, TV Jamaica, November 11, 2005.

[36]   Michael Kuelker, *Book of Memory: A Rastafari Testimony* (St. Louis: CaribSound, 2005); Russell Banks, *The Book of Jamaica* (Harper, 1996); Robert Roskind, Rasta Heart: A Journey into One Love (One Love Press, 2001).

[37]   Stephanie Black, dir., *Life and Debt* (New Yorker Video, 2003); J. Michael Seyfert, dir., *Rent a Rasta* (Cinepobre, 2006), http://www.rentarasta.com/. The practices seen in *Rent a Rasta*, see Julia Connell Davidson and Jacqueline Sánchez Taylor, "Travel and Taboo: Heterosexual Sex Tourism to the Caribbean," in Elizabeth Bernstein and Laurie Schaffner, eds., *Regulating Sex: The Politics of Intimacy and Identity* (Routledge: 2004). Benedict Anderson,*Imagined Communities: Reflections on the Origin and Spread of Nationalism* (London: Verso, 1983/1991).

[38]   Margaret Prescod interview with Hugo Chávez on Democracy Now,*September 20th, 2005*; http://www.democracynow.org/article.pl?sid=05/09/20/1330218, my emphases.

[39]   Aurora Levins Morales, *Getting Home Alive* (Ithaca: Firebrand, 1986), p. 50, quoted in Suzanne Bost, "Transgressing Borders: Puerto Rican and Latina Mestizaje," *MELUS*; 6/22/2000.

[40]   Carole Boyce Davies, *Black Women, Writing and Identity* (Routledge, 1994), quoted in Suzanne Bost, "Transgressing Borders."

[41]   Carole Boyce Davies, "Beyond Unicentricity: Transcultural Black Presences," *Research in African Literatures* (1999); my emphasis.

[42]   Los Van Van, "Somos Cubanos," *Llegó Van Van* (Atlantic/WEA, 1999).

[43]   David Hackett Fisher, *Historians' Fallacies* (Harper, 1970), 3-39.

[44]   Norman   Kelley,   "Black   Cultural   Criticism,   Inc.,"   July   17,   2004; http://www.dissidentvoice.org/July2004/Kelley0717.html. A blatant expression of the theology of black victimization is Albert Cleage's *The Black Messiah* (New York: Sheed & Ward, 1968). In *Black Theology and Black Power*, James Cone also uses collective black victimization as a starting point, although his perspective is more nuanced than that of Cleage. See also James H. Cone, "Black Theology in American Religion," *Theology Today* 43:1 (April 1986). There have been many critiques of the blind spots in this theology. Rosemary Ruether argues that Cone's "kind of theology primarily addresses *white* people," i.e., it centers on its other. "Black Theology vs. Feminist Theology," *Christianity and Crisis* (April 15, 1974).William Jones criticizes an over-reliance on theological reflections inspired by the "oppression and slaughter of Jews in WW II," which, in calling into question the faith in "God as active in *and* sovereign over history," leaves unanswered an implicit question: "Is God racist and an anti-Semite?" "Theodicy and Methodology in Black Theology: A Critique of Washington, Cone and Cleage," *The Harvard Theological Review* 64.4, Theology and the Black Consciousness (Oct., 1971), pp. 541-557.

[45] militancy, Ralph Ellison, "The World and a Jug," *Shadow and Act* (Random House, 1964), 124.

[46] schema, Sigmund Freud, *Standard Edition* Vol. 17, p. 119; in Michael Vannoy Adams, *The Multicultural Imagination: "Race," Color, & the Unconscious* (Routledge, 1996), 45.

[47] Inter-relatedness, Ralph Ellison, "Change the Joke and Slip the Yoke" (1958), in *Collected Essays*. Anti-miscegenation laws, see my chapter "Interraciality in historical context," in *On Racial Frontiers* (Cambridge UP, 1999), 36-37; "The very fact that laws had to be passed after a while to forbid such relations indicated the strength of that [interracial] tendency": Howard Zinn, *A People's History of the United States* (Harper & Row, 1980), 31.

[48] Sleeping, robbing, and rebelling together: Edmund Morgan, *American Slavery, American Freedom: The Ordeal of Colonial Virginia* (Norton, 1975), 327.

[49] Herbert G. de Lisser, *The White Witch of Rosehall* (Macmillan Caribbean, 1929/1958/1962). "To be a model of virtue here would be merely to make oneself ridiculous," Rutherford reflects, in the midst of affairs with women of two colors.

[50] I discuss black nationalist rap in "Interracial Dialogue in Rap Music," *New Formations* 16 (Spring 1992).

[51] James Cone, *Black Theology and Black Power* (New York: Seabury, 1969);

psychologically correct. C.J. Jung, *Seminar on Dream Analysis*, ed. William McGuire (Princeton UP, 1984), 706.

[52] Growing consensus against racial categories, Brent Stapes, "On Race and the Census: Struggling with Categories that no longer Apply," *New York Times* Feb. 5, 2007.

[53] For a revisisionist view of Bolívar's attitudes towards race: Marilyn Grace Miller, *Rise and Fall of the Cosmic Race: The Cult of Mestizaje in Latin America* (University of Texas, 2004).

[54] Ernesto "Che" Guevara, *The Motorcycle Diaries: Notes on a Latin American Journey* (Melbourne: Ocean Press, 2004), 149; "quintessentially," 154.

[55] Dr. Leahcim Semaj, The 10th Annual Bob Marley Lecture, University of West Indies-Mona, February 8, 2007.

[56] Spanish-speaking Jamaican culture: see for example Cubena, *Chombo* (Miami: Ediciones Universal, 1981). Cubena is the pen name of Dr. Carlos Guillermo Wilson, who taught Afro-Latino literature at Loyola University in Los Angeles. *Chombo* describes the experience of people from Jamaican during the construction of the Panama Canal. The spirit of political resistance which one hears in 1970s Jamaican reggae continues to be an enormous influence across a broad spectrum of music in contemporary Latin America.

[57] Florencia Mallon, "Constructing Mestizaje in Latin America: Authenticity, Marginality, and Gender in the Claiming of Ethnic Identities." *Journal of Latin American Anthropology* 2:1 (Fall 1996), 171-72. Latin American uses and abuses of the ideology of *mestizaje* manifest an ambiguous duality, Mallon asserts. As a form of resistance, *mestizaje* helps pry open colonial and neo-colonial racial categories. But as "an official discourse of national formation, a new claim to authenticity," it also sometimes serves as a form of "social control" which can marginalize populations perceived as outside the mestizo norm.

Black Authenticity, *Racial Drag,* and the Case of Dave Chappelle

Joy Viveros

The question of whether there is or can be such a thing as black authenticity begins for me with the question of whether there can be any racial authenticity at all; and if so, whence does it originate? I restrict my inquiry here to the case of so-called racial minorities in the United States, because the cultures that support the reproduction of race here cannot be considered apart from our domestic racisms, which I know more intimately, and about which I feel myself more qualified to speak, than the varieties that have taken root elsewhere.

So far it appears that race as datum that can be discovered in a body to definitively establish its dissimilarities from all other human bodies outside of a racial group cannot be verified without the interpreter of data first "looking for" race. Thus, whatever geographic and historical similarities do bind individuals to group statuses, and whatever genetic differences do exist among bodies that generate geographically and historically linked genotypes and phenotypes, it appears that race as a fixed and verifiable object upon which any analysis can be built does not in fact exist. Race as a biologically discreet event is a cultural phantasm.

My account thus far of race—and by extension racial membership—fails to address, of course, that historically distinct minority groups have produced cultures that thrive and make the world over as a result of their commonly generated meanings, and that these groups—and the subjects who comprise them—suffer and resist ideas about them generated from without. To say that race is not a physical fact capable of legitimizing the cultural productions that rely on its facticity is not to say that nothing about race is real: the horrors perpetrated and ideologically justified, and the suffering inflicted and endured in its name, the abundant gifts of racially inflected culture, including language, visual art, music, literature, all are real, as is the sense of group belonging for racial minorities produced in part by this society that in relation to its minorities at once rejects and is curious, ghettoizes and invites assimilation and class mobility, damns and borrows from.

My own account thus far is also, as most discussions of race inevitably are, ponderous: weighted down with all its own import. This tonality common to most treatments of race suggests, I argue here, a special significance for comedic and camp interpretations of race. For the moment, however, let us dwell on the predominant sense of race—in which the vast history of historical wrongs, violence, captivity, and death appears to make it impossible to conceptualize race and its effects with anything but the sincerity attendant on respect. The regime of sincerity in respect to race is also produced, it would seem, by the freight of guilt generated by belonging. To belong, after all, is to commit affirmatively, and equally to have one's membership assigned by another. At the core of belonging there is always, for the one who has been claimed as the legitimate and worthy subject of incorporation, the potential for chafing at the terms of membership and for recoil from the group itself. And for the group claiming a right to possess and name, there is always a potential for misidentification and misapprehension of the one annexed as its own. If we look back to the early literature of passing in the United States, we see not only a calling out of the unverifiability and instability of race, but also a high degree of ambivalence on the part of the racial passer toward that marginalized racial group to which she or he "belongs." It would be reductive to view that ambivalence as merely disidentification with an abused and degraded social status. The autobiographies and novels of passing, from Nella Larsen's *Quicksand* and *Passing* to James Weldon Johnson's *Autobiography of an Ex-Colored Man*, to Rebecca Walker's contemporary post-passing memoir *Black and Jewish and White: Autobiography of a Shifting Self*, do not simply anatomize the crucible of outsider status, or even their authors' ambivalence about racial identity but also a determination to render visible their alienated gaze at the in-groups that claim them.

This ideologically problematic intention could only be acknowledged in a minor key in literary and cultural studies as evidence of internalized racism— the disease that is the subject of the story apparently having compromised the storyteller—so long as the incursion of African Americans in large numbers into the middle class had not been effected in cities, suburban tracts, and malls, in corporate workplaces and academic campuses. With shifting demographics has come bit by bit a fraying of the boundaries of African American culture and all of the racial certainties that accompanied those boundaries.

This is not to say, of course, that the limit signified by the epithet "nigger" will not be a touchstone to which the racially privileged will refer into the foreseeable future. But as greater numbers of African Americans and mixed-race Americans have a cultural experience of self that diverges from inherited ideas of so-called blackness, the meaning of race is increasingly muddy in many quarters, muddy even for subordinated racial groups for whom the idea of an authentic racial essence is so often the thing that grounds racism in an accessible and transparent logic: we are different from that other who oppresses us, not only by habitus and culture and choice, but in some way that makes us essentially different from that other, and bound to our own racial compatriots by a natural fact.

The racially neutralized subject purveyed in popular advertising refers to some extent to the actual subject position of many African Americans living in so-called white communities who—notwithstanding whatever racially exclusionary behaviors they endure in these communities—are incorporated with them, albeit perhaps as a body seals off and contains a threatening foreign substance. The habitus of the black middle class, that is, particularly those who are racial minorities in white communities, is intimately related to and resembles, at least, that of their peers. My concern here is not whether any single individual can be rightly accused of historical amnesia—of forgetting "where he comes from," "who her people are," etc.—but to observe that when color and culture, ideologically constructed as a seamless continuity, lift away from one another, the certainties surrounding race itself slip for most interpreters.

We understand, of course, why the dominant culture might want to produce a neutralized African American subject so divorced from history that assimilation and consignment to the status of replica is the limit of its imagination. As for racially subordinated cultures, the spectacle of a racial minority who cannot be behaviorally distinguished from a white subject resurrects that primal fable of eternally warring peoples which produces a sensible calculus. From thence issues the contemporary notion of the "Oreo." According to the terms of this epithet, "blackness" (skin color, the inescapable distinguishing mark) is a destiny to which self-understanding must conform. Behaviors linked with the dominant culture are at such moments rhetorically produced by the African American community as pointing to a disturbance of identity. But as greater numbers of African Americans live in social worlds at a distance from those African American cultures nurtured in part by racial segregation and containment, what are the stakes in constituting identity for this growing population as a thing outside the self: an alien knowledge each member approaches as a stranger? My interest here is not to evaluate the benefits or sensibleness of any individual's quest to find a "lost" connection to communities of African Americans which they have missed out on knowing by living in predominantly white communities, but rather to question the premise implicit in such quests, and in the epithet Oreo, that racial authenticity is something a member of a racial minority in the U.S. could ever be without.

While self-knowledge in the context of race relations and racial inequality is certainly something one can acquire or deepen, I would suggest that racial authenticity is built on the one foundational experience that no person of color can escape: a legal and social tradition that has set the person of color as a thing apart, an object of consideration, inquiry, legislation, contempt. Even barring direct encounters with people who harbor especially racist attitudes, the society in which we live is populated by countless folks—many with various kinds of bureaucratic, academic, judicial, and social authority—who do not grant us the same premise in humanity as their own. Further, we live knowing that in a previous age, we would have been even more unlike our peers: more vulnerable than others to disease and weather and other privations, and superadded to this, subject to harm and persecution, to the point of death, by the general citizenry.

This knowledge is, I would argue, the essential ground of racial authenticity. Perhaps such a proposal seems perverse in that it suggests that such authenticity is a negative effect of a thing set in motion by the dominant culture. But I would argue that this irreducibly personal encounter with history and the intersubjective ground of racism—with the fact that sociohistorically, at least our bodies can never be more or less purely a form of self-expression, that they mark us (or might, if our genetic origins were widely known) as those whose humanity is or has been diminished by our group membership, by our very bodies—is the foundational, universal, and therefore authentic experience of the racially subordinated subject.

· · · · ·

I have so often heard African Americans speak of their early lives in pre-lapsarian and post-lapsarian terms: of the days before they understood themselves to "have" a race—and the awakening, on the date when the epithet "nigger" was applied to them (or when equivalent language signaled their preexisting and nonnegotiable racial status) to the existence of a racial hierarchy, and their unfortunate position within it. I remember my own dawning sense of racial hierarchies, the only non-white child in my precious little grade school; there was something they withheld, something I didn't have a name for—a haunting world of access, approval (love?) outside my sphere. Another world was moving at a different speed than my own—

commonly held understandings I was too young to name were already at work in the air that our teachers and parents and other adults breathed out.

When my son was four, I decided that the world would not find him alone, stranded on a playground or street, the word "nigger" shattering the protection of my boundless love. This word, when he heard it, would not be the revelation of a shameful open secret about the self—but only something to know about the speaker, he or she a host to a contagion. It seemed necessary to bring the news then, for the malicious heart of this word seeks out its quarry at tender ages—enjoying the special lifelong relationship it develops, in memory at least, between perpetrator and victim. So I told him. The short version. Africa. Slavery.Dark skin, light skin.Difference.The Niger.*Niger*. Negro.Nigger.The whole linguistic flow of history. My aim was this: to float the sound out there with "sky," and "boat," and "mad," and other words. To interrupt what must be for the uninoculated an inevitable circuit that makes the term mean something profound and intimate, something from which the self must seek to resurrect.

I hoped to bring into view that the resort to racial hierarchies as a basis for identity betrays a powerful delusion, related to all disturbances of identity. As such it participates in the whole unintentional realm in human relations: the self bolstering itself and its wishes by its various unconvincing means. The testicle-tucked transvestite; the race man or woman.The costumery of life and the frailty of insight. The accident of identity—and our multifarious means of denying all this is so.

Regarded this way, perhaps all racial identities gain a delusional aspect. All depend on overdetermined social codes whose stylized forms cannot help but bespeak the construction of the natural. From this vantage, is not racial identity itself—whatever the ilk—a bit of a spectacle? Are not the imperfectly persuasive certainties of identity and group belonging, encoded through a righteous regime of behaviors—a little, an ever so little bit funny?

This is exactly the ground that stand-up and sketch comedy over the past several decades has been invested in mining. From Margaret Cho to Sara Silverman, from Richard Pryor to Eddie Murphy, Cedric the Entertainer to Dave Chappelle, each *displays* for popular audiences that voice, inflection, vocabulary, posture, bodily movements, and the apparent self-evidence of the proper parameters of morality, pleasure, and truth are each the predictable effects of racially generated ideas about social reality. The uncanny impersonations of African American male comics, in particular, of their racial others—that is, of "white folks"—are a riveting spectacle of the extent to which ideology produces the self. As they slide, with barely a transition, from the race men they were raised to be to the white men they might have become, it is increasingly difficult to sustain the ordinarily unbroken sense of one's own identity as an effect of reasoned reflection and insight.

Contemporary stand-up and (to a lesser extent) sketch comedy, wherein performers are invited to bring into focus surreal aspects of reality and shock audiences with an ideologically diverse range of insights, are perhaps the forms of theatre best suited to disrupting the viewer's habituated identification with performers—to generating that "alienation" or "defamiliarization" effect (*Verfremdungseffekt*) Bertolt Brecht suggests is a precondition to "all understanding."[1] Both genres are interested in a style of impersonation that at once inhabits a character and renders impossible any satisfying identification with her or him. This strategy informs both the stockinged and bewigged but incongruously male-voiced impersonations of women by *The Kids in the Hall* and the pancaked and bewigged impersonations of white men by Dave Chappelle in which he makes no attempt to disguise his own skin color and features. In the former case, a destabilized gendered subject comes into view, tottering about in little pumps amongst the various but eerily consistent archetypes of suburban female identity; in the latter case, a hybrid subject appears, making both inside claims to racial superiority and, indelibly, blithely, to outside racial privilege. The shared strategies of these bemused transvestitisms are in keeping with Brecht's description of the acting technique he proposes for epic theatre:

> [T]he technique which produces an A-effect is the exact opposite of that which aims at empathy. . . . The actor does not allow himself to become completely transformed on the stage into the character he is portraying. He is not [his subjects]; he shows them. He . . . puts forward their way of behaving . . . but he never tries to persuade . . . others . . . that this amounts to a complete transformation. (136-37)

Thus when Chappelle plays a white television commentator being booed by the audience on Season One of *Chappelle's Show*, he captures the conservative position in the culture wars with his "Excuse me. Pardon me. Hey, will you cut the malarkey? Okay, I'm talking. There's a white man talking up here"[2] (think a skinny, tightly reined in, corporate, inconsequential Harold Bloom) and simultaneously refers, with his incompletely lightened skin and pancake dusted eyelashes, to the very different man behind the performance. This incomplete transformation yields *"racial drag"*: the display of an embodied racial identity, the purpose of which is not to ridicule "the other race," but rather to parody race itself. The mismatch between performer and performance in Chappelle's comedy, and the fluid movement between racial sensibilities constructs race as a wished for rather than actual certainty. Thus in Chappelle's oeuvre, a deadly earnest racist receives roughly the same sincerity in representation as do Nazis in Mel Brooks's musical dance number, "Springtime for Hitler." Both flaunt the absurdity of our invented knowledge.

Is this not the joke in Dave Chappelle's blind white-supremacist black man Clayton Bigsby, unaware of his own race? Racial identity peeled away from its social inevitability—and just the delusion naked and stranded? In the Clayton Bigsby sketch, one of the first of Season One of *Chappelle's Show* (2003), Bigsby's rants against African Americans captures perfectly the antisemitic, anti-immigrant and racist sensibility of Klan and Neo-Nazi rhetoric. In his answers to exploratory questions by a reporter on the overall thesis of his six books, Bigsby replies, "Sir, my message is simple: Niggers, Jews, homosexuals, Mexicans, A-rabs, and all kinds of different Chinks stink— and I hate 'em."[3] As for the specific "problem" he has with "Niggers," he goes on:

> How much time you got, Buddy? Where would I start? Well, first of all, they're lazy good-for-nothing tricksters. Crack smokin' swindlers. Big butt-havin', wide-nosed, breathin'-all-the-white-man's-air. They eat up all the chicken. They think they're the best dancers. And they stink! Did I mention that before?

The sketch's spot-on impersonation of white supremacist logic emphasizes its cockeyed aspect. Bigsby's accusation that blacks are "breathin' all the white man's air" is a succinct, if absurdist, rendering of white supremacist discourse on the need to protect the so-called white race against the expansionist behaviors of "colored races."[4] What makes the "Blind Supremacy" sketch groundbreaking is not so much Chappelle's ridicule of white supremacist ideology, but that he denaturalizes its logic, lifting it away from its ordinary associations. Instead of the congested hate filled aspect of an Aryan spokesman, we have a man whose psychological comforts are preposterously mismatched with his social identity. As with much of the best sketch and stand-up comedy, a rhetorical form is emptied of its usual content—but in this case not because the usual form of hate speech is replicated with incongruous particulars, but because the wrong party is speaking. Chappelle drives home the rickety but tenacious logic of racist identity in the final coup of the sketch in which, in an afterward, we are told that Bigsby has at last "accepted that he is a black man," but has also "filed for divorce from his wife . . . [b]ecause she's a nigger lover."

Much of Chappelle's work deconstructs the edifice of the near tribal aspect of racial identifications. In his "*Roots* Outtakes"[5] sketch, for example, the interracial tension invoked by the searing if sentimental iconography of the shirtless Kunta Kinte, arms pinned above his head, absorbing the slave driver's blows suddenly transforms into something else when Chappelle breaks character to give the improbably short white actor "Steve" playing the overseer a hard time for overdoing the application of the whip (which, it turns out, has been intercepted by a shield strapped to the actor's back). As Chappelle turns away from the camera, the divisive scene of interracial violence is revealed to be a theatrical staging that at once reminds us that none of the actors have personal experience with slavery, and underscores the not insignificant power differential between black star (of the *Roots* spoof, of *Chappelle's Show*) and white bit actor that is close to the inverse of the historical scene. In gesturing toward the changing contexts of race relations, Chappelle resurrects and then disappears the grudges that are so central to group identity. *Chappelle's Show* makes a similar move in a sketch which imagines a nationally televised "racial draft"[6] aimed at definitively "sett[ling]" the "racial standing" of mixed race celebrities. The negotiation among racial groups evolves, during the course of the sketch, to a baseball cards-like acquisition and trading of public figures who have either lost their racial caché for their "people" or inspired the admiration of another racial group. Thus by sketch's end, Colin Powell has been acquired by the white delegation, but only on the condition, proffered by the black delegation, that whites also take Condoleezza Rice who is given away (unloaded) as "part of the deal."[7] Here, the racially ambiguous figure is not invoked to suggest the psychosocial struggles of a subject torn by multiple racial allegiances (as it would be in most interracial memoirs and the literature of passing), but rather to parody the discomfort shared by all racial communities at the spectacle of a racial compatriot sidling too close to the enemy.

Chappelle pursues his troubling of racial affiliation in his 2004 stand-up concert in San Francisco, *Dave Chappelle: For What It's Worth: Live at the Fillmore*. In its opening bit he announces that "I've stopped smoking weed— with black people." He goes on:

> I'm sorry black people to break the news so publicly, but I can't smoke with you anymore. Every time I smoke weed with my black friends, all you talk about is your *trials* and tribulations. I'm sick of that shit; I got my own problems, nigger. It's a waste of weed: I'm smokin' weed to get away from my problems, not takin' away yours."[8]

Here Chappelle flouts two of the most longstanding taboos in African American artistic production: making public its persistent and ubiquitous *ressentiment* and airing to a general (i.e., "white") audience any sense of racial disaffiliation. We are certainly a long way, in such moments, for example, from the "group consciousness" prescribed for African Americans by Alain Locke in "Enter the New Negro"[9] and the nationalist injunctions of Richard Wright who proclaims in "Blueprint for Negro Writing" that the "Negro writer's," "loyalties" must be "toward all those forces which help shape the consciousness of his race toward a more heroic cast."[10] But Chappelle's goal is not simply to assert the right to map the shifting racial affiliations of a life, but also to speak the name of race as culture. Thus he follows the delight caused in some quarters of his audience by his proclamation that "From now on, I smoke weed exclusively with white people," with a gesture that both holds whites close and keeps them at a critical distance: "Calm down, mother fuckers—you win by default. You got good weed conversation. All white people talk about when they get high, is other times that they got high. I could listen to that shit all night....That shit is great." Chappelle's backhanded compliment to the white tribe pointedly refers to the very different psychohistorical contexts that produce African American and Euroamerican subjectivity. While Chappelle makes no argument for an essential difference between so-called whites and blacks (on his "racial commentaries": "[o]ur differences are just cultural, that's it"[11]) his depiction of cultural difference is attentive to the surreal dissimilarities in psychosocial accommodations to reality among the two racial groups.

That difference includes, of course, for an African American community held in thrall for in the U.S. for over two centuries and long besieged by racial discrimination, a sense of persecution that thrives (Chappelle: "Some people say all black people look alike.....We normally just call those people police"), independently at times, of any "authenticatable" racial conspiracy. Thus one of Chappelle's bits in *For What It's Worth*, in which he asserts that "[e]very black person needs an alibi,"moves from his fear and distrust of police to speculating half-seriously that there must be a conspiracy behind the Michael Jackson child abuse prosecution and attendant media frenzy. At the same time, he concedes the paranoia of the conceit when he takes on the persona of an anonymous white authority figure asking Michael to "jerk off another child" in order to distract the country from the state of the economy and our misadventures in war.

Distrust of the American legal system runs throughout Chappelle's oeuvre, from *Chappelle's Show* Season 2 "Law and Order" episode which renders an absurdist comparison of the treatment of blacks and whites by police and the courts and ends with the observation, "I got to get in on this being white thing. It's like there's two legal systems, damn near,"[12] to his speculation in *For What It's Worth* that the current spate of arrests of black celebrities is the effect of a cultural backlash against African Americans resulting from their widespread celebration of the O.J. Simpson acquittal:

> We shoulda been quiet about that shit. Soon as it was 'not guilty,' niggers was dan—
> [*Chappelle dances*]. 'All in your face, nigger. In your face! It hurts don't it? It hurts.

Burns, doe'n't it? Ooh, that justice system burns, doe'n't it? Welcome to my world, mother fucker.'"

But Chappelle's interest is not merely to show that the America inhabited by Euroamericans is fundamentally different from the one inhabited by African Americans, nor even to show the psychic consequence for the latter of this difference. He does investigate these virtually unrelated Americas quite aggressively when, for example, he envisions what time travel back to the 18th century would be like for him and a white peer:

> If I went back in time with a white person, and we saw George Washington walk in front of our time machine, my white friend would probably be like, "Oh, my God, Dave, look, there's George Washington, . . . the father of this great nation. Let me go shake his hand." I'd be on the other side, like, "Run, nigger! George Washington!"

> And we'd both be right. We like him because he wrote the *Declaration of Independence* and all that shit. *[Miming writing thoughtfully]* "We hold these truths to be self-evident . . . all men are created equal." *[Turning as if to address someone behind him]*–"Go get me a sandwich nigger, or I'll kill you!"– *[turning back to the imaginary writing pad]* ". . . liberty . . . justice for all."

And he points repeatedly to the impossibility of an entirely healthy adaptation to racial marginalization, including in his discussion of Michael Jackson's plastic surgery which moves from talking about the pop star to inhabiting his subjectivity to addressing him directly:

> . . . Mike . . . is a freak–he's a freak: his face is all cut up. But just remember when you look at that thing he calls his face, that he did that for you somehow. Somehow he thought maybe you might–, "Maybe it will help, maybe people will like me more if I turn myself into a white . . . ghoulish-like creature; I don't know what the fuck it is. But he did it for you. And I appreciate the gesture, Michael Jackson, if you're watchin' this. I appreciate that gesture. And I want you to know, fuck everybody: Dave Chappelle understands.[13]

In fact, in much of his comedy, Chappelle depicts himself as equally beset as his racial compatriots by the sense that nothing can deliver African Americans from the seemingly inescapable trap of race.

Thus a sequence in *For What It's Worth* that begins with mapping the contemporary circumstance of poor African Americans onto the classic American narrative of self-making quickly devolves into a certainty that nothing but the most abject pandering to racist ideology will do:

> I spoke at my old high school and I told them kids straight up, "If you guys are serious about making it out of this ghetto, you got to focus, you got to stop blamin' white people for your problems. And you've–, you've got to learn . . . how to . . . rap, or play basketball or somethin', nigger! You're trapped. *You are* trapped! Either do that

or sell crack. That's your only options, the only way I've ever seen it work. You better get to entertainin' these white people, nigger—get ta dancin'! Go on out there and *be* somebody! . . . (I just hope they listened.)

But the overall sensibility of Chappelle's work is not so much invested in demonstrating that racial injustice persists, but in clearing out a space for nuancing the proliferating effects of race in culture.

I argue here that the hegemonies of race are enforced equally by ideologically driven prescriptions and proscriptions within racially ostracized communities about acceptable identities, perspectives, and representational strategies, as it is by discrimination and censorship from without. And I see in much stand-up comedy by racially marginalized people, and in Chappelle's oeuvre, an impish resistance to every regime of the unsayable. Thus in the very first episode of *Chappelle's Show*, he welcomes the audience with

> I . . . haven't been cancelled yet. But I'm workin' on it. And I think this next piece might be the one to do it. . . . I showed it to a black friend of mine. He looked at me like I had set black people back with a comedy sketch. *[Shrugs]* Sorry!! Let's roll it.

In this introduction, Chappelle casts the black community as no less a taboo enforcing body than the presumably predominantly white television network producing his show. The African American artistic tradition has developed with a strong sense of being watched by white America, and the stultifying self-censorship that results therefrom is part of what Chappelle would resist.

The work of opening up of what it is possible to say and observe—and better, to know for oneself about race—is being accomplished by Chappelle and others working in stand-up. The genre permits these writer-performers to extricate themselves from a suffocating sincerity that most discourses anatomizing the operations of race seem unable to map a way out of. Some of this work proceeds in proliferating and nuancing the representation of the so-called black experience of race. Consider, for example, the stand-up of Kamu Bell and Regi Steele, two African American comics working on the West Coast. Kamu Bell has a fascinating set piece in which he bemoans the passing of an era when whites could be relied on to fear blacks.[14] In this bit, Bell treats wistfully the sociologically well documented fact that white women have habitually crossed to the other side of a street, gripping their pocketbooks against their bodies, to avoid a face-to-face encounter with a black man. Instead of the relief one might expect at the diminishing reach of a racial stereotype, he delivers a whimsical gaze at an historically imperiled intersubjective perk that has hitched itself to the protean damage unleashed on marginalized racial identity. Regi Steele, who grew up in a suburb and speaks in a voice that is mainstream in the extreme (i.e., unrecognizably "black"), confides that he can only deliver on the archetypal figure of the fearsome black man by assuring folks he wishes to intimidate that he knows a few, has a few in his extended family.[15]

Chappelle's Show too conjures the figure of the black person who has lived in white communities his entire life and whose cultural ways and tastes are out of sync with received ideas of the African American experience. In "White People Can't Dance Experiment,"[16] a skit about the kinds of music that move different racial communities, a fair skinned, dreadlocked African American cop begins dancing in a stereotypically "white" way to a folk rock song performed by John Meyer. Raising the specter of the race traitor, Chappelle queries the officer suspiciously with "Hey man, how you know that song?" The dancing cop, seemingly having lost control of his own body, replies, "I'm from the suburbs, man! I can't help it. I can't help it!" At this, Chappelle, who spent part of his childhood in Ohio and lives there now, looks in the camera, shrugs, and starts dancing fluidly, in a way culturally coded as "white."

Chappelle's playful gaze at the physical memories and stylized movements encoded in bodies of various races participates in a Sontagian campiness that understands race as an "aesthetic phenomenon"[17] rather than an argument whose rightness can be evaluated against that of other races. At the same time, the brief spike in racial paranoia embodied in the sketch reminds the viewer that in African American culture the boundaries of authentic racial identity are regulated by a "stylized repetition of acts"[18]—and that, much like gender, the "ritualized production" of race is produced "under and through the force of prohibition and taboo, with the threat of ostracism . . . compelling the shape of the production."[19]

The taboos effected by "black American national consciousness," Robert Reid-Pharr argues, are a defense against the "inchoate [black] subject" produced by "modern (slave) culture." [20] In shoring up the ideological boundaries of a reactively conservative black identity, he observes, African American literature and culture deploy against the threat of the "marginal and ambiguous" (389), the figure of what Angela Davis has termed the "culpable slave" (387). The juggernaut of American slavery thus pursues its extortions centuries after its demise. Race slavery—having entered into an original relationship with each of its subjects, enslaving each for an allegedly essential identity and indicting and living in each as a primal failure of autonomy— inevitably engenders in its subjects and descendants cultural expressions that play at the edges of or are absorbed in incrimination and questions of guilt. The African American community's gaze at its own violated boundaries is apparent throughout its literary production, including DuBois's ruminations on the "red stain of bastardy"[21] and Wright's proposed policing of an ideologically sound black artistic production that would not go "a-begging to white America." [22] But African American stand-up, interested, as is much stand-up, in the incalculable remainders from ideologically directed lifeworlds, is less concerned with the integrity of its group's boundaries than with the peculiar conventions of identity-in-race. Thus Chappelle's "White People Can't Dance Experiment" dismisses the profound threat of illegitimacy associated with the figure of the race fugitive and instead trains a campy gaze on the proliferation of racialized subjectivities that "relishes, rather than judges, the little triumphs and awkward intensities of 'character.'"[23]

Chappelle does not exempt himself from the irrationalities he teases out of virtually everyone's accommodations to the surreal landscape of domestic race relations, including the essentialist mantras of race. In a Season 1 stand-up routine that segues into a sketch, he identifies himself as a "genetic dissenter"[24] through an imagined history in which he appears as himself in earlier and earlier eras, moving backward from 2004 to 1978, 1945, 1863, to the antebellum era, and finally to Africa on the cusp of European contact. In each scene he criticizes the ruling political elite, so that his opening "Man, Bloomberg is fuckin' up!" winds down in 1863 to "Man, Lincoln is fuckin' up!" and ultimately to a pre-Civil war scene in which, as a slave, he comments, "white folks in general is fuckin' up." The ultimate payoff to his conceit comes later when his status as incisive social critic cannot withstand an imagined return to the motherland. In the penultimate scenes—"1695: Africa"—he is criticizing his tribal leader ("Man, the chief's fuckin up!"), and finally, having gone to investigate an approaching ship, in shackles in the hold of a slaver saying, "Man, I fucked up!" In this piece, Chappelle, in captivity in a slave ship by dint of his "genetic" resistance to authority, suggests that the central insights of African American racial identity are more fragile and contingent than they appear. The special sociopolitical perspective produced by racial marginalization yields an identity that experiences itself as transcultural and transhistorical, but is of course, the skit concedes, neither.

His "Man, I fucked up!" radiates outward to the limits of anyone's project of imagining an identity outside the terms given by one's society—and generously, self-disclosingly, to the irrational guilt of the scapegoat. In the skit's return to the "beginningest of beginnings[,] . . . the first morning of Eden," [25] Chappelle visits the racially marginalized subject's wish to wake up from the long dream of race. Instead of an awakening, he (Chappelle, always himself) is returned, by his own historically generated subjectivity—and thus, in the skit, by the grinning Möbius strip of history—to an encounter with racial identity that appears inescapable. At the same time, the skit retains, by its sense of "Being-as-Playing-a-Role,"[26] a sense of the arbitrariness, absurdity, and fixity of any identity at all, and thereby at once acknowledges that there can be no cure for the racial ambiguities of contemporary life, and disengages from—one might even say, in its own way transcends—the subjective limits of racialized identity.

Notes

1.   Bertolt Brecht, *Brecht on Theatre: The Development of An Aesthetic*, ed. and trans. John Willett (1964; New York: Hill and Wang, 1966) 71, 122.

2.   *Chappelle's Show*, Season 1, Episode 1, January 22, 2003, originally aired on Comedy Central.

3.   *Chappelle's Show*, Season 1, Episode 1, January 22, 2003, originally aired on Comedy Central.

4.   This rhetoric is from a website associated with white supremacist David Lane, antisemitic murderer and author of the slogan, "We must secure the existence of our people and a future for white children." http://www.churchoftrueisrael.com/the-order/lane1.html

5.   Dave Chappelle, *Chappelle's* Show, Season 1, Episode 3, February 5, 2003, originally aired on Comedy Central.

6.   Dave Chappelle, *Chappelle's Show*, Season 2, Episode 1, January 21, 2004, originally aired on Comedy Central.

7.   It is perhaps not accidental that "Racial Draft," which draws its explicit structure from the televised sports draft also bears some residual similarity to the antebellum auction block. *Chappelle's Show* openly plays with slavery's iconography, from its spoof of the 1970s T.V. miniseries *Roots* to the closing image of every show featuring the image of *Pilot Boy Productions*: Chappelle as a slave with dollar bills fanned in each shackled hand with the audio trademark, "I'm rich, Biatch!" Chappelle's postmodern cosmos not only draws attention to the instability of racial positionalities, but also indulges in sprightly, flippant speculations about what it might be like were whites to receive treatment historically reserved for blacks.

8.   Dave Chappelle, *Dave Chappelle: For What It's Worth—Live at the* Fillmore (2004), Columbia TriStar, release date: August 16, 2005.

9.   Alain Locke, "Enter the New Negro," The *Survey Graphic:* "Harlem Mecca of the New Negro," Vol. VI, No. 6, March 1925.

10.   Richard Wright, "Blueprint for Negro Writing" (1937), John A. Williams and Charles F. Harris, eds., *Amistad 2: Writings on Black History and Culture* (New York: Random House, 1971).

11 Dave Chappelle, *Chappelle's Show*, Season 2, Episode 3, February 4, 2004, originally aired on Comedy Central.

12 Dave Chappelle, *Chappelle's Show*, Season 2, Episode 5, February 18, 2004, originally aired on Comedy Central.

13 Dave Chappelle, *Dave Chappelle: For What It's Worth–Live at the* Fillmore (2004), Columbia TriStar, release date: August 16, 2005.

14 W. Kamu Bell, routine performed at *The Punchline* in San Francisco, August 27, 2006.

15 Regi Steele, routine performed at *The Punchline* in San Francisco, Summer 2007.

16 Dave Chappelle, *Chappelle's Show*, Season 2, Episode 3, February r, 2004, originally aired on Comedy Central.

17 Susan Sontag, "Notes on Camp," *Against Interpretation and Other Essays* (1996; New York: Routledge, 1993) 277.

18 Judith Butler, *Gender Trouble: Feminism and the Subversion of Identity* (New York, Routledge, 1990) 136.

19 Judith Butler, *Bodies That Matter: On the Discursive Limits of "Sex"* (New York: Routledge, 1993) 95.

20 Robert F. Reid-Pharr, "Tearing the Goat's Flesh: Homosexuality, Abjection and the Production of a Late Twentieth-Century Black Masculinity," *Studies in the Novel*, Volume 28, number 3, Fall, 1996, 373.

21 W.E.B. DuBois, *The Souls of Black Folk* (Chicago: A. C. McClurg & Co., 1903) 9.

22 Richard Wright, "Blueprint for Negro Writing," *Portable Harlem Renaissance Reader*, ed. David Levering Lewis, 200.

23 Susan Sontag, "Notes on Camp," *Against Interpretation and Other Essays* (1996; New York: Routledge, 1993) 291.

24 Dave Chappelle, *Chappelle's Show*, Season 1, Episode 1, January 22, 2003, originally aired on Comedy Central.

25 Zadie Smith, *White Teeth* (2000; New York: Vintage International, 2001) 322.

26 Susan Sontag, "Notes on Camp," *Against Interpretation and Other Essays* (1996; New York: Routledge, 1993) 280.

How Black Do You Want It? Countee Cullen and the Contest for Racial Authenticity on Page and Stage

Jonathan Shandell

L angston Hughes' most renowned statement on racial authenticity in African American writing is his landmark 1926 essay "The Negro Artist and the Racial Mountain" which begins in this manner:

One of the most promising of the young Negro poets said to me once,

"I want to be a poet—not a Negro poet," meaning, I believe, "I want to write like a white poet"; meaning subconsciously, "I would like to be a white poet"; meaning behind that, "I would like to be white." And I was sorry the young man said that, for no great poet has ever been afraid of being himself. And I doubted then that, with his desire to run away spiritually from his race, this boy would ever be a great poet. But this is the mountain standing in the way of any true Negro art in America. (692).

The "young Negro poet" under discussion, never named in the essay, is Countee Cullen. Following Hughes in his climb up the "racial mountain" of self-prejudice against black subjects and themes toward a vista on "true Negro art" requires some scrutiny of the declaration he attributes to his contemporary and the series of assumptions he derives from it. Does Cullen's statement truly indicate some deep-seated desire to "run away" from his race and a fear "of being himself" as an African American? A newspaper profile of the young poet by pioneering black journalist and drama critic Lester Walton (published a few months before Hughes' essay) quotes Cullen proclaiming something slightly different: "I want to be *known as* a poet and not as a Negro poet" (my emphasis). A small difference in syntax has major implications. Hughes' unattributed quote implies an interior, ontological struggle with racinated identity. Walton's rendering of the same statement speaks to Cullen's discomfort not with blackness *per se* but with the cultural prejudices that attach to it, with the manner in which America *knows* its Negro poets: through restrictive and often falsifying demands for "racial" writing.[1] "I do not see any reason why we should be expected to do any particular kind of writing, painting or singing," Cullen elaborates. "The artist should feel free to get and use those materials for which he has the largest capabilities, whether those materials be within the confines of his particular group or outside" (qtd. in Walton).

However Cullen might have declared himself to one listener or another, the difference between these two quotations speaks to a wider contest among Harlem Renaissance artists and critics over definitions of black authenticity in creative expression. What makes a work of art authentically "Negro"? How might the African American artist faced with a national imperative "to pour racial individuality into the mold of American standardization" ("Racial Mountain" 692) create works that faithfully and honestly reflect a distinctive experience of being black in America? Such questions divided leading African American artists and intellectuals of the 1920s and have persisted within critical discourse on black culture ever since. This essay will revisit that critical divide in order to challenge the variously articulated charges of "in-authenticity" leveled regularly against Cullen—indictments beginning with Hughes and continuing throughout decades of later scholarship. I will argue that Cullen's inter-racialist stance—his various efforts through cultural criticism, poetry and drama to articulate African American subjectivity through the filter of Euro-American artistic forms and traditions—does not deprive his voice of racial authenticity; on the contrary, Cullen deserves renewed consideration as an authentic African American voice straining against white cultural hegemony from within its formal boundaries.

Rehabilitating Cullen's voice in the name of racial authenticity first requires separating questions of content and meaning from those of formal tradition. As will be expounded below, Cullen's techniques as a writer and his tastes as cultural critic owed much to the Euro-centricity of American culture. He neither attempted to hide his admiration for favorite poets Chaucer and Keats, nor offered any apologies for the extent to which these and other white European authors and Western literary conventions influenced his own poetry. Such tendencies offer enough incriminating evidence for many of Cullen's critics—i.e., if his poems look "white" on the surface, he must not be an "authentic" black poet. But such a verdict sidesteps any specific consideration of the ends to which a poet might use a chosen form, and of what (if anything) Cullen's poetry communicates about blackness. Notwithstanding the poet's various debts to European literature, and irrespective of what kind of poet Cullen might have wished to "be" or to "be known as" to the public, is there genuine truth in what his verses articulate about his subjective experience inside a black body? This is the standard for authenticity that Cullen's writing demands if it is to be analyzed sincerely rather than dismissed with a cursory glance.

Earnest evaluation of Cullen also requires discarding the bias against inter-racialism that colors much literary criticism, particularly within the crowded field of Harlem Renaissance scholarship. For instance, Nathan Irvin Huggins finds Harlem writers of the 1920s to have been "bound to an emulation of whites" and thus compromised by "enslavement to white forms and values" (305-6). In a similar vein, Henry Louis Gates, Jr. concludes that "the New Negroes of the Harlem Renaissance ... erased their racial selves" (148) to the extent they respected or adopted white influences. From another perspective, those disputing suggestions that the Harlem Renaissance was a "failure" tend to read the presence of inter-racialism within the movement as a game of misdirection designed to manipulate white patrons and audiences while undermining European and Euro-American standards. Houston Baker labels this sport of artistic bait-and-switch as a process of "formal mastery" (50) and "radical marronage" (75). Both lines of criticism—for and against the "failure" of Harlem Renaissance efforts—center on an inherent distrust of inter-racialism as a legitimate and authentic objective for African American artists.[2]

In truth, this contest for "real Negro art" was as much about class distinctions as it was about ethnicity. Hughes' essay illustrates J. Martin Favor's observation that, from the Harlem Renaissance to the turn of the 21st century, African American writers have habitually "felt the necessity of writing themselves into a privileged discourse on black identity" (3) which posits that "the best way to understand blackness in America is to scrutinize the lower classes, where ... the most authentic blackness is to be found" (4). Hughes' stance on Negro poetry rejects bourgeois American acculturation and root itself in what he calls "the low-down folks, the so-called common element" ("Racial Mountain" 693) of black communities. He promotes his own "jazz poetry" as a genre which is genuinely "racial in theme and treatment" in that it attempts "to grasp and hold some of the meanings and rhythms of jazz" (694)— the vernacular music of those "low-down folks." By contrast, no Harlem Renaissance figure was more notoriously bourgeois than Cullen—the son of an Episcopal minister, and a Phi Beta Kappa scholar at NYU and Harvard. Thus, Hughes argues, a writer like Cullen who employs traditional white poetic cadences betrays both an embarrassment in sharing a heritage with "low-down folks" and a deep-seated desire to become "Nordicized" (693). "I am ashamed for the colored artist who runs from the painting of Negro faces to the painting of sunsets after the manner of academicians. ... So I am ashamed for the black poet who says, 'I want to be a poet, not a Negro poet,' as though his own racial world were not as interesting as any other world" (694). Implicit here is an unspoken charge of commercialism—the accusation that a poet like Cullen rejects the black masses and writes "white" to support a comfortable standard of living, currying the favor of audiences more able to fund their efforts with publication contracts and book purchases. Thus "white comes to be unconsciously a symbol of all the virtues ... [of] beauty, morality *and money*" (693, my emphasis).

But must it necessarily follow that Cullen's middle-class background, elite education, college-groomed admiration for English poets, and the palatability of his work among white consumers render his writing inauthentic as "real" Negro poetry? Is the poet's formal conservatism truly an indication that Cullen "fears the strange un-whiteness of his own features" (694), as Hughes concludes? Though these charges are popular points of attack for Hughes and other critics of Cullen, it is clear—as I will illustrate—that whatever the realities of the marketplace, this poet conceived of his own work as directly defiant of (rather than acquiescent to) prevailing demands on Negro poets and unashamedly expressive of his self-identification as an African American.

As both leading poet and cultural critic of the Harlem Renaissance, Cullen promoted a divergent perspective from Hughes on racial authenticity in art. He believed that no Negro poet would be free to articulate any genuine sense of himself or herself when restricted in form or subject matter by white America's pervasive demands for "racial" writing. For Cullen, the primary challenge facing black poets was the realization of an undiluted freedom of self-expression that American culture had historically denied to its African American artists. A yearning to venture outside the accepted confines of "racial" subject matter and aesthetic forms need not be inconsistent with honest appreciation for one's own racial identity or heritage. In the June 1927 installment of "The Dark Tower," his monthly column of cultural criticism for *Opportunity*, Cullen writes:

> Without in the least deprecating the beauty of Negro spirituals or the undeniable fact that Negro singers do them, as it were, to the manner born, we have always resented the natural inclination of most white people to demand spirituals the moment it is known that a Negro is about to sing. So often the request has seemed to savor of the feeling that we could do this and this alone. (18)

Thus it was not (despite Hughes' strident rhetoric) inherent racial qualities of art and by extension the race itself that Cullen feared, but rather an excess of racial fixation in the American public imagination.

As Cullen saw it, American preoccupation with "racial art" threatened to replicate in the cultural sphere the injustices of Jim Crow segregation. Cullen repeatedly protested such bias as perpetuated by the white public. To a wealthy white French Negrophile who scolded the poet over his admiration for Keats, he responds, "May we not chant a hymn to the Sun God if we will, create a bit of phantasy in which not a spiritual or a blues appears ... in short do, write, create what we will, our only concern being that we do it well and with all the power in us?" ("On Miscegenation" 373). He also posed a similar challenge to well-intentioned black critics like Hughes with the poem "To Certain Critics," which begins:

> Then call me traitor if you must,
>
> Shout treason and default!
>
> Say I betray a sacred trust
>
> Aching beyond this vault.
>
> I'll bear your censure as your praise,
>
> For never shall the clan
>
> Confine my singing to its ways
>
> Beyond the ways of man. (206)

Writing as literary critic, Cullen afforded more respectful treatment to Hughes than he receives in return. Reviewing Hughes' published volume *The Weary Blues* in February 1926, Cullen praises his contemporary as "a transcendently emancipated spirit among a class of young writers whose particular battle-cry is freedom" and "a remarkable poet of the colorful; through all his verses the rainbow riots and dazzles, yet never wearies the eye." But his review also sounds a note of hesitation:

> I wonder if jazz poems really belong to that dignified company, that select and austere circle of high literary expression which we call poetry. ... I find myself straddling a fence ... There is too much emphasis here on strictly Negro themes; and this is probably an added reason for my coldness toward the jazz poems—they seem to set a too definite limit upon an already limited field. ("Poet on Poet" 73-4)

Far too much is made by commentators over Cullen's expressed concern for "high literary expression," and not enough attention paid to how his unease with jazz poetry results from an unmistakable admiration for the boldness of Hughes' voice. In this review, Cullen wrestles with some vital critical questions: Do the preponderance of "Negro themes" and formal innovations within Hughes' poetry play into the hands of those who would deny the African American poet the freedom to write in other modes? Will the strength of one battle cry for liberation *from* poetic traditions drown out the efforts of those black writers pursuing a different type of autonomy to work *within* those same traditions? Can and should the struggle for literary emancipation be fought on two fronts at once? These were questions that consumed Cullen throughout his career. Though he favored a less radical aesthetic approach both as artist and commentator, his reservations about jazz poetry and other models for "racial art" were always qualified and uncertain, never polemical nor reactionary.

In Cullen's view, exploring diverse forms and traditions (besides being the rightful province of any writer so inclined) could actually serve the black poet as a powerful means of affirming the self. Just as Chaucer did not compromise his Englishness when versifying about Troy nor Shakespeare in dramatizing Verona or ancient Rome, Cullen saw no inviolable bond between the milieu for art and the authentic expression of race, nationality or identity. Indeed, for African Americans separated from the memory, cultural heritage and language of their ancestry, the correlation between the surface appearance of art and who the artist truly is becomes highly problematic. "As heretical as it may sound," Cullen writes in the 1927 anthology *Caroling Dusk*, "there is the probability that Negro poets, dependent as they are on the English language, may have more to gain from the rich background of English and American poetry than from any nebulous atavistic yearnings toward an African inheritance" (xi). Cullen was deeply ambivalent about his era's upsurge in Africa-worship—a movement encouraged in part by a white-driven vogue in Negro primitivism and perpetuated by black artists with little or no first-hand experience of the continent. "What is Africa to me ... One three centuries removed," Cullen asks in the ballad "Heritage"—a poem that articulates both attraction to and alienation from iconoclastic notions of Africa and its "Heathen gods" (104) as well as an equally tortured skepticism with the alternative offered by Christianity and Western society.

In light of too many critics like Michael L. Lomax who dismiss Cullen's poems as "essentially fatuous literary artificialities" (246) rather than the expression of an authentic African American voice, it is worth underscoring that ambivalence is not the same as outright rejection. Huggins notes what he sees as an irony in Cullen's poetry: "No other Negro writer of the 1920s was more anxious to use primitive and atavistic motifs than the poet Countee Cullen. It is a bit ironic, because none of the Harlem writers was more formally schooled, none more genteel in inclination and taste." Thus, for Huggins it is "strange" and "out of character" (161) for a poet as formally conservative as Cullen to concern himself with inner subjectivity, for his erudite verses to strain with the weight of viscerality. Such a critique simply rehashes Hughes' position that Cullen was essentially an imitator of a tepid white poetics rather than a sincere voice of black subjectivity. But it was precisely in the friction between external restraints of American acculturation and the more elusive interior pangs of Africanist consciousness where Cullen located the essence of his African American identity.   One of his most notorious statements of self-analysis posits that his "chief problem" as a poet "has been that of reconciling a Christian upbringing with a pagan inclination" (*Caroling Dusk* 179).   His poetry articulates this tension in myriad ways, particularly in familiar versus such as the Petrarchan sonnets "Yet Do I Marvel" and "From the Dark Tower," as well as longer ballads such as "Heritage" and "The Black Christ."   Here I will illustrate the point using a less familiar poem:

> Atlantic City Waiter
>
> With subtle poise he grips his tray
> Of delicate things to eat;
>
> Choice viands to their mouths half way,
> The ladies watch his feet.
>
> Go carving dexterous avenues
> Through sly intricacies;
>
> Ten thousand years on jungle clues
> Alone shaped feet like these.
>
> For him to be humble who is proud
> Needs colder artifice;
>
> Though half his pride is disavowed,
> In vain the sacrifice.
>
> Sheer through his acquiescent mask
> Of bland gentility,
>
> The jungle flames like a copper cask
> Set where the sun strikes free. (85).

The stringency of Cullen's iambic verse—a chosen form for centuries of English balladeers—mirrors the social confinement in which his waiter character must operate; the poem's structure mirrors its theme of "colder artifice."   Within those formal confines, Cullen taps veins of race consciousness: the "jungle clues" transmitted through a long and painful African diaspora to guide the footsteps of black Americans, and the generations-old disavowal of pride that white society exacts on its darker subjects.   The antiseptic world of lunching ladies and genteel diction of "choice viands" and "dextrous avenues" give way to vibrant golden imagery of copper, flame and sunshine.   While the same "acquiescent mask / Of bland gentility" shrouding the waiter's proud face covers the poem itself, Cullen offers furtive glimpses at something bolder—even primal—lurking behind the facade.

This tension between cultural imprisonment and inner rebellion was for Cullen (though not the product of an *exclusively* black cultural heritage) an authentic rendering of the psychic division between an elusive African genealogy and the forces of Euro-American cultural hegemony. This quality of his poetry was not lost on some perceptive critics of the era. James Weldon Johnson saw through the paradox in 1931 by writing:

> Some critics have ventured to state that Cullen is not an authentic Negro poet. ... there is in [this criticism] a faint flare-up of the old taboo which would object to the use of "white" material by the Negro artist ... Yet, strangely, it is because Cullen revolts against these "racial" limitations—technical and spiritual—that the best of his poetry is motivated by race. He is always seeking to free himself and his art from these bonds. He never entirely escapes, but from the very fret and chafe he brings forth poetry that contains the quintessence of race-consciousness. (220).

Jessie Fauset, too, found in this poet "the feelings and the gift to express colored-ness in a world of whiteness" (238). Cullen's poetic articulation of his "colored-ness" and "race-consciousness" was of a much different nature than the jazz aesthetic advanced by Hughes, but no less authentic. Its expression was not geared to deny, evade or camouflage blackness but rather to mark its precarious position within the restraints of a bourgeois, Eurocentric and Christian-bound American culture.

The intersection of white literary traditions and "darker" racial sensibilities informs Cullen's only major solo work for the theater: his strikingly modern 1935 translation of *TheMedea*.[3] Cullen's treatment of the play transposes Euripides' high tragic verses into colloquially flavored prose (with choral odes in verse). A few of Creon's outbursts to Medea during their first confrontation early in the play encapsulate the contemporary idiomatic flavor of the dialogue: "I'm not one for beating about the bush, Medea ... Forewarned is forearmed ... You are wasting your breath, as well as my time ... I must think of my own flesh and blood. Charity begins at home" (*The Medea* 270-1). Cullen wrote the play for Rose McClendon to enact the title role opposite a white actor playing Jason. Whatever racial overtones the drama evokes are not a direct function of the text itself, but rather the by-product of historical circumstance and critical ascription. Kevin J. Wetmore explains:

> Cullen made no attempt to 'Africanize' the play, the characters, the setting or the message in any way—the prose language is straightforward American dialect of the 1930s with no indication of ethnicity. ... Nevertheless, critics responded (and still respond) to the text with Cullen's own ethnicity and the fact that Rose McClendon was to play the role in mind. ... [Cullen's] play is perceived and received as being an

Afrocentric translation of *Medea*, linked to black American culture in spite of the lack
of a black cultural presence or African American references in the play (145-7).

A 1925 review of the published script in *Opportunity* illustrates the type of
response that Wetmore describes. Reviewer Mildred Boie argues of *The Medea*
"[t]hat he chose a play dealing with a woman who [is] ... the victim of unfair
efforts to cut her off from her rightful position in society signifies Mr. Cullen's
ability to objectify by putting off in time and situation the problem of social
discrimination to which, in a special form, he too is subject" (381). More
recently, Lilian Corti reads *The Medea* as "a complex and significant synthesis
of ancient Greek, contemporary American and African nationalist elements,"
disputing what she finds to be an inherent "racial bias" against the play "not
only from white critics ... for whom the idea of a black Medea was evidently a
tiresome curiosity, but also from black critics who assume that Greek myths
cannot possibly be relevant to African American experience" (622).

Extending Corti's analysis of the play, I propose that the culture
immediacy of *The Medea* springs most directly from its engagement with the
"theme of alien-and-exile"—a motif that Arthur P. Davis identifies as a both a
central motif of Cullen's "race poems" and as a literary topos "common to all
New Negro writing [with] its origins in that movement's attempts to make
Africa a literary homeland for the Negro creative artist" (390). When cast and
staged in the manner originally intended, *The Medea* articulates in time and
space—in a way that printed words alone could never accomplish—how a so-
called "barbarian" tragic heroine makes for an appropriate surrogate cultural
ancestor for blacks ostracized by white American society and stranded in
perpetual exile from their true African roots. Such a theatrical appropriation
of Ancient Greek myth aligns with Anthony Tatlow's analysis of intercultural
performance: "Sometimes the only way of engaging with one's own cultural
past lies in its alienation not just by but through the foreign" (78).

Though *The Medea* never saw the inside of a theater until the 1950s, the
play is noteworthy for Cullen's era as a work that links this writer's
employment of "white" artistic modes with a larger critical debate permeating
the American theater at the time. Throughout the 1920s and 1930s, theater
artists and critics both black and white wrestled with a sticky racial taboo
against casting African American actors in classical roles associated exclusively
with white performers. The first notable challenge to this proscription was the
Shakespearean work of Ira Aldridge, James Hewlitt and the African Grove
Players during the 1820s. About a century later, an unaffiliated nationwide
network of amateur dramatic societies, university clubs and semi-professional
companies developed to continue the practice we now call "non-traditional
casting." One troupe achieving particular visibility in this respect was the

Ethiopian Art Theatre of Chicago. Founded under the leadership of Raymond O'Neil, a white director who had previously led the Cleveland Playhouse, the Ethiopian Art Theatre became most notorious for making Willis Richardson the first black playwright on Broadway with their staging of *The Chip Woman's Fortune* at the Frazee Theater in April 1923. But the Ethiopian Art Theatre's repertoire also featured all-black productions of plays by Shakespeare, Molière, Hugo von Hofmannsthal, and other European playwrights. *The Chip Woman's Fortune* shared the bill at the Frazee with Oscar Wilde's *Salome* and an "à la jazz" treatment of Shakespeare's *The Comedy of Errors*.

It was these latter two offerings that sparked the most public debate during the Ethiopian Art Theatre's visit to New York. While reactionary white reviewers tended to assert "a mental parallelism of white art for white folk, and black art for black folk" in their assessments, African American commentators responded in lockstep: "The great works of Shakespeare, Molière and others are not the indisputable heritage of the white man which constitute his forbidden territory of drama upon which none but Caucasians should trespass" (Harris 775). Joining the chorus in support of the Ethiopian Art Theatre's integration of the Western canon was W.E.B. Du Bois, who writes in *Theatre Magazine*, "we may think of the Negro actor ... as one who gives to the world an interpretation of the same great plays which white actors have portrayed. Despite singular prejudice on the part of some people, this is a practical and legitimate role for black men and women" ("Can the Negro" 68).

Only three years after this pronouncement, DuBois crafted his famous and oft-cited definition of black authenticity in drama—which leaves no room for so-called "color blind" treatments of European dramatic classics:

> The plays of a real Negro theatre must be: 1. *About us*. That is, they must have plots which reveal Negro life as it is. 2: *By us*. That is, they must be written by Negro authors who understand from birth and continual association just what it means to be a Negro today. 3: *For us*. That is, the theatre must cater primarily to Negro audiences and be supported and sustained by their entertainment and approval. 4: *Near us*. The theatre must be in a Negro neighborhood near the mass of ordinary Negro people. ("Krigwa" 134)

Clearly the mounting of Shakespeare and Wilde by African American actors on a Broadway stage fails to meet the standards of authenticity Du Bois set down for the Krigwa Players—an amateur ensemble he founded in the basement of the Harlem Library.[4] So can the efforts of the Ethiopian Art Theatre be a "practical and legitimate" undertaking for black artists but still not measure as "real Negro theatre"? And what, then, might Du Bois have made of a work like *The Medea*—a European classic reinterpreted by a Negro poet that looks to carve out a distinctive African American foothold behind the hegemonic lines of western theater history? If nothing else, these two somewhat conflicting pronouncements from Du Bois speak to the limitations of setting *a priori* standards of black authenticity in the theater that can serve for all situations. What seems "legitimate," "real," or racially authentic for African American artists and audiences of one particular time and place may resonate quite differently in other contexts—as different civic, economic and artistic forces come into play.

It is difficult now—especially in light of the obvious biases of critics of the 1920s—to reconstruct exactly how the artists of the Ethiopian Art Theatre interpreted *Salome* or *The Comedy of Errors*, and whether they found in this material possibilities for expressing some authentic truth about themselves. But it is enough to acknowledge that the potential was there, just as it was for other black artists of the era (including Countee Cullen) who chose to work within rather than reject the white Western canon of drama. An *Opportunity* column of 1928 highlights how the theater as an artistic medium creates new possibilities for self-expression in every age and cultural context: "Just as the traveler in a foreign country can sometimes see beauty in surroundings to which the native has become dulled, other dramatic gifts may pick up new high lights which native talent fails to catch" (Jelliffe 214).

On stage, as on the page, we must never assume a simple correlation between the surface appearance of a work of art and who the artist or artists involved truly wish themselves to be. The writings of Countee Cullen, and the work of groups like the Ethiopian Art Theatre, should be seen not as mere imitations of white cultural hegemony, but also as holding the power to embody what Langston Hughes seeks when he surveys the nation's cultural landscape—namely, a "real Negro art in America." Ultimately, as Favor reminds us, any gesture of defining black literary authenticity becomes "a pointedly political act in a racialist society" (6). The agenda informing such an act is in most instances valiant and commendable for its anti-racist, anti-classist and anti-hegemonic aims. Still, pursuit of these objectives must not cloud our vision of other paths to authenticity that should also remain discernable from the summit of the racial mountain.

Notes

[1] In his introduction to the anthology of Cullen's writing *My Soul's High Song*, Gerald Early offers this quote from an article in the *Brooklyn Daily Eagle* (February 10, 1924): "If I am going to be a poet at all, I am going to be POET and not NEGRO POET. That is what has hindered the development of artists among us. Their one note has been the concern with their race. That is all very well, none of us can get away from it. I cannot at times. You will see it in my verse. The consciousness of this is too poignant at times. I cannot escape it. But what I mean is this: I shall not write of negro subjects for the purposes of propaganda. That is not what the poet is concerned with. Of course, when the emotion rising out of the fact that I am negro is strong, I express it" (*My Soul's High Song* 23). Here, too (though the words "known as" are not present), Cullen's concern is not with his own identity but with public expectations for the "NEGRO POET", and the desire not to restrict himself to them.

[2] For an extended discussion of the critical bias against inter-racialism among Harlem Renaissance critics, see Hutchinson 14-28.

[3] Cullen's other theatrical writings are: the 1946 musical *St. Louis Woman*, written with Arna Bontemps (based on Bontemps' 1931 novel *God Sends Sunday*); and the one-act *The Third Fourth of July*, written with Owen Dodson, published in *Theatre Arts* in 1946.

[4] See Walker for an account of the history and repertoire of the Krigwa Players.

Works Cited

Baker, Houston A. *Modernism and the Harlem Renaissance*. Chicago: University of Chicago Press, 1987.

Boie, Mildred. "The Proof of the Poet." Review of *The Medea and Some Poems* by Countee Cullen. *Opportunity* 13 (Dec. 1935): 381.

Corti, Lillian. "Countée Cullen's *Medea*."*African American Review* 32 (Winter 1998): 621-33.

Cullen, Countee. "Atlantic City Waiter." Early, *My Soul's High Song* 85.

_____, ed. *Caroling Dusk*. New York: Harper & Bros., 1927.

_____. "Countee Cullen on Miscengenation."*Crisis* 36 (Nov. 1929): 373.

_____. "The Dark Tower."*Opportunity* 15 (June 1927): 181.

_____. "Heritage." Early, *My Soul's High Song* 104-8.

_____. *The Medea*. Early, *My Soul's High Song* 261-303.

_____. "Our Book Shelf: Poet on Poet." Review of *The Weary Blues* by Langston Hughes. *Opportunity* 4 (Feb. 1926): 73-4.

_____. "To Certain Critics." Early, *My Soul's High Song* 206.

_____, ed. *Caroling Dusk*. New York: Harper & Bros., 1927.

Davis, Arthur P. "The Alien-and-Exile Theme in Countée Cullen's Racial Poems." *Phylon* 14.4 (4ᵗʰ Q. 1953): 390-400.

Douglas, Ann. *Terrible Honesty: Mongrel Manhattan in the 1920s*. New York: Farrar, Straus and Giroux, 1995.

DuBois, W.E.B. "Can the Negro Serve the Drama?" *Theater Magazine* 38.1 (July 1923): 12, 68.

_____ . "Krigwa Little Negro Theatre," *Crisis* 32 (July 1926): 133-6.

Early, Gerald. "Introduction." Early, *My Soul's High Song* 3-73.

_____, ed. *My Soul's High Song: The Collected Writings of Countee Cullen, Voice of the Harlem Renaissance*. New York: Doubleday, 1991.

Favor, J. Martin. *Authentic Blackness: The Folk in the New Negro Renaissance*. Durham, NC: Duke University Press, 1999.

Fauset, Jesse. "Our Book Shelf."*Crisis* 31 (1926): 238.

Gates, Henry Louis, Jr. "The Trope of the New Negro and the Reconstruction of the Image of the Black."*Representations* 24 (1988): 129-55.

Harris, Abram L. "The Ethiopian Art Players and the Nordic Complex."*Messenger* 5 (1923): 774-7.

Huggins, Nathan Irvin. *Harlem Renaissance*. New York: Oxford University Press, 1971.

Hughes, Langston. "The Negro Artist and the Racial Mountain."*The Nation* 122(23 June 1926): 692-4.

Hutchinson, George. *The Harlem Renaissance in Black and White*. Cambridge, MA: Harvard University Press, 1995.

Jelliffe, Roweena Woodham ."The Negro in the Field of Drama."*Opportunity* 6 (July 1928): 214.

Johnson, James Weldon. *The Book of American Negro Poetry*. New York: Harcourt, Brace & World, 1931.

Lomax, Michael M. "Countee Cullen: A Key to the Puzzle." *Harlem Renaissance Re-examined*. Eds. Victor A. Kramer and Robert A. Russ. Troy, NY: Whitson Publishers, 1997. 239-47.

Tatlow, Anthony. *Shakespeare, Brecht, and the Intercultural Sign*. Durham, NC: Duke University Press, 2001.

Walker, Ethel Pitts. "Krigwa, A Theatre By, For, and About Black People." *Theatre Journal* 40.3 (October 1988). 347-56.

Walton, Lester. "... Protests Holding Negro Artists to Racial Themes" [title incomplete], *New York World* 15 May 1927. In Schomburg Clipping File, microfiche 001,298—"Cullen, Countee."Schomburg Center for Research in Black Culture, New York, NY.

Wetmore, Kevin J. *Black Dionysus: Greek Tragedy and African American Theatre*. Jefferson, NC: McFarland & Co., 2003.

Peculiar Irresolution: James Baldwin and Flânerie

Monika Gehlawat

"The most crucial time in my own development came when I was forced to recognize that I was a kind of bastard of the West...I was an interloper; this was not my heritage. At the same time I had no other heritage which I could possibly hope to use - I had certainly been unfitted for the jungle or the tribe."

- James Baldwin, "Autobiographical Notes"

"To be away from home and yet to feel at home anywhere; to see the world, to be at the very centre of the world, and yet to be unseen of the world, such are some of the minor pleasures of those independent, intense and impartial spirits, who do not lend themselves easily to linguistic definitions."

- Charles Baudelaire, "The Painter of Modern Life"

James Baldwin reflects above on the special attitude he brought to Western culture, identifying himself not as a native son, but an interloper. A century earlier, Baudelaire described the liberating qualities of this paradox of homelessness by invoking the flâneur. This figure provides a fresh way to challenge the notion of black authenticity as an inherited or intrinsic quality and illuminates Baldwin's dynamic urban subjectivity. His essay "Autobiographical Notes" was written and published in 1955 when Baldwin was thirty-one years old and just back in America from nearly a decade spent in Paris. This moment in his career is crucial to understanding his particular mode of flânerie that most emphasizes the qualities of liminality and movement as the precursors to identity. Baldwin's unrelenting awareness that he did not fit in anywhere helps to critique the sense that black authenticity originates in a particular place, community, or a priori self-knowledge. I will argue that Baldwin resists *both* an ontological definition of individual authenticity *and* a prescribed relationship to group identity. His writing emphasizes the productive interaction of the individual and culture in order to dissolve the myth of *belonging* altogether. Rather than exhibiting "black authenticity," he fiddles with the term; for Baldwin, contradiction is better than complacency. Conflict, resistance, and visual agency characterize the way he tests this notion via flânerie.

The highly individualistic experience Baldwin represents in his writing on the city is based in a fundamental sense of alienation. What makes him a flâneur is not only his alienation in white America but also his slightly incongruous relationship to the black community. Cornel West describes the marginalist tradition of African-American literature he believes Baldwin belongs to:

> The Afro-American marginalist tradition promotes a self-image of both confinement and creativity, restriction and revolt. It encompasses a highly individualistic rebellion of Afro-Americans who are marginal to, or exist on the edges of, Afro-American culture and see little use in assimilating into the American mainstream.[1]

This category of African-American literature seems fitting for Baldwin, especially its image of creativity in the face of restriction. However, my reading of Baldwin as a flâneur complicates the intentions of marginalist writers as West describes them. In particular, he writes that this type of individual sees "little use in assimilating into the American mainstream," but I think Baldwin walks a finer line in his critical approach. Specifically, his form of "individualistic rebellion" engages urban social life; it is, in fact, exercised vis-à-vis its encounter with both African-American and American cultural forms. His participation in politics, enthusiasm for American movies and musical art forms, and dominant voice in urban social debates put his writing in constant dialogue with contemporary culture. As a flâneur, Baldwin articulates curiosity, desire, and skepticism for the conflicting social forms he encounters, while deliberately refusing affiliation with any of them.

In his book *Black Autobiography in America*, Stephen Butterfield has criticized Baldwin for his "political detachment," explaining that in black autobiography, "the self is conceived as a member of an oppressed social group, with ties and responsibilities to the other members."[2] According to this definition, he argues that Baldwin fails to create the kind of work that can effect social change because he writes from an individualistic viewpoint. I would agree that Baldwin's writing comes from a profoundly alienated place, a precarious independence that is aware of a community but also afflicted with a sense of un-belonging, an agitated relationship not only to his own racial community but to others as well. Throughout his writing, he maintains both tension and proximity to Christianity, heterosexuality, European cultures and America. Though formative, his ties to various groups and places was touch-and-go; any attempt to absorb him into their cause was met with resistance or else a stubborn, firsthand rendering of the cause itself.[3]

At the same time, Baldwin demonstrates considerable contradiction, self-questioning, and a keen awareness of his own vulnerability. He does not reject communal notions of black authenticity for some implicit faith in the self or individual authenticity. His writing is full of phrases like "I failed to see," or "I tried but couldn't hack it," or "I think all theories are suspect," or "reassessment, though painful, is valuable." At times, he is almost willfully paradoxical, resisting absolute points of view to show that he has the energy to think creatively. In his essay, "The Black Boy Looks at the White Boy," Baldwin writes, "The world tends to trap and immobilize you in the role you play; and it is not always easy – in fact, it is always extremely hard – to maintain a kind of watchful, mocking distance between oneself as one appears to be and oneself as one actually is."[4] Despite the simple binary presented here, Baldwin never actually provides a sustained definition of the self. The sense of "oneself as one actually is" is problematized repeatedly in this essay (most perceptibly in the relationship between Baldwin and Norman Mailer) as well as other written works, showing how Baldwin is always speaking and un-speaking his positions. Indeed, there seems to be a way in which Baldwin uses the very complexity of "what one actually is" to befuddle the world and maintain a vigilant, ironic exposure to it. Any claims to individual or socially-based authenticity would only undermine his independent play which, like the flâneur, "seeks refuge in the crowd."[5] The payoff for Baldwin is not simply to escape appropriation, but to sustain, amidst false starts and hyperbole, a personal and spontaneous sense of risk-taking. The world is never far from Baldwin's artistic or philosophical experience, and what he seems to despise most in it is the potential for indifference.

I want to read James Baldwin as a postwar American flâneur because I find in the bulk of criticism that exists on this writer little that theorizes his relentless mobility and purposeful marginality to urban life. Actually, much has been said of Baldwin as a cosmopolitan traveler, an exile or expatriate, but these narratives are usually based on the notion of escape rather than protest. It is common to hear of Baldwin referred to as an artist with a "divided mind,"[6] a social critic, a gay writer, an African-American writer, a gay African-American writer. Is it really necessary to supply this body of criticism with yet another label? Perhaps in this case, for the flâneur provides us with a way of thinking productively, rather than descriptively, about Baldwin's relationship to postwar American culture. Flânerie is an expansive practice that challenges black authenticity to emerge as a varied, even contradictory, presence in contemporary life. Any attempt to categorize Baldwin, as the list above shows, deteriorates as ideologies compete to claim him as their own. Some critics consider this slipperiness or adaptability cause for censure; they label Baldwin an agnostic, a detached or self-involved critic whose emphasis on the personal never achieved the political scope expected of him.[7] Reading Baldwin as a flâneur enables us to contemplate how his intense commitment to the personal, to movement and the moment, and to the appropriation of public space make him not only political but, in Benjamin's sense, revolutionary. In order to do this I look to thinkers like Henri Lefebvre and Walter Benjamin, as well as post-colonial critic Homi Bhabha. These thinkers allow me to emphasize Baldwin's status as an outsider and to understand his critique of cultural confinement alongside his own trans-Atlantic mobility. I argue that Baldwin's marginal relation to various (racial, religious, economic, political, and sexual) groups and his vigilant refusal to be identified with any of them paradoxically informs his social praxis. From the borders, he can transgress and agitate, while remaining open, vulnerable and proximate to the crowd.

In *Absolute Bourgeois*, T.J. Clark describes Baudelaire in 1848: he was "...shadowy, open, confused: fluid in his allegiances, hysterical in his enthusiasms, claiming the right to contradict himself. It is Baudelaire *in the interlude*, in a space between two poses, two closures on the world outside."[8] The archetypal flâneur, Baudelaire predates James Baldwin by a century, yet his fluidity and contradictory presence in urban life are quite relevant to understanding Baldwin's relationship to America, in particular New York. New York is Baldwin's birthplace as Paris was Baudelaire's, and they share the paradoxical sense of being estranged from home. This liminality has political leanings--it is both idealistic and critical, but most of all it is characterized by an intensity that energizes the "interlude" itself. This consciousness of the moment rejects inherited assumptions about authenticity in order to *produce* forms of social behavior that challenge the status quo. By accepting one's alienation from birthplace, race, and even a fundamental self-certainty, the flâneur truly opens out to the world. Homi Bhabha explains the "unhomely" resistance to closure thus:

> the intervention of the 'beyond' that establishes a boundary: a bridge, where 'presencing' begins because it captures something of the estranging sense of the relocation of home and world...to be unhomed is not to be homeless, nor can 'unhomely' be easily accommodated in that familiar division of social life into private and public spheres.[9]

Bhabha speaks to the condition of the diasporic subject, but I argue that Baldwin, like Baudelaire, articulates his sense of the "beyond" against the traditional grain of his community and cityspace. For him, it was necessary to leave New York for Paris and, in a sense, perform the sense of exile twice-removed in order to return to New York and generate power out of alienation. Indeed, he becomes a flâneur only at the point when he converts his marginality into a defiant mobility in metropolitan life. Furthermore, Baldwin's writing challenges "that familiar division of social life into private and public" by suggesting that estrangement in the world is ever-present, yet awareness of this fact might facilitate the integration of one's own inner and outer self. Rather than trying to "fit in," one might fit *within* oneself, making private and public life whole, while one's presence in the world and self-development may continue to produce friction or struggle.

In order to develop this reading, I engage Baldwin's essays and his collection of short stories, *Going to Meet the Man*. This collection, though published in 1965, includes stories that were written as early as 1948. Consequently, the span of Baldwin's first trans-Atlantic movement finds its aesthetic articulation in these works. The combined pursuits of essayist and artist also serve to align Baldwin with the hybrid identity of the flâneur as dandy, artist, and social critic. His integration of private and public space via these roles facilitates an understanding of Baldwin as flâneur. Baldwin did not want separate and protected spheres of private and public life, he wanted to experience private life *in* public space. That is, he refused to see expatriation or art practice as a refuge from racial discrimination or oppression in public policy. It was important to revolutionize total experience so that the public self could coexist with private life and aesthetic pursuits. Otherwise, individual life becomes "parceled-out," as Henri Lefebvre puts it: "The ordering into perspective is also a "staging" of everyday life; it organizes it: the scene is what determines the *ob-scene*, what is not here."[10]

Harlem

Prior to his departure in 1948, Baldwin's life in New York far from resembled the idyllic image of the flâneur strolling about town, a "prince incognito."[11] But then, part of my project here is to dispel simplistic narratives of flânerie, which fail to consider what Susan Buck-Morss calls "the other hellish side of the urban phantasmagoria."[12] For Baldwin, this was Harlem, but also the experience of being black in New York City. The glorified sense of the flâneur as dandy or aristocrat seem superficial, for it stops at the *image* most commonly associated with this figure rather than the modes of experience that one *performs*. Indeed, the more flânerie can be thought of as a practice rather than a privilege, the more we can reject ontological assumptions about authenticity. The flâneur does not transcend complexity or danger but maintains a kind of proximity to shock-producing effects through constant immersion, attention, and play. Although Baldwin experienced many shock-intensive conditions, he was not able to express their revolutionary potential until he left New York and activated his alienation. I will begin by discussing ways in which Baldwin felt the African American subject in postwar New York City suffered from paranoid, self-mechanizing modes of behavior.

Baldwin's experience in Harlem creates a double sense of homelessness: first, the shared truth that home is never one's own nor secure and second, the deep disgust with the enforced conditions of that home. Locating a secure claim for authenticity in that space becomes impossible for the critical flâneur. Baldwin writes extensively on the quality of life experienced in neighborhoods like Harlem whose most visible features are the housing project and the policeman. These elements restrict freedom spatially and psychically; the cramped, bleak quarters of the projects induce a kind of claustrophobic rage which is kept in check by the double pressure of the policeman's gaze and his billy club. Baldwin argues that black people living in the ghetto lack the security to move freely in the public sphere while, at the same time, suffering from administrative control in their private lives. He writes, "Even if the administration of the projects were not so insanely humiliating (for example: one must report raises in salary to the management, which will then eat up the profit by raising one's rent; the management has the right to know who is staying in your apartment; the management can ask you to leave, at their discretion), the projects would still be hated because they are an insult to the meanest intelligence."[13] Notice how here and elsewhere Baldwin critiques the conditions in Harlem according to a basic human standard. He refers to even "the meanest intelligence" and "the desire to make hovels habitable" to invoke universal standards and then to reveal their flimsy aspect in the material conditions of Harlem. In the late 1940s and 1950s, any attempt to flee the menial imprisonment of this life rarely met with success in other parts of the city.[14] Indeed, black people were discouraged from living downtown and were often asked to leave apartment buildings because of neighbors' complaints. Specifically, these spatial conditions show how Baldwin's identity as an artist (seeking a community downtown) and a black man (from uptown) had begun to require greater mobility.

In his story "Previous Condition," published the same year Baldwin left New York for Paris, he describes a day in the life of a young black actor lost between the white world and that of "his people." The protagonist is staying in an apartment leased by a white friend downtown and the story begins as he is thrown out by the landlady:

> "You get outa my house!" she screamed. "I got the right to know who's in my house! This is a white neighborhood. I don't rent to colored people. Why don't you go on uptown, like you belong?"

> "I can't stand niggers," I told her, I started to close the door again but she moved and stuck her foot in the way.[15]

Many forms of anger manifest in this scene--the landlady's anger at the intruding black body and the protagonist's anger at being viewed as such. The latter, however, is more complicated than it seems. His rage is due to frustrated mobility, as well as the way in which black people are expected to live, as "niggers," in cramped projects uptown where they "belong." In fact, it is his very lack of belonging, his private suspicion that no one should *belong* to such a home that characterizes his paralysis and sense of loss in the story. Baldwin demonstrates how indignation at the status quo renders the marginalized individual homeless; rejecting where society wishes him to be, he is barred from accessing any other domain. He writes, "The city didn't love us. They looked at us as though we were zebras, and you know, some people like zebras and some people don't. But nobody ever asks the zebra."[16] The passivity expected of the black city dweller is implicit in this provocative example; he or she must accept dehumanizing conditions. Immediately recognizable and potentially dangerous, black people in the city are the fixed object of others' gaze and can be corralled, if need be.

Toward the end of "Previous Condition," the narrator takes the subway uptown after a wretched day in the city. He heads toward Harlem without thinking about it, escaping to the place where he has been ordered to go. Baldwin writes, "I got off in Harlem and went to a rundown bar on Seventh Avenue. My people, my people. Sharpies stood on the corner, waiting. Women in summer dresses pranced by on wavering heels...There were white mounted policemen in the streets. On every block there was another policeman on foot."[17] The repressive presence of state authority does not reduce the tension in the neighborhood but rather bottles it up and intensifies the anger. The sharpies who stand on the corner are waiting--what for is suggestive--one cannot miss the theater of a social conflict, the standoff that Baldwin represents-- sharpies on the corner and policemen on the street. For the author, the policeman "represent the force of the white world, and that world's real intentions are simply...to keep the black man corralled up here, in his place. The badge, the gun in the holster, and the swinging club make vivid what will happen should his rebellion become overt."[18] Spatially, it is significant that while the policemen patrol the street, the sharpies lurk in the corner, neither moving nor occupying a visible and legitimate zone. They have already been, in a sense, cornered.

The detached voice Baldwin uses in his essays has been criticized for its dissociative tone toward African Americans. That is, he speaks about the black man as outside of himself, just as he does about the police or politicians. I'd like to suggest that this voice is neither apolitical nor indicative of self-hatred but can be understood as the voice of the flâneur whose proximity to the crowd is laced with an awareness of his marginal status. It also exhibits how Baldwin formally challenges authenticity as an immediate or intrinsic claim. The third-person voice reflects a position of attentive resistance, deliberately illuminating the alienation Baldwin experiences. David Frisby reminds us that for Benjamin, "the flâneur is an uprooted person. He is at home neither in his class nor in his birthplace but rather only in the crowd. Such marginality creates a distance between the figure and that which is being observed."[19] This distance is self-imposed, though not cold. It is a mode of survival that allows the flâneur to remain open to the shocks of daily urban life while also writing of them. Furthermore, Baldwin's despair with the quality of life suffered by African Americans is too easily read as despair with the community itself. His critical stance involves empathy toward what he sees. It is no wonder that most, if not all of Baldwin's essays about Harlem were written after he had returned to New York from Paris. His development toward flânerie required that he simulate actual physical distance from the site of his investigations before he could practice it in proximity to its threats.

In his essay "The Flâneur in Social Theory," David Frisby writes:

> Benjamin refers to "the dialectic of flânerie: on the one hand, the man who feels himself observed by everyone and everything, the totally suspicious person, on the other, the completely undiscoverable, hidden person." This hidden figure, who is totally at home in the urban milieu, however strange it may appear in the course of his explorations, possesses the capacity for reading the signs of the...metropolis.[20]

This dialectic of exposure and invisibility approximates the black city-dweller who finds himself, in the case of Baldwin, simultaneously inspected and overlooked by administrative power. He is not, however, "totally at home in the urban milieu." The gaze that objectifies also fails to see him, and this paradox creates a deep sense of alienation from oneself and the city. Benjamin's description of the "completely undiscoverable, hidden person" carries a different valence when applied to the experience of the African-American in New York. The latter may be ignored, but never hidden; the advantage of being hidden, the flexibility of remaining incognito is not extended to the individual who is visually tagged by the color of their skin, no matter how elusive their presence may be. This visual discrimination restricts mobility, for it marks the black subject as transgressive if seen outside of segregated domains.

The transformation required to practice flânerie is marked by agency. Prior to leaving New York, Baldwin describes how he reacted, almost automatically, but always in obedience to the standards set into place by "the man." He refers to these reactions as a kind of talent at survival, a version of Benjamin's "man of the crowd" who, "when jostled, bows profusely to his jostlers." Unlike the flâneur who demands elbow room, the man of the crowd is overrun by the crowd. In fact, Benjamin adds, the man of the crowd "exemplifies, rather, what had to become of the flâneur once he was deprived of the milieu to which he belonged."[21] Baldwin describes the humiliating skill of submission African Americans learn in order to survive. He writes, "A Negro learns to gauge precisely what reaction the alien person facing him desires, and he produces it with disarming artlessness. The friends I had, growing up and going to work, grew bitter every day."[22] In "Previous Condition," the narrator echoes:

> Like a prizefighter learns to take a blow or a dancer learns to fall, I'd learned how to get by... After the first few times, I realized that I had to play smart, to act out the role I was expected to play...When I faced a policeman I acted like I didn't know a thing, I let my jaw drop and let my eyes get big. I didn't give him any smart answers, none of the crap about my rights. I figured out what answers he wanted and I gave them to him.[23]

The protagonist mimics the offensive caricature of the doltish black man with rolling eyes and open mouth in order to legitimate the authority who created the stereotype in the first place. However, the appearance of passivity evoked by the narrator is just that, a mask. Underneath, hostility and resentment grow against the intended audience of these studied performances. Having no outlet, the disconnection between action and desire, the self-protective psychic repression contributes to the most painful alienation of all, which is not the alienation of the black man from the world, nor even his alienation from his own community, but an internal and deeply felt alienation from himself. This compulsory performance differs greatly from the flâneur's willful play with appearances. The latter demonstrates agency and daring in the crowd; hardly defensive, the flâneur's openness allows for the emotional life of people to interpenetrate.

The submissive survival tactics that Baldwin describes operate as a protective shield, altogether opposing the bold practice of the flâneur who lays himself open to the danger in the crowd. This turning-against-oneself is an act of discipline that Foucault describes as the real power of state authority. Once a subject becomes self-regulatory, the state need not flex its muscles with threatening violence because it has created an atmosphere of paranoia and objectification. The policeman need only to stroll by for the ghetto-dweller to know what is expected of him and to deliver it. Moreover, each performance of this expectation works to undermine his sense of dignity and independence while securing the power of the other. Eventually, this dynamic creates an environment where the authority of the state may even be able to *perform* the mask of liberal generosity. Having trained the black subject into self-regulatory submission and corralled him into an economically-deprived neighborhood, state power builds housing projects and offers welfare in order to appear not a hostile, killing force, but a benefactor.

Baldwin punctuates this point when he writes, "The people in Harlem know they are living here because white people do not think they are good enough to live anywhere else. No amount of "improvement" can sweeten this fact. Whatever money is now being earmarked to improve this, or any other ghetto, might as well be burnt. A ghetto can be improved in one way only: out of existence."[24] Baldwin has no interest in preserving what he considers to be the confining spatializations of contemporary urban life. Again, he has been critiqued for his harsh attitude toward Harlem for, unlike both black and white liberals, he did not glorify the neighborhood as an authentic, culturally rich enclave but pointed to its deprivation and sub par living conditions. His frustration with these immobilizing forces led to his departure from this home and, shortly thereafter, New York. The conditions, both psychic and social, that he describes, help to lay the groundwork for the flâneur's revolutionary potential. In particular, this figure challenges domesticated imprisonment, segregated social space, restricted movement, and the threatening power of the gaze. Next we will the see how the flâneur struggles against these forces by coopting their weapons: Baldwin accesses visibility and mobility in order to challenge traditional notions of black authenticity that bar his own emergent presence in social space.

Paris

James Baldwin wrote extensively during his years in Paris, mostly about the experience of being an American. The anonymity he discovered in Paris made it possible for him to explore the isolation and anger he felt privately in New York. In an essay about exile, James Dievler explains this situation:

> The reality of not "fitting in" at home allows for a certain naturalness about living in a different country. And further, the psychological sense of exile, the disconnectedness from one's home, loses its crisis nature when one is truly disconnected.[25]

For Baldwin, being out of place was, for the first time, a natural feeling. In Paris, this displacement was coupled with a profound sense of space which, as Dievler notes, transforms the "crisis" nature of exile. By deliberately performing the exile he felt at home, Baldwin develops a sense of detachment from the condition itself. In another country, the sense of disconnection seems not tragic but matter-of-fact, and Baldwin was free to be simply alone.

Baldwin did not find utopia in Paris, nor do I think was he looking for it. Indeed, he quickly found that France had its own "niggers" and wrote extensively about the discrimination directed against North Africans and Algerians in Paris. Although the most violent confrontations between Algerians and the French occurred after he left Paris in the late 1950s, Baldwin witnessed much of the building racial tension while he was there and returned often in the 1960s to report on the Algerian War. He struggled to understand how he related to the victims and oppressors in France, and found that his identification with the Africans was complicated in ways he had not anticipated.

In "Encounter on the Seine: Black Meets Brown," Baldwin writes:

> The African has endured privation, injustice, and medieval cruelty; but the African has not yet endured the utter alienation of himself from his people and his past...They face each other, the Negro and the African, over a gulf of three hundred years...This alienation causes the Negro to realize that he is a hybrid. Perhaps it now occurs to him that in this need to establish himself in relation to his past he is most American, that this depthless alienation from oneself and one's people is, in sum, the American experience.[26]

Before discussing the content of this passage, I want to underscore once again the detached third person voice with which Baldwin talks about both the African and the African-American. His critical stance represents the liminality of his hybrid position while formally representing the "depthless alienation" he discovers. The breach between past and present appears to Baldwin as the most telling distinction of African-Americans from their African counterparts. It also suggests a lonely challenge to claims of both national and racial authenticity. The spatial and temporal divide experienced by the American cause a compulsive longing, a search for one's native home which, he suggests, the African does not experience. This awareness helps us to understand why, for Baldwin, the moment, the activity of the moment, generates the possibility of self-development. There is a lack of ontological certainty evident in Baldwin's writing: the question "Who am I?" is replaced with "Who can I become?" Black authenticity, as a claim stemming from one's ancestral past or presumed cultural affiliation, is tackled by the complex unhomeliness of the flâneur.

Baldwin's marginality in Paris relates him to various groups – Africans, Europeans, other expatriates - and he moves freely among them. This mobility was not available to him in New York, and if practiced, resulted in discriminating censure. In Paris, Baldwin's liminality, his not-quite-fitting identity, actually proved to be an advantage for it qualified him for a kind of floating engagement with various communities. He writes exuberantly about this free access to difference:

> I was born in New York, but have lived only in pockets of it. In Paris, I lived in all parts of the city – on the Right Bank and the Left, among the bourgeoisie and among *les miserables*, and knew all kinds of people, from pimps and prostitutes in Pigalle to Egyptian bankers in Neuilly. This may sound extremely unprincipled or even obscurely immoral: I found it healthy...This perpetual dealing with people very different from myself caused a shattering in me of preconceptions I scarcely knew I had.[27]

Baldwin's detachment and mobility makes him willing to shed affiliative tendencies and expands his imaginative range. Openness results in a symbiotic relationship which also allows him to identify and disrupt his own latent preconceptions. Baldwin sees those preconceptions as impediments to growth rather than inherent values that prove black (or other forms of) authenticity. Consequently, exposure to difference creates the self rather than isolating it. Some of the groups he mentions might not have been so accessible to a white American, a straight man, a European, or an artist. The particular combination of labels which he long suffered in New York grants him in Paris a kind of chameleon aspect, much like the flâneur's ease with the crowd. Indeed, I would argue that Baldwin comes close to describing the psychic effects of innervation when he writes that his "perpetual dealing with people...caused a shattering in [him]." Susan Buck-Morss defines innervation as "Benjamin's term for a mimetic reception of the external world, one that is empowering, in contrast to the defensive mimetic adaptation that protects at the price of paralyzing the organism, robbing it of its capacity of imagination, and therefore of active response."[28] Innervation and the stimulation of haptic energy contrast with the paranoid self-regulation Baldwin suffered in Harlem. The more mobile and fluid Baldwin's flânerie, the more expansive his sense of self.

Both Baldwin and Lefebvre's spatial theory demonstrate how individual appropriation of space begins at the street level. As we have seen in his writing on Harlem, Baldwin argues that the presence of policemen, patrolling in twos and threes, refuses the right of the people to their own street. Further, the theater of conflict and violence is present on the street corner, where sharpies stand, waiting, and policeman ride by on horses. Lefebvre hopes, rather, that "the street is appropriated, and thus 'socialized' space, within the setting of the city, for the benefit of multiple open groups without exclusivity or the need for membership."[29] For Baldwin, Harlem is not a socialized space for, although neighborhood inhabitants populate the street, they can't appropriate it and, due to police presence, are denied free movement.

In Paris, although Baldwin is quick to point out the presence of gendarmes and hostility toward North Africans, there is nonetheless a greater sense of the public sphere and generative social space. In his story "This Morning, This Evening, So Soon," he describes a street scene outside a café where the narrator sits with a Frenchman and several African-American students. He writes:

> We have taken a table at the Deux Magots and Pete strums on his guitar and begins to play a song...The waiter looks a little worried, for we are already beginning to attract a crowd, but it is a summer night, the gendarmes on the corner do not seem to mind, and there will be time, anyway, to stop us.

A few moments later, the narrator continues:

> In the crowd that had gathered to listen to us, I see a face I know, the face of a North African prize fighter, who is no longer in the ring. I used to know him well in the old days, but have not seen him for a long time. He looks quite well, his face is shining, and he is quite decently dressed. And something in the way he holds himself, not quite looking at our table, tells me that he has seen me, but does not want to risk a rebuff. So I call him. "Boona![30]

This scene is productive in several ways. First, Baldwin is careful not to create a utopic street scene; this is not an idyllic landscape, but a contradictory one that is in the process of subtle negotiation. Spontaneity characterizes the tenor of the scene and suggests a form of temporal authenticity that resists essential definition through ephemerality. The narrator and his friends play music, drawing a crowd and also the worry of the waiter. Gendarmes are present, but this time, state authority occupies the corner rather than sharpies. The North African emerges from the crowd and wishes to join the group but not to draw attention to himself; his presence represents the vulnerable visibility inherent in urban space. Boona wishes to see, and even to be seen, but approaches the scene as a marginal spectator, exposed with averted eyes. The social space allows for his tangential entry due to the proximity of the crowd and the focus on Pete's song. The primacy of vision is temporarily destabilized and other bodily senses are allowed to activate spatial experience. Pete's song creates intimacy with the crowd, rather than alienating them with the coldness of the gaze. This is Lefebvre's street – appropriated by various people, temporarily flexing their right to this domain, but most importantly, "for the benefit of multiple open groups without exclusivity or the need for membership." The narrator in the story seems just as sensitive to the presence of his old friend Boona as he is to the anxiety of the waiter, but his social imagination allows for both of them, as well as the crowd and the gendarmes. Baudelaire reminds us, "The crowd is [the flâneur's] domain...his passion and profession is to merge with the crowd."[31] And so we witness a gradual transformation: Baldwin maintains the detached perspective of the observer, just as he had in Harlem, but now, his membership in the visual field is generative not paranoid; he acts imaginatively and does not wait.

We can begin to see how Baldwin's experience of public and private space operates along the axis of visuality. He makes the flâneur's bargain to see and be seen within the field of visibility. Visuality plays an instrumental role in gauging how the city dweller enjoys freedom based on anonymity. It also suggests the way in which surfaces and exposure do more to test claims of authenticity than presumed ties to group identity or inherent definitions of the self. Baldwin's view of personal independence transforms the fixed binary of public and private space because it yearns for the private to be made visible, embedded within and carried out through the public. In "This Morning, This Evening, So Soon," Baldwin presents two instances of love in order to demonstrate how the most intimate emotion between people is rendered possible or not depending on the potential for private life *in* public space.

The narrator in the story falls in love with and marries a white Swedish woman while living in Paris. Baldwin writes:

> It was on a bridge, one tremendous, April morning, that I knew I had fallen in love. Harriet and I were walking hand in hand. The bridge was the Pont Royal...we had been quarreling...I wanted to pull her to me and say *Baby, don't be mad at me*, and at that moment something tugged at my heart and made me catch my breath. There were millions of people all around us, but I was alone with Harriet. She was alone with me. Never in all my life until that moment had I been alone with anyone. The world had always been with us, between us...and now, for the first time I had been quarreling with my girl. It was our quarrel. It was entirely between us, it had nothing to do with anyone else in the world.[32]

This moment, with its simple set of terms–me, my girl, the world, love, a quarrel– actually structures a sophisticated social equation. In order to fall in love, the narrator needs the world–that is to say, he needs the world to be present, aware of his affairs, and then to stay out of them. His emotional discovery is significant on three levels: first, he realizes that he is in love with Harriet. Second, he finds that this emotion has emerged without any interference from society, and third, he discovers that this emergence is visible and experienced within shared social space. Because of the past discrimination he experienced in America, his love for a white woman has to take place in public or else it will seem like a violation, unlawful because private. Baldwin shows how the Pont Royal Bridge and its passing crowds sustain his personal discovery because they create a secure site for it, marked by their passing indifference.

Earlier in the story, the narrator reveals an experience his unmarried sister had in America. Baldwin does not explicitly contrast the siblings' fates, but the highly visual quality of both stories allows for a productive critical dialogue. The narrator recounts:

> Years ago, [my sister] Louisa and the boy she was going with and two friends of theirs were out driving in a car and the police stopped them. The girl who was with them was very fair and the police pretended not to believe her when she said she was colored. They made her get out and stand in front of the headlights of the car and pull down her pants and raise her dress – they said that was the only way they could be sure...none of the men could do anything about it. Louisa couldn't face that boy again and I guess he couldn't face her.[33]

In this scene, the roles of public and private are distorted; a private experience (both on the social and bodily level) is made hyper-public by the aggressive intrusion of state authority. As a result, the private realm collapses, rather than, as in the case of the narrator's love for his wife, growing vis-à-vis its encounter with the public. Not only does Louisa's friend suffer the humiliation of her body being made into a spectacle (in order to "prove" its authenticity), but Louisa's own private life fails to survive the role of playing public witness. The policemen in this episode violate the girl with their own gaze and force the moment of visualization on the others in the car, thereby implicating them in its transgression and undermining the sanctity of private life. As a result, Louisa and the boy *cannot face one another* – that is to say, they cannot bear to see the beloved, nor allow themselves to be seen – this erasure of the visual field due to shame forecloses on love.

The fear of returning to a life of repression kept Baldwin from returning to New York for almost a decade. But the independence he gained in Paris seemed illusory unless he was able to access it elsewhere. Agency, individual empowerment, and mobility were deeply personal necessities for Baldwin and he gradually decided that they must be tested in New York under less "indifferent" conditions. In "The Discovery of What It Means to Be An American," He writes, "The freedom the American writer finds in Europe brings him, full circle, back to himself with the responsibility for his development where it always was: in his own hands."[34] The self-sufficiency implied in this statement is based both on the confidence and the alienation of the flâneur, whose aim it is to maintain liminality without falling into a comfort zone of domesticity or static security. Baldwin also echoes this when he writes, "Havens are high-priced. The price exacted of the haven-dweller is that he contrives to delude himself into believing he has found a haven."[35] Indeed, Baldwin may perform exile in order to understand his permanent state of alienation, but he will simultaneously dispel any illusion of having found security.

Baldwin as Flâneur

In order to understand how Baldwin counters both inherent and communal claims to black authenticity, I want to take a moment in order to theorize the strategies and conditions for his flânerie. We have already seen how Baldwin practiced mobility without paranoia while in Paris, due in large part to the absence of surveillance and social boundaries. It is also necessary to study how the transitions from New York to Paris and back again locate Baldwin within the spatial margins that mirror the liminal condition of the flâneur in the city. In order to do this, I want to consider Homi Bhabha's work on hybridity and diasporic subjects. In *The Location of Culture*, he writes:

> What is theoretically innovative, and politically crucial, is the need to think beyond narratives of originary and initial subjectivities and to focus on moments or processes that are produced in the articulation of cultural differences. These 'in-between' spaces provide the terrain for elaborating strategies of selfhood–singular or communal–that initiate new signs of identity, and innovative sites of collaboration, and contestation, in the act of defining the idea of society itself.[36]

Bhabha's argument that notions of selfhood occur in "sites of collaboration, and contestation" provides a possible terrain for Baldwin whose critique of authenticity refuses binding forms of affiliation. His alienation from any kind of originary past requires that identity be dynamic and creative. Bhabha suggests that the development of the self need not rely on a fixed lineage, that it might in fact be "politically crucial" for that self to be formed otherwise. His focus on "in-between" spaces speaks to Baldwin's flânerie as a trans-Atlantic practice. Just as Baldwin was able to theorize "what it means to be an American" when he was in Paris, so too, the experience there prepares him to practice flânerie in New York and resist the stultifying effects of haven-dwelling.

The dissolution of rigid categories must begin on the level of individual experience and occurs particularly when the flâneur travels freely from one part of the city to another while refusing any sense of belonging. The recognition of Baldwin as flâneur does not alter the threatening landscape of New York, but it empowers the individual to combat restrictive forces by presenting a form of social practice based on bold movement in the face of indifference, fear, or spatial discrimination. The combination of alienation and openness is fundamental to flânerie. Bhabha writes:

What is at issue is the performative nature of differential identities: the regulation and negotiation of those spaces that are continually, *contingently*, 'opening out', remaking the boundaries, exposing the limits of any claim to a singular or autonomous sign of difference – be it class, gender or race. Such assignations of social differences – where difference is neither One nor the Other but *something else besides*, *in-between* – find their agency in a form of the 'future' where the past is not originary, where the present is not simply transitory. It is, if I may stretch a point, an interstitial future, that emerges *in-between* the claims of the past and the needs of the present.[37]

The critical desire to co-opt Baldwin into various ideological or identity groups may find its resistance here, in the simultaneous sense of unity and dispersion performed by a "differential identity." One's being in the world, particularly through the practice of flânerie, is grounded in exposure to many forms of difference (some of which it takes on), and cannot be isolated or identified as just one kind of difference. In Baldwin's case, when he returns to America, he inhabits many kinds of difference–his identity as an exile, a black man, an artist, and a public intellectual refuses social assignation despite the highly politicized calls for solidarity in the 1960s. Perhaps the closest he comes to authenticity is to be, as Bhabha puts it, "neither One nor the Other but *something else besides, in-between*" and as a result he negotiates space "contingently, opening out, remaking boundaries" through the principles of mobility, independence, and marginality so central to the flâneur. Some critics like Eldridge Cleaver view this ambivalence and individuality as a sign of Baldwin's racial self-hatred. Bhabha, however, demonstrates how the past need not determine identity formation, how by abandoning its restrictive authority (as Baldwin discovers he must), the individual is free to challenge the very limits of social difference. When Baldwin considers himself, most of all, an American, he simultaneously recognizes that identity as a "site of contestation." The relationship requires the vigilant and everyday practice of flânerie within the public sphere.

Lefebvre helps me to better articulate this immediacy of experience in terms of time. His "theory of moments" offers a way for us to integrate our earlier discussion of the private and public domains of experience with the contingency of time and space. For one thing, his theory of moments locates itself squarely in the public domain of the everyday, not in a "safe space" of reflection. This proximity, therefore, requires participation and a proactive approach to maintaining autonomy. It also occupies a necessarily shared territory of private and public. Any given moment the everyday is experienced by a multitude of people, even those alienated from one another in a common environment. This collective quality can be converted into a tactical opportunity to facilitate empathy, or when necessary, resistance. Lefebvre explains how this conception goes beyond both pluralism and totalitarianism:

> Individual consciousness opens onto 'moments' that are also part of social
> consciousness. Conflicts are always possible, as individual consciousness may reject
> the form that has been developed socially or historically. It may aspire to other
> forms…It also alters – adapts, amends – their forms. The unity of the individual and
> the social is manifested in these very conflicts. This dialectical unity can only tend
> towards an overcoming.[38]

The narrator's epiphany of falling in love on the bridge is one such moment. He simultaneously discovers the personal emotion felt towards his lover and the implications of this feeling for the larger social consciousness, a connection that "alters – adapts, amends" habitual ways of thinking, in this case about race and the public sphere. The moment punctuates for him the conflict he faces as a black man in love with a white woman and offers the potential to aspire otherwise. This "overcoming" occurs because of the ongoing dialectics of public and private experience. Lefebvre encourages such an exchange of alienation into immediacy with the elements of the material world. The expatriate, in particular the African-American in Paris, must transform the rootless impermanence of his status into a position of power, risk-taking and resistance.

Briefly, I want to consider this dynamism in terms of what Walter Benjamin might classify as a "dialectical image" in Baldwin's story. For Benjamin, a dialectical image occurs in the moment when an object becomes visible to spectators and is "brought to a standstill." He believes that radical discoveries are possible when our own "flight through life may be likewise sheltered in the presence of onlooking strangers."[39] One such moment occurs at the end of "This Morning, This Evening, So Soon" when the narrator returns to his Parisian home: "I walk into our dismantled apartment. It stinks of departure. There are bags and crates in the hall which will be taken away tomorrow, there are no books in the bookcases, the kitchen looks as though we never cooked a meal there, never dawdled there in the early morning, or late at night, over coffee."[40] This *moment*, this *image*, captures the narrator's "flight through life"; the dismantled apartment reveals the illusion of haven-dwelling, and stresses the ephemerality present in the story's title: "This Morning, This Evening, So Soon." The past seems to vanish and the narrator can ascertain no trace of it as an anchor to assure him of a fixed identity. This liminal moment occurs literally in the in-between space of moving; it approaches authenticity as the here-and-now that constitutes the "specialness" of flânerie. Ultimately, Baldwin's view of Paris recalls the delight of Benjamin's urban poet: "Love, not at first sight, but at last."[41]

I have been trying to suggest that Baldwin's flânerie is in fact deeply political, due to his very resistance to ideological appropriation. From an alienated and marginal place, he nonetheless expresses the need for a totalizing human condition in which public and private life no longer suffers from rigid compartmentalization. He resists the abstraction of everyday life through sensitivity to the moment and desire for social innervation. He wrote that his primary aim was, and always had been, "to achieve...a viable, organic connection between [his] public stance and [his] private life." The sincerity of this aim nonetheless refuses resolution when considered alongside Baldwin's earlier admission in the Mailer essay that he must always maintain a watchful distance between his inner and outer self. I want to suggest that these statements are not mutually exclusive, but they help to articulate Baldwin's complexity. Despite his desire for an organic connection between private and public life, he remains agitated, talkative, even contradictory about how to make such a change manifest. This dialogue allows personality to emerge vividly through actual praxis rather than being absorbed by larger communities and ideologies.

Baldwin suspects that when the public sphere dictates private desire, total integration, if successful, comes at the expense of critical capacity and real understanding between people. When personal ideas are seen as threats to group authenticity, the interior life of individuals simply empties out. In "This Morning, This Evening, So Soon," his narrator observes the antiseptic but heavily guarded sense of privacy most Americans practice. He discovers upon meeting new Americans that

> their friendliness did not suggest, and was not intended to suggest, any possibility of friendship. Unlike Europeans, they dropped titles and used first names almost at once, leaving themselves, unlike Europeans, with nowhere thereafter to go...any suggestion that there might be further depths, a person...behind the name, was taken as a violation of that privacy which did not, paradoxically, since they trusted so little, seem to exist among Americans. They apparently equated privacy with the unspeakable things they did in the bathroom or the bedroom, which they related only to the analyst, and then read about in the pages of the best seller.[42]

Here surfaces fall flat without the dialectical energy of private and public engagement. This fragmentation painfully aborts the organic flow of everyday life so that there cannot be a total revolution of mind and body space. Intimacy is hollow when fearful of real understanding. The Americans Baldwin describes here believe they have something to be ashamed of and so they use friendliness as a way to avoid lowering their protective shields. Unlike the flâneur, they are not open to the shocks of daily living. Baldwin's praxis was based upon the kind of principle for integration that Lefebvre details in his *Critique of Everyday Life*. Lefebvre writes, "The unique life, life as a totality present in its every form, which remains the goal and meaning of revolutionary culture~all this is incomprehensible to the bourgeois. His life is parceled out. Action is one thing...thought is something else."[43] Oddly enough, what Lefebvre describes here is the alienation of man from himself, from the possible integration of his private/public life, whereas Baldwin, ever open to critique and alienation from various ideologies, struggles to keep himself whole. His efforts remind us of the flâneur who "stabs away at the crowd," and makes of it, at once, his refuge. "The streets become the dwelling place~walls are the desk upon which he presses his book, newsstands his library, café terraces his balconies from which he looks down on his household after work."[44]

The "impossibility" of Baldwin's identity emerges in the public realm as a way of challenging what is or can be considered black authenticity. His refusal to be secretive about his sexual practices, his direct protests about the social conditions of blacks in America, and his slippery presence along the margins of conventional lines of race and community all work to intervene unpredictably in the exercise of authority. This practice must be vigilant in each moment, for selfhood is produced erstwhile and in the face of social contestation. Baldwin's mobility is maintained by sustaining a critical tension within and against the various spatial structures and ideologies, including traditional definitions of authenticity. This detachment coexists with the empathy of the flâneur, transforming the coldness of the 3rd person narrative voice with aesthetic strategies that devise possibilities for change. This intimacy is substantiated by revelations of his own private life in public space. Exercising mobility in the field of visibility overturns the power of the gaze; no longer paranoid or secretive, Baldwin is free to look. The feverish vision and mobility of the flâneur challenge conventional abstraction in daily life, reinstall love, and totalize revolution. This always~temporary, constantly~articulated resistance is captured by Michelet who writes, "I sprang up like a pale blade of grass between the paving stones."[45]

Notes

1   Cornel West.*Prophecy Deliverance!*(Philadelphia: Westminister Press, 1982) 71.

2   Stephen Butterfield.*Black Autobiography in America* (Boston: University of Massachusetts Press, 1974).

3   A good example of this subjectivity can be found in the essay "Nobody Knows My Name: A Letter from the South." Here, Baldwin uses a highly visual language to describe how his involvement in the Civil Rights Movement generated personal revelations about his alienation from his people, even as he witnessed and personally experienced the injustice suffered by all African-Americans. In addition to using terms like "reflection," "mirror," "others' eyes," and "angles" to describe his tangential approach to the movement, he also changes perspective from first person singular to first person collective, to third and second person.

4   James Baldwin. "The Black Boy Looks at the White Boy."*Collected Essays.*(New York: Literary Classics of the U.S., 1998) 271.

5   Walter Benjamin. "Paris, Capital of the Nineteenth Century." *Reflections.*ed. and intro. Peter Demetz, trans. Edmund Jephcott. (New York: Harcourt Brace Jovanovich, 1978) 156.

6   C.W.E. Bigsby. "The Divided Mind of James Baldwin," *Journal of American Studies* 13.3 (1979). Bigsby derives his model from Lionel Trilling's belief that certain individuals in the postwar period contain both the "yes and no" of their cultures. While this liminality is helpful in thinking about Baldwin, I argue that his writing is less ambivalent than it is purposeful about inhabiting this marginal position.

7   See Irving Howe's "Black Boys and Native Sons" *Dissent* (Autumn 1963); Eldridge Cleaver. "Notes on a Native Son," *Soul on Ice.* (New York: Delta, 1968); Stephen Butterfield. *Black Autobiography in America* (Boston: University of Massachusetts Press, 1974).

8   TJ Clark.*Absolute Bourgeois.*(Princeton: Princeton UP, 1988) 141-2.

9   Homi Bhabha.*The Location of Culture.* (London: Routledge, 1994) 9.

10 Henri Lefebvre. "The Other Parises" *Key Writings*, ed. Stuart Elden, Elizabeth Lebas, Eleonore Kofman(London: Continuum, 2003) 156.

11 Charles Baudelaire. "The Painter of Modern Life," *Selected Writings on Art and Literature.* trans. and intro. P.E. Charvet (London: Penguin, 1972) 400.

12 Susan Buck-Morss."The City as Dream-World and Catastrophe" *October*, 73 (Summer 1995) 8.

13 Baldwin."Fifth Avenue, Uptown, A Letter from Harlem" 175.

14 One of the most well-known critiques of urban renewal projects in postwar New York comes from Jane Jacobs.Attacking "low income projects that become worse centers of delinquency, vandalism, and general hopelessness than the slums they were supposed to replace," Jacobs notoriously added, "This is not the rebuilding of cities. This is the sacking of cities." Jane Jacobs. *The Death and Life of Great American Cities* (New York: Random House, 1961) 4.

15 James Baldwin."Previous Condition," *Going to Meet the Man* (New York: Vintage, 1995)

91.

[16]   Fred Standley. "James Baldwin's Literary Milieu," *The City in African-American Literature*. ed. Yoshinobu Hakutani and Robert Butler. (London: Associated University Press, 1995) 142.

[17]   Baldwin, "Previous Condition" 99.

[18]   Baldwin, "Fifth Avenue, Uptown, A Letter from Harlem" 176.

[19]   Frisby 92.

[20]   David Frisby."The Flâneur in Social Theory" *The Flâneur*, ed. Keith Tester (London: Routledge, 1994) 92.

[21]   Walter Benjamin."On Some Motifs in Baudelaire" *Illuminations*.ed. and intro. Hannah Arendt, trans. Harry Zohn.(New York: Schocken, 1988) 171-2.

[22]   Baldwin, "Harlem Ghetto" 50.

[23]   Baldwin, "Previous Condition" 88.

[24]   Baldwin, "Fifth Avenue, Uptown, A Letter from Harlem" 175-6.

[25]   James A. Dievler. "Sexual Exiles: James Baldwin and *Another Country*" *James Baldwin Now*, ed. Dwight A. McBride. (New York: NYU Press, 1999) 168.

[26]   Baldwin. "Encounter on the Seine: Black Meets Brown" 89.

[27]   Baldwin "The Discovery of What It Means to Be an American" 140.

[28]   Susan Buck-Morss. "Aesthetics and Anaesthetics: Walter Benjamin's Artwork Reconsidered." *October* 62, (Fall 1992): 3-41.

[29]   Lefebvre131.

[30]   Baldwin, "This Morning, This Evening, So Soon" 183.

[31]   Baudelaire 399.

[32]   Baldwin, "This Morning, This Evening, So Soon" 158.

[33]   Baldwin, "This Morning, This Evening, So Soon" 174.

[34]   Baldwin "The Discovery of What It Means to Be an American" 141.

[35]   Baldwin Intro –*Nobody Knows My Name* – 135.

[36]   Bhabha 1.

[37]   Bhabha 219.

[38]   Henri Lefebvre."The Inventory," *Key Writings*.(New York: Continuum, 2003) 173.

[39]   Walter Benjamin.*Briefe*.Volume 1.Gershom Scholem and Theodor Adorno, eds. (Frankfurt: Suhrkamp Verlag, 1996) 446.

[40]   Baldwin."This Morning, This Evening, So Soon." 155.

[41]   Walter Benjamin."On Some Motifs in Baudelaire," *Illuminations* (New York: Schocken, 1969) 169.

[42]   Baldwin, "This Morning, This Evening, So Soon" 159.

[43]   Lefebvre, "Mystification: Notes for a Critique of Everyday Life," ed. Stuart Elden, Elizabeth Lebas, Eleonore Kofman(London: Continuum, 2003) 76.

[44]   Walter Benjamin."The Paris of the Second Empire in Baudelaire."*Selected Writings Volume Four*, Howard Eiland and Michael W. Jennings.(Cambridge: Harvard UP, 2003), 19.

[45]   Cited in Benjamin's *Arcades Project*, 444.

"Many forces at work": Clarence Major's Early Fiction and the Critique of Racial Economy

Benjamin D. Carson

In his early, experimental novels—*All-Night Visitors* (1969), *NO* (1973), *Reflex and Bone Structure* (1975), *Emergency Exit* (1979), and *My Amputations* (1986)—Clarence Major turned away from the tradition of social realism that so many African American writers before him had adopted and opted for a radically disjunctive, fragmented, non-representational style of writing that forces readers to "discover alternative, non-logical ways of knowing and being in the world with others" (Bell, Introduction 3). By adopting such a style, Major sought to show the contingent nature of identity and, concomitantly, to call attention to the limitations of theories of identity formation "based solely along racial lines" (Bunge 3). In contradistinction to Ann DuCille, bell hooks, and Henry Louis Gates, Jr., whose work is highly, if not solely, invested in the political economy of race, I argue that Major, in *Reflex and Bone Structure* and *Emergency Exit*, makes a case for renouncing race-thinking altogether. Major's (anti-)aesthetic project is to invent "a new way of seeing" (Bunge 43), a new way of perceiving that transports readers "into [...] alternative realities" he hopes are (Klinkowitz, "Innovative" 155), in the words of Paul Gilroy, free from "all racializing and raciological thought, from racialized seeing, racialized thinking, and racialized thinking about thinking" (41-2).[1] Major's early fiction, in short, demonstrates a desire to create imaginatively a political culture beyond the color line.[2]

While both *Reflex and Bone Structure* and *Emergency Exit* arguably fall under the rubric of postmodernist fiction, to overcome race-thinking, *Emergency Exit* at times takes refuge in humanism, or the idea that despite ostensible differences, human beings are essentially all the same.[3] This tension between Major's humanism and his postmodernist (anti-)aesthetic in *Emergency* is not finally resolved, but his desire to renounce race-thinking is never in doubt. *Reflex and Bone Structure* is a full-blown postmodern novel in which characters— or subjects—are in a constant state of dismantling. As Phillip Brian Harper argues, "dismantling suggests the division of an assembled entity into its constituents parts [...] [It] suggests the demonstration of essential discontinuities rather than the disintegration of essential integrated wholes" (48). Ontologically, the subjects or "personalities" in *Reflex* are not "integrated, stable entit[ies]" but an "endless play of differences and incongruities" (48-9). While their tactics differ, *Emergency Exit* and *Reflex and Bone Structure* both demonstrate Major's commitment to a "deliberate wholesale renunciation of race" (Gilroy 41).

Throughout his literary career, Major has consistently downplayed the importance of race. He, for example, has been a long time critic of the notion of a "black aesthetic," or the "idea that African Americans produce art in a certain way" (Bunge x), and has stated explicitly that he does not "write racial literature" (50).[4] Unlike Henry Louis Gates, Jr., he "has trouble understanding how race can dictate aesthetic principles" and does not "see any objective way of dealing with the work an artist does, solely along racial lines" (x, 3). He argues that "black poets, for instance, are going in many different directions. There are many forces at work" (3). Major knows, though, that denying the notion of a black aesthetic "will upset a lot of people who like to write about The Black Novel and The Black This or That. It's too bad. It's just one other category that, unfortunately, allows for a lot of subtle racism to pass for scholarship" (34).

Major's early novels[5] "do not abide by traditional rules of racial representation and therefore do not make racial politics their centermost concern" (Tate 7).[6] Rather, they attempt to account for those many forces–gender, class, education, sexuality, region, nationality, "implicit wishes, unstated longings, and vague hungers" (178)–that shape and reshape an elusive subjectivity, one which is always at risk of being reduced to a single defining characteristic.[7] Major's work, as Bernard Bell argues, "moves beyond black sites of cultural production and consumption, as well as beyond thematic and structural concerns with racial and political consciousness, to a preoccupation with exploring the boundaries of language and imaginative consciousness" (Bell, Introduction 6). In this sense, then, Major's early fiction, in its "obsession for indeterminacy" (Soitos 185), and its "tendency to minimize representational effects" (Bunge 29), can be read as a critique of racial reductionism and the allure of political projects grounded in race-thinking *and* as a response to those who "agree that 'race' is invented but are then required to defer to its embeddedness in the world and to accept that the demand for justice requires us nevertheless to enter the political arenas it helps to mark out" (Gilroy 52).[8]

While race theorists like Ann DuCille, bell hooks, and Henry Louis Gates, Jr. are cognizant of the pitfalls of racial reasoning,[9] they still posit race as the central category within which individual gestures become intelligible, often at the expense of those other "forces at work." DuCille, hooks, and Gates recognize race as a socially constructed category yet choose not to abandon it even when its usefulness as an explanatory category has been exhausted or is dangerously delimiting.[10] When the lens of race and ethnicity is the *only* one through which one sees, the possibility of self-representation is foreclosed and the meaning of social acts is overdetermined. In other words, everything you do, you do not just for yourself but for your race, and what you do is always already racially coded. If Major denounces the notion of an identifiable black aesthetic, he equally denounces all-inclusive representations (of people, groups, etc.), whatever their "strategic or inventionary value" (Fuss 20), preferring to "look at people on a one-at-a-time basis" (Bunge 9). Major argues, "we can't oversimplify when we're trying to be sincere" (9).

In *Skin Trade* Ann DuCille displays an initial desire but finally an unwillingness to transcend racialized thinking and seeing. In "Toy Theory: Black Barbie and the Deep Play of Difference" DuCille addresses the controversy surrounding Barbie and Mattel's attempt to create "real dolls," or "would be multicultural versions" of Barbie (17, 30). In what way do these multicultural versions of the original doll look "like me," in the case of DuCille, a "black" woman (16)? DuCille asks,

> What does it mean when similarity and difference—even allowing for the power of metaphor—are calculated according to a like-me or an unlike-me that is not only a code for race but a code for race as skin color? Just what are we saying when we claim that a doll does or does not look like me, does or does not look black? How does black look? How does woman look? What would make a doll look like a "natural woman"? What would make a doll look authentically African American or realistically Nigerian or genuinely Jamaican? (16)

DuCille's critique of Mattel is based on racial reductionism, Mattel's reducing (while attempting to reproduce) heterogeneity to "stereotyped forms and visible signs of racial and ethnic difference" (37). But, DuCille goes on to ask,

> could any doll manufacturer or other image maker—advertising and film, say—attend to cultural, racial, and phenotypical differences without engaging the same simplistic big-lips/broad-hips stereotypes that make so many of us—blacks in particular—grit our (pearly white) teeth? What would it take to produce a line of dolls that would more fully reflect the wide variety of sizes, shapes, colors, hairstyles, occupations, abilities, and disabilities that African Americans—like all people—come in? (37-8)

The issue facing Mattel is the difficulty of representing difference. A "black" doll isn't enough, because what constitutes blackness is as elusive as what constitutes whiteness or brownness. Blackness, even when it attempts to be inclusive, that is, to represent someone "like me," is always short of the mark. Whatever blackness is is always mitigated by factors irreducible to skin color. DuCille reminds us that we "have to ask what authentic blackness looks like. Even if we knew, how could this ethnic or racial authenticity ever be achieved in a doll" (50)? The answer is: It can't.

In Mattel's inability to represent "racial and ethnic alterity," DuCille suggests there is something to be learned, and that is "the degree to which difference is an impossible space—antimatter located not only beyond the grasp of low culture but also beyond the reach of high theory" (56). But here, in this moment of racial unrepresentability, what Gilroy calls a "crisis in raciology," rather than seizing an "important opportunity" that "points toward the possibility of leaving 'race' behind," DuCille reinscribes race into the impossible space rather than "preventing its rehabilitation" (Gilroy 29). Unwilling to take the next difficult step of renouncing race thinking altogether, DuCille ends up employing, even while deconstructing, "the concepts and categories" used by "the beneficiaries of racial hierarchy," the rulers, owners and persecutors whose position within the social structure, depends on race thinking (12). She argues we "need to theorize race and gender not as meaning*less* but meaning*ful*—as sites of difference, filled with constructed meaning that are in need of constant decoding and interrogation" (DuCille 58; emphasis original). DuCille vacillates between wanting to downplay race as a descriptive category and wanting to maintain it, while arguing that it must be constantly decoded and interrogated. Rather than arguing for the impossibility of representing complexity "in the face of real bodies" and renouncing race as an analytical category, she wants the admittedly inadequate category to stay, as long as we recognize the impossibility of its representation (58).

Similarly, in "Representations of Whiteness in the Black Imagination," hooks, while acknowledging "this thing we call 'difference,'" still speaks without reservation about the "black imagination" and "the black experience" (166).[11] She writes, "this projection [of the 'fantasy of whiteness' that 'the threatening Other is always a terrorist'] enables many people to imagine there is no representation of whiteness in the black imagination" (174). She suggests "it is useful, when theorizing black experience, to examine the way the concept of 'terror' is linked to representations of whiteness" (174-75). hooks makes clear here and elsewhere, e.g. "Postmodern Blackness," that the "black experience" is a heterogeneous one—that there is not simply "one"—though she goes on to suggest that behind the "black experience" is a "black imagination" that represents "whiteness" in (a) particular way(s). When hooks writes, "to name that whiteness in the black imagination is often a representation of terror," she reduces heterogeneity to a singular racial imagination—one that is identifiable and shared. And she risks such reduction when she says, "collectively black people remain rather silent about representations of whiteness in the black imagination" (169).

hooks, despite her own admonitions, reduces the complexity of human experience and the production of subjectivity to race and the racial imagination, as though it were the primary arbiter of human perception and interaction. hooks acknowledges, though, that observing the "world from the standpoint of 'whiteness'" or blackness "may indeed distort perception" (177). A moment in hook's *Killing Rage*, which is strikingly similar to a scene in Major's *Emergency Exit*, provides a telling example of the danger of the racial imagination—and its ability to "distort," if not overdetermine, perception. This moment comes when hooks and K, her "friend and traveling companion," board an airplane (*Killing* 8). Before boarding the plane, though, hooks and K were involved in a "case of racial harassment," one in which "two young white airline employees" rudely continue a personal conversation rather than assisting them with their first-class upgrade (10, 9).

When hooks and K finally board the plane, K discovers a mistake with her boarding pass. K is called to the front of the plane where she is "publicly attacked by white female stewardesses who accuse her of trying to occupy a seat in first class that is not assigned to her. Although she had been assigned the seat, she was not given the appropriate boarding pass" (8). What is clear is that the airline, and the two rude young white airline employees who were talking rather than doing their job, are responsible for the mix up, not K and not the "white man" who currently occupies the seat. hooks, now in a killing rage, does not want to hear the white man's apologies—and hooks does note that "the anonymous white man [...] quickly apologizes to K"—or his "repeated insistence that 'it was not his fault'" (9). hooks shouts at him, saying "it is not a question of blame, that the mistake was understandable, but that the way K was treated was completely unacceptable, that it reflected both racism and sexism" (9).[12] She argues that the "white man" should have intervened "in the harassment of the black woman" rather than choosing his "own comfort," and that doing so would have been a way for him to avoid complicity "with the racism and sexism that is so all-pervasive in this society" (9). For hooks, everything this "white" man does he does not just for himself, but for his race (and his sex). Whiteness, in this instance, has become monolithic, and this "anonymous white man" has come to stand in, as a synecdoche, for white male culture writ large.

Whether this case is one of racism and sexism is less clear than hooks' conflation of employee incompetence and the representation of whiteness in the black imagination, wherein this anonymous man is stripped of his subjectivity and becomes synonymous with "terror" and a "system of domination" (hooks, "Representation" 166).[13] What hooks fails to acknowledge is that "to know that [someone] is a white male is not necessarily to know what he thinks—about white males, about [black women], or about anything else" (Krupat 4).

Henry Louis Gates Jr.'s project to uncover the black literary tradition—a tradition based on signifyin(g) on the literary work of a black author's foreparents—is race-based to its very roots. His work, like that of hooks' and DuCille's, is "not merely an arbitrary intellectual endeavor, but rather a strategic assertion of [black] cultural pride and [black] political power" (Favor 6). The recovery of the black literary tradition is an attempt to contest the hegemony of the Western and Anglo-European literary tradition, and to stake claim to a tradition that is not simply mimetic of the master's tradition. Gates argues that the central signifier of the black literary tradition is "Signifyin(g)": "Repetition and revision are fundamental to black artistic forms, from painting and sculpture to music and language use [...] Whatever is black about black American literature is to be found in this identifiable black Signifyin(g) difference" (*Signifying* xxiv).

In Gates' formulation, signifyin(g) is a practice which seemingly does "not include persons other than African Americans (unless by some circumstance they were raised in African American culture)" (Favor 5). That "unless" suggests that signifyin(g) isn't easily contained within a specifically identifiable race or culture. And as J. Martin Favor asks, "doesn't even a single nonblack raised in an African American culture begin to modify the notion of what constitutes African American culture" (154)?[14] Favor's question raises the issue of cultural hybridity and in doing so problematizes Gates' formulation of a pure African American literary tradition. Gates himself seems to acknowledge as much when he writes, "Lest this theory of criticism, however, be thought of as only black, let me admit that the implicit premise of this study is that all texts Signify upon other texts, in motivated and unmotivated ways" (*Signifying* xxiv).[15]

Despite Gates' desire to uncover an originary black aesthetic practice, a specifically racialized signifying practice would imply that only African Americans practice signifyin(g), and that the license to "signify" is issued by skin color—and that a certain signifying practice, when traced to its roots, will uncover a person of color, in this case, an African American. For Gates, theorists of the black tradition "must analyze the ways in which writing relates to race, how attitudes toward racial differences generate and structure literary texts by us *and* about us. We must determine how critical methods can effectively disclose the traces of ethnic differences in literature" ("Canon-Formation" 176).[16] This task is a formidable one and rests on the idea that race and ethnicity are recoverable when the structures generated by them are identified.[17] All of which presupposes that race and ethnicity are static and identifiable, that they have a recognizable, transcendental signified.[18]

The strategy to elevate race to the central signifier of identity, cultural belonging, and a source of pride, rather than to renounce it as a historically destructive and delimiting category that has been the source of much suffering has often been employed to "resist the destiny that 'race' has allocated" to those "who have been subordinated by race-thinking and its distinctive social structures" and to "dissent from the lowly value it placed upon their lives" (Gilroy 12). Oppressed groups, as Gilroy argues, "have built complex traditions of politics, ethics, identity, [...] culture" and literature, within the strictures of race-thinking and racist cultures (12). But "[t]he currency of 'race' has marginalized these traditions from official histories of modernity and relegated them to the backwaters of the primitive and the prepolitical" (12), even as these traditions have, through "elaborate, improvised constructions," fought to defend themselves from abuse (12). But as Gilroy makes clear, these constructions

> have gone far beyond merely affording protection and reversed the polarities of insult, brutality, and contempt, which are unexpectedly turned into important sources of solidarity, joy, and collective strength. When ideas of racial particularity are inverted in this defensive manner so that they provide sources of pride rather than shame and humiliation, they become difficult to relinquish. For many racialized populations, 'race' and the hard-won, oppositional identities it supports are not to be lightly or prematurely given up. (12)

DuCille, hooks, and Gates invoke race to counter race-thinking, and thus remain within the logic of a racial economy. While DuCille acknowledges the impossibility of representing the "heterogeneity of the world," and the singularity of individual bodies that exist in the "impossible space" of difference, she is unwilling to renounce the category of race (DuCille 38, 56). hooks, who is equally willing to acknowledge difference within experience, still holds on to a racial imagination that stands behind and mitigates experience and perception. hooks, like DuCille, holds on to an identity politics grounded in race in an attempt to "find new strategies of resistance" to what she sees as a "pervasive politic of white supremacy which seeks to prevent the formation of radical black subjectivity" (hooks, "Postmodern" 423). Race, for hooks, forms the basis of an oppositional identity, while Gates sees race as the basis for an oppositional literary tradition. For these theorists, then, race, as the primary constitutive factor in identity formation, will not, as Gilroy puts it, "be lightly or prematurely given up." Thus their projects remain within the logic of a racialized politics, necessitating the invocation and employment of the self-same categories of the "rulers, owners, and persecutors," the protectors and beneficiaries of race-thinking (Gilroy 12).

Reflex and Bone Structure and *Emergency Exit* work to counter the reductive logic of raciological thought. Gates, for example, argues that the practice of "signifyin(g)" is identifiably "black," and serves to identify an African and African American tradition or black aesthetic, but Major is unconvinced. In a 1973 interview with John O'Brien Major remarked:

> But as far as some kind of all-encompassing black aesthetic is concerned, I don't think black writers can be thrown together like that into some kind of formula. Black writers today should write whatever they want to write and in any way they choose to write in. No style or subject should be alien to them. We have to get away from this rigid notion that there are certain topics and methods reserved for black writers. I'm against all that. I'm against coercion from blacks and from whites. (Bunge 12)

We are reminded of this sentiment when in *Reflex and Bone Structure* (1975) we hear the narrator (and author of the book we're reading) assert,

> I want this book to be anything it wants to be. A penal camp.A bad check.A criminal organization.A swindle.A prison. Devil's Island. I want the mystery of this book to be an absolute mystery. Let it forge its own way into the art of deep sea diving. Let it walk. I want it to run and dance. And be sad. And score in the major league all-time records. I want it to smoke and drink and do other things bad for its health. This book can be anything it has a mind to be. (61)

And again, later, the narrator tells us that "this novel has to keep changing [...] A novel is anything. Fiction is a stained glass window" (112). In both form and content *Reflex and Bone Structure* challenge not only static notions of individual identity, but the identity of a recognizably black literary tradition. Identity is many hued, a stained glass window.

Reflex and Bone Structure is what Stephen F. Soitos calls an "anti-detective novel" (177). Like conventional detective novels that are written "in the first person" and give "the narrator complete control over the story," *Reflex* is written from the perspective of the narrator (177). However, in "this anti-detective novel the first-person format, which was traditionally used for clarity of expression and easy reader identification, is used to confuse and alienate the reader" (177). By challenging the form of the conventional detective novel, Major is drawing attention to the "issue of control and authorial authority" (177), as well as the "process of epistemology or the nature of understanding itself" (179-80), which in *Reflex* is "subverted at every turn" (178). The indeterminacy that results from this subversion challenges the reader's perception; it calls attention to the way s/he thinks, and, through the process of experiencing "epistemological fragmentation," forces open the mental fetters that bind him/her to rigid, categorical thinking, in this case, race-thinking (184). This radical indeterminacy challenges the reader's cognitive faculties, while allowing the reader a chance to "seize control of the world and reshape it to [his or her] liking and benefit" (184), rather than simply imitate "the old tested ways of seeing the world" (Bunge 43).[19]

In *Reflex* the reader experiences the narrator struggling not to represent reality, but to create the reality of Cora, Canada, and Dale, as well as a host of minor characters who come in and out of the action or non-action of the novel, often with little or no impact, e.g. the Puerto Rican boy in a green shirt. The narrator makes it clear that he is the controlling force behind the actions of the characters in the novel, and that these actions are the "workings of his imagination, as it conjures up characters and incidents" (Bradfield 121). As Larry D. Bradfield argues, "by simple, spontaneous reflex action his imagination can create characters who have sufficient reality, or bone structure, to generate responses, or further reflexes to be recorded" (121). At one point the narrator alludes to his creative license, his ability to create or extend a complex, fluid reality:

> Cora is away being interviewed by Cecil B. DeMille. I'm here, on the bed, thinking about my future. I want to blur the distinctions between it and the past. I'll make up everything from now on. If I want a commercial airline to crash with Cora and Dale on it doing it in the dark, I'll do that. Or have them go down at sea in a steamer caught in a violent typhoon near Iceland, or in an exploration vessel off the West Indies. I'll do anything I like. I'm extending reality, not retelling it. (49)

While the narrator is the controlling force behind the actions of his characters, he still struggles to creatively imagine them, especially Dale, a character who seems always just beyond his imaginative powers. If the impossibility of representation and the irreducibility of identity are the primary subjects of Major's early fiction, then the narrator's struggle to control and codify Dale's identity is hardly surprising. Of Dale the narrator writes,

> I used to imagine Dale was a fly and I, a cartoon character with a swatter sneaking up behind him, ready to get him and his stinking flyspeck. Too often, I'm tortured by a sense of dread caused by the fear that I do not really hate Dale, but respond this way to him out of a lack of interest. I mean, I *should* be interested in him since he's one of my creations. He *should* have a character, a personality. And it is strange that I'm jealous of him since he's formless. (11-2)

The narrator's inability to capture Dale's form is frustrating; but Dale's formlessness, the result of an ontological dismantling, suggests a kind of liberation from the reductiveness of a representable identity. Dale slips beneath the radar that seeks to reify his bone structure. The narrator's frustration is apparent when he writes,

> I shouldn't spend time and energy trying to understand and explain anybody. I should spend time in myself. Or in Canada, looking out through his eyes. Try to do something useful from his point of view. I could get a fresh look at Cora maybe. (62)

The narrator's attempt to shift perspectives, in order to get a better sense of Dale's ontological status, suggests his realization that his perspective, while limited, is all he has. The opening scene of *Reflex* equally makes this point:

> Immediately we're at another party. The lights are pink. All the people are well-dressed and drunk. Healthy cows and chickens are standing around in the living room, mooing and clucking. The people do not seem to be aware of them and they're not aware of the people. I'm the single exception. Even Cora, Dale and Canada can't see the animals. A red hen flies to the back of a fat, red and white cow. The chicken says, "Cluck, cluck cluck, cluck, cluck cluck, cluck cluck." (3)

That the guests at this (post-humanist) party morph into and then appear as barnyard animals is "an indication that subjective perception lies at the heart of the story" (Klinkowitz, "Innovative" 155). By stressing the singularity of perception Major avoids generalizing, or replacing the complexity that comes with looking "at people on a one-at-a-time basis" (Bunge 9) with the notion that everything you do, you do not for yourself but for your race, your class, or your gender.

Like Dale, Cora eludes the grasp of the narrator's imaginative powers. Cora, who may or may not have been killed when a bomb in a brief case exploded or after being "run over by a speeding taxi" (Major, *Reflex* 111), moves through the novel like a will-o-wisp. She's fragmented, and Cora "thinks that when she sees herself in fragments she's wrong. It destroys the beauty, the entity, of her being. She hates herself for it" (72). In a moment of anxiety Cora struggles even to identify herself. Her identity splinters and she becomes, in her own words, "schizy." Cora

> talks quietly to herself. "I have an obsessional personality."
>
> "No, Cora. You're cyclothymic."
>
> "I'm schizo."
>
> "You're Black and Marginal, emotional and fearful."
>
> "No. I'm schizy." (106)

Cora's fragmentation, here, is both frightening and liberating.[20] Being "schizy,"[21] she is free from representation—from being Black and Marginal—and yet the loss of a coherent self creates an anxiety Derrida reminds us "is invariably the result of a certain mode of being implicated in the game, of being caught by the game, of being as it were at stake in the game from the outset" ("Structure" 279).[22] Cora's identity is as fluid as her cyclothymic mood swings, and the narrator, after trying to "center" Cora, finally admits the impossibility of basing her identity "on a fundamental ground" or the "concept of a centered structure" (84). "She's elusive," the narrator concedes (Major, *Reflex* 10). "Cora moves up and down the spirit of her coiling self. She has an endless meaning" (42).

Cora's "meaning" is deferred/differed because the "situations and scenes" (122)—what Derrida calls "repetitions, substitutions, transformations, and permutations" (84)—in which she exists are constantly shifting, and, as the narrator reminds us, "the real point is to deal with the situations and scenes," individually (Major, *Reflex* 122). If the situations and scenes in *Reflex* repeat, they do so with a difference. This repetition with a difference is Major's way of showing how meaning and identity change when situations and scenes are re-imagined, signaling not only the power of the imagination to create "reality" but also the randomness that is ever present in that reality. Bradfield argues that Major's fiction is a "fiction of contingency," and one of the ways contingency is evidenced in *Reflex* is in the way scenes are revised (122). "Each time the bomb scene appears," for example, "it is imagined anew. There is no chronological line to the police investigation at the scene and after; there are imagined presentations of the scene, the police, and the investigation" (121). Like the lack of "chronological line to the police investigation," there is a lack of a chronological narrative in *Reflex*. The novel moves in stops and starts, and, in its indeterminacy, eludes our imaginative grasp, while at the same time allowing us, as readers, to participate in its making.

The shifting situations and scenes, and the protean, fluid nature of the characters' identities, open up an imaginative space in which the reader can participate in the creation of the novel. The narrator invites such participation when he admits that "he refuses to go into details. Fragmentation can be all we have to *make* a whole" (Major, *Reflex* 17; emphasis mine). As Soitos argues, "given this fragmentation and refusal to accept order, there is only one consciousness left that is capable of making sense out of the book: the reader's. It is the reader who in the end becomes the [...] real creator of the text" (182). The reader is given the task of putting the fragments together, knowing, though, that the "whole" created out of these fragments is, as Harper reminds us, finally one of "essential discontinuities" that can once again be dismantled (48).

Reflex, then, in "its willing inability to construct a linear plot and recognizable characters," refuses to link "known and accepted hierarchies of word and visual clues" that we, as readers, depend on for "visual and linguistic perceptions" (184). As Soitos cogently argues,

> The ultimate dissolution of this Euro-American hierarchy seems to be one of the aims of *Reflex*. With its nonlinear time frame, its character and plot dissembling, and its epistemological fragmentation, the novel forces a new perception [...] [It] attacks Euro-American control of literary genres and standards of literary excellence, forcing a new awareness of how cultural identity is taught and perceived. Out of this comes a new sense of self and renewal of identity. (184-85)

By forcing a new awareness of how identity is perceived and can be imagined anew, and by "trying to show all the shifting elements of the so-called self," Major is calling attention to the irreducibility of identity, and how the many forces constituting our protean identities always elude our imaginative, and therefore, our representative grasp (Bunge 18).

In *Emergency Exit*, Major includes a number of his own abstract paintings, and thus, in contradistinction to *Reflex*, challenges us to link "word and visual cues" to guide our "visual and linguistic perceptions" (184). These paintings function not as "illustrations [...] but as extensions of the narrative action, *additions* to the text" (Roney 163; emphasis original). As Lisa Roney argues, the "faceless male and female figures" are "alienated and disconnected," and suggest misperception and "the racial misunderstanding that is reflected in passages on either side of the paintings" (164). Major seeks not only to write his characters out of the color codes that seek to confine them but to paint them out. Early in *Emergency* the narrator asserts: "This person that is me is reaching out in contradictions. I want to paint my way out of this. Write my way out" (7). As Roney rightfully suggests, "through the visual image and the written word," Major is "searching for a colorful, but color-blind existence" (162), and by foregrounding visual perception, *Emergency Exit* calls attention to the inability, in an increasingly hybrid world, to maintain, visually, "stable racial categories" (Gilroy 22).[23] And by exposing the limitations of "racialized seeing," then, *Emergency Exit* offers, through the power of the imagination, an emergency exit out of raciology—"a shorthand term for a variety of essentializing and reductionist ways of thinking that are both biological and cultural in character" (40, 72)—and a way toward a "colorful, but color-blind existence" (Roney 162).[24]

Emergency Exit is the story of the Ingram family: Jim and Deborah Ingram and their children, Julie, Barbara, and Oscar. *EmergencyExit*, in form, is

Major's most disjunctive novel; yet its plot, if one could call it that, is rather straightforward.[25] While Jim and Deborah are married, Jim is having an affair with Roslyn, his secretary. Jim and Deborah's daughter, Julie, is dating Allen Morris, a drug-dealer from Harlem who, like the rest of the characters in this novel, is struggling with issues of identity. Deborah, who is still in love with Jim, on more than one occasion, expresses a sexual interest in Allen, and Julie struggles with her own sexual attraction for her father. But *Emergency Exit* is less about the Ingram family and their prurient desires than the personalities who move in and out of a myriad of shifting situations and scenes that demonstrate the inadequacies of the "old visual signatures of 'race'" (43).

Jim, who is a light-skinned black man, is having an affair with his white secretary, and this causes Deborah, his wife, great anxiety. She thinks Jim's attraction to Roslyn has something to do with her being white, though it is clear that that is not the case: "Besides," Deborah says,

> Roslyn is very attractive any man would enjoy lifting her across a threshold or two and thought she's no spring chicken she's younger than me and well you know how some Black men are about white women and how some white women are about Black men and I'm afraid Jim is like that and Roslyn is like that then on the other hand they might be attracted to each other on a purely human level who knows why any two people are attracted to each other any way anyway Jim maintains that her color has nothing to do with it he says he loves her for the person she is and wants a life with her which leaves me where all by my lonesome. (237)

In Deborah's admission that Jim might be attracted to Roslyn "on a purely human level," coupled with Jim's claim that "color has nothing to do with it," we hear Major's desire to subordinate race to the "stuff that truly counts" (Bunge 101). As Major has made clear,

> even from the first, I kept writing about the human condition, not necessarily the black condition [...] I do not write racial literature; I am a human being first, and then a black man. I write books about people who are black, yes, but they are human beings first. Of course, I am a member of my family, my race, my culture, but I feel a kinship with people of good will and integrity, no matter their color or background. (50)

Major's desire to subordinate race to the human condition is evident in a particularly absurd situation that transpires when Jim enters a bar and is confronted by a white man with a gun. While this scene could be read as a "racist" moment, Major humorously undercuts the racial implications by reducing the encounter to absurdity:

> Jim stood with his elbows on the brass. Bartender Kute smiled said sorry don't serve niggers here Jim said that's all right I never drink them. Give me a scotch and soda.

> Kute reached under the counter and brought out his Colt. It galloped down the bar
> and out the place into the dusty main road. Everybody in the joint fell out laughing
> said to the light complexioned black man where you from pal. Rudo said drinks on
> me set him up Kute. We all God's own. (196)

Major resolves this situation—and prevents the violence that stems from race-thinking—by subordinating race to the human condition, the fact that "we all God's own" (196).

In a particularly striking scene in *Emergency Exit*, one that recalls hooks and K's encounter on the airplane, Major once again exposes the danger of invoking those "outmoded principles of differentiation" (356). While Al and Julie are spending the weekend at the Ingram family's cabin at Duck Pond, Al and Julie decide to take a canoe ride and then enjoy a picnic. In the presence of nature Al, once again, feels out of place. "Harlem," he muses, "was never like this" (*Emergency* 119). So Al announces to Julie that he is "going for a walk" (119). As soon as he is alone he "sees coming this way from the mouth of the river a motorboat. Hears its constant groan. White people pink faces" (119). Al sees that the two white men, one of whom has a shotgun, have spotted the canoe and are coming "closer now" (119). While Al is squatting behind a bush, one of the white men "aims the gun at the bush where Al is hiding and pulls the trigger" (119). The men disappear, but Al "feels a huge mixture of rage fear and shame as he crawls back away from the cliff and the bush toward the clearing where Julie apparently is asleep" (119). Al attempts to recount his encounter with these white men to Julie, but she "just can't believe that" (120). Her "mouth hung opened [sic] in disbelief" (120). Julie's disbelief rattles Allen, and he responds, "You can't believe it because you're too white yourself. And the minute he said it he knew it was the beginning of their separation" (120). For Allen, Julie's light complexion has served as a buffer from the reality of racism—that is, from a system of thought that values and judges people not on the content of their character but on the color of their skin.

However, Major contests Allen's racial imagination. As we have seen, Major takes situations and scenes and re-imagines them, and, accordingly, the scene in which Allen encounters the two white men is re-envisioned later in the novel. While Al "sat on a large rock near the edge of the water" he heard the "bluntness of a motorboat's motor" (177). Before long Al "saw the boat, in far too close for a motorboat. Could it be. Al moved back into the shade of the path. One person. A man. It *is* the same boat: red white and blue" (177). If the boat Al sees "*is* the same boat," the man in the boat is *not* the same man, though Al is unable to see that: "Be sure now man yeah I'm sure all right he's yours get ready you ain't got nothing but your bare hands so work fast then there's still the chance that within minutes you can be a dead duck, a dude with a bullet in his head. The man has the rifle standing up in the empty seat beside him. Is he the one are you sure you sure (177). Having convinced himself that this white man is the same man who tried to kill him, "Al leaped up onto the rock in one solid motion and almost in the same motion jumped from the rock into the boat when it was close enough. The character in the boat, a young white man who is startled and who reaches for his rifle, loses control of the boat. Al kicked the rifle into the water" (177-78). Soon enough, though, Al "realized that he was not the one who had shot at him that day in Little Duck Pond. He was not even the one who had been with the one who shot at him. This realization took away some of his anger and drive" (178).

For bell hooks, the white man on the airplane who chose his own comfort over K's stands in for all white men, and by extension, white culture. Similarly, Al conflates all white men with the one man who took a shot at him at Little Duck Pond. Like hooks', Al's racial imagination paints a wide swath and rather than looking at individuals on a one-at-a-time basis, he reduces the complexity of identity to a singular criterion, skin color. By revising Al's confrontation with the two white men on Little Duck Pond, Major is cautioning us against the kind of reductive logic that follows from a racial imagination. In this scene, Al, like hooks, denies an "other" the right to "activate self-identity," and instead imposes—through the veil of the racial imagination—a representation that subsequently denies the autonomy of an individual who is the contingent product of many forces in a complex social matrix (Goldberg 182).[26] Focusing on race as the primary constitutive factor in identity formation has led to the idea that there is something called the "black experience," a notion which Major has spent his career challenging.

In *Emergency Exit* the "Black Professor," who is obviously a subject of critique, "was consumed by his racial identity," and the only aspect of Inlet's history "he cared about was that of the experience of its Black people" (198). At Inlet College, he taught "Introduction to The Black Experience and a five-hundred level course called, The Sense of the Black Experience," and we are told that "his students thought he was a drag" (198). While "he introduced them to Drag Gibson[,] [t]hey still thought he was a drag" (198). "To get away from his troubles," we learn that

he spent evenings at home reading Black history books. He had a secret ambition. One day he would go beyond these works in the field of the Black Experience. He would write and publish the definitive work on the Black Experience, especially in Inlet, Connecticut. Perhaps Wesleyan University Press would publish it [...] Meanwhile, he spoke only to Black people and for sure did not hang out with white faculty. (198)[27]

Major makes clear how we are to take the kind of thinking the Black Professor clings to by undercutting it with humor and the Black Professor's own one-dimensional view of "blackness." The narrator tells us that "on weekends" the Black Professor "went to Harlem, New York, and cut the rug. He also got drunk a few times and got ripped off. On one such occasion he was left standing in an alley in his drawers. But he still loved his people and swore by them" (198-99). The Black Professor never attends plays at the Inlet Playhouse "because it was white owned and the Black Auction Block Playhouse never had anything going. He did not know that it was also white owned" (199).

While in this scene the Black Professor has an unflinching devotion to "his people," and an ambition to write the "definitive work on the Black Experience," in an earlier situation, one in which he is speaking to his American History 101 class, he urges students "to remember [that] history is primarily fiction. Don't trust anybody who claims to know what happened. Nobody you know was there. And very likely [...] even those who were there did not know what was going on" (56). Knowing that Major constantly re-imagines situations and scenes in order to remind us of their contingency and the fluidity of subject positions, it should not surprise us that the Black Professor's advice to his students contradicts his own position on the "Black Experience."

Major's early fiction reminds us of—and forces us to experience—the many forces or "surrounding influences" that work to produce subjectivity (Bunge 109). Unlike hooks, DuCille, and Gates, Major renounces race as the primary, constitutive factor in identity formation and aesthetic production, and by adopting a style that minimizes "*representational* effects" (29), he is attempting to force a "crisis of raciology" (Gilroy 41). When confronted by this crisis, or the uncertainty of how to define or categorize people (or texts) in terms of skin color, rather than abandoning race as an analytical tool, hooks, DuCille, and Gates, recuperate it and defer to its "embeddedness in the world" or its spectral presence in a text (52). Major, like Gilroy, sees this crisis of representation as a liberating moment when, through the power of the imagination, we can create a culture premised not on racial categories but on "face-to-face relations between different actors—beings of equal worth" (41).

Major is at odds with "black writers" who get "hung up in militant rhetoric," and suggests "it has always been the novel or poem that begins from and spreads all across the entire human experience" and "ends up liberating minds" (Bunge 24-5). In *The Dark and the Feeling* he writes, "[t]he novel not deliberately aimed at bringing about human freedom for black people has liberated as many minds as has the propaganda tract, if not more" (24). What Major understands and is attempting to communicate in his early fiction is that "imaginative and spiritual freedom precede social liberation" (Klinkowitz, "Innovative" 157), or, as Gloria Anzaldúa says, "nothing happens in the 'real' world unless it first happens in the images in our heads" (109). Whether by subordinating race to the human condition, as he does in *Emergency Exit*, or by dismantling subjectivity to expose radical alterity, as he does in *Reflex*, Major boldly uses imaginative literature to fashion a "world that is undivided by the petty differences we retain and inflate by calling them racial" (Gilroy 356). At a time when pathological problems stemming from race-thinking are on the rise, the more *ethical* world Major envisions—a world beyond the color line—is prophetic and worth taking seriously. It has been a long time coming.

Notes

[1]   The term "racialized" was introduced by Robert Miles in *Racism and Labour Migration* (1982), a study of immigration to Britain after WWII.

[2]   On the dust jacket of Major's *Come By Here: My Mother's Life* (2002), the publisher's blurb reads, "An extraordinary woman dreams of a world beyond the color line."

[3]   This essay will not attempt to tease out nor resolve the tension between Major's postmodern (anti-) aesthetic and his humanism. This tension, as Hutcheon has argued, is inherent in postmodernism. My use of humanism here follows Kate Soper's definition in *Humanism and Anti-Humanism* (1986). Humanism, she writes, "appeals (positively) to the notion of a core humanity or common essential feature in terms of what human beings can be defined and understood" (11-2).

[4]   As Klinkowitz argues, for Major, "using race as the dominant critical concern disallows appreciation of works by black authors, and in the meantime fosters a style of very limited social realism" (*Fiction* 102).

[5]   By "early novels" I am referring to those published before 1987. *My Amputations* (1986) was the last of his experimental novels, and *Such Was the Season* (1987) marked a shift toward a more conventional style.

[6]   Claudia Tate's *Psychoanalysis and Black Novels: Desire and the Protocols of Race* (1998) specifically addresses novels by African Americans that do not "fit the Western hierarchical paradigm of race as exclusion, vulnerability, and deficiency. These works depict what [she] call[s] a 'surplus,' a defining characteristic not generally associated with African American personality and culture" (7). While Major's work could, of course, be read in light of Tate's important study, I would argue that Major would be unconvinced by Tate's admittedly

sophisticated argument. In *Emergency Exit*, Major seem to mock psychoanalytic readings of race when he writes: "Listen: Inlet Research Company reports: purity deep in the psyche racism deep in the psyche cleanliness and proper conduct both deep in the psyche" (9). Similarly, Major, I suggest, would not be moved by Gates' assertion that "now, we must, at last, don the empowering mask of blackness and talk *that* talk, the language of black difference" ("Canon-Formation" 178). The notion that all blacks talk in a certain way, that they talk "*that* talk," suggests a kind of non-essentialist essentialism: what makes blackness black is the "language of black *difference*" (emphasis mine).

[7]   As Hilary N. Weaver argues, "identity may actually be a composite of many things such as race, class, education, region, religion, and gender [...] Identities are always fragmented, multiply constructed, and intersected in a constantly changing, sometimes conflicting array" (240). For Major, what is called the self "is really a nonexistent thing, or something that is in a constant state of becoming" (Bunge 17). The "self," in other words, is not "organically united" but is constituted by "essential discontinuities" (Harper 48).

[8]   It is curious that so little scholarly attention has been paid to Major's works, many of which have gone out of print. While his career as a writer spans more than forty years, and has resulted in the publication of more than two dozen books, as of 2006, serious consideration of his work amounts to scattered references, primarily in studies of African American literature, to his first four novels; a roughly five page general treatment of his early fiction in Bernard Bell's seminal work *The Afro-American Novel and Its Tradition* (1987); and the indispensable collection *Clarence Major and His Art: Portraits of an African American Postmodernist* (2001), the only collection of scholarly essays available devoted solely to certain of Major's works. This dearth of scholarship may be due to the difficulty of appropriating his work for "political and ideological needs" (Hogue 193). In *Psychoanalysis and Black Novels*, Tate makes a similar argument. She writes, "Because these works do not conform to the protest agenda of black modernism, they are repressed in the traditional black canon" (11-2). On this point, see also Walter Mosley's "Black to the Future," 34, and Madhu Dubey's *Signs and Cities* (2003), Chapter 1.

[9]   I allude here to Cornel West's essay "The Pitfalls of Racial Reasoning" in *Race Matters* (1994). There West argues that "the undermining and dismantling of the framework of racial reasoning—especially the basic notions of black authenticity, close-ranks mentality, and black cultural conservatism—lead toward a new framework for black thought and practice. This new framework should be a *prophetic* one of moral reasoning with its fundamental ideas of a mature black identity, coalition strategy, and black cultural democracy [...] [A] prophetic framework encourages *moral* assessment of the variety of perspectives held by black people and selects those views based on black dignity and decency that eschew putting any group of people or culture on a pedestal or in the gutter" (43). West's piece is prophetic indeed. But here, too, West insists upon "black identity" and a "black cultural democracy," while the vision Major articulates in *Emergency Exit*, for example, makes common cause with Paul Gilroy's "multicultural democracy," or what elsewhere in *Against Race* he calls "cosmopolitan democracy" (41, 243), a vision that renounces solidarity based on race in favor of "planetary humanity" (356).

[10]   It could be said that DuCille, hooks, and Gates are putting race "sous rature" or "under erasure." As Spivak explains in her Preface to Derrida's *Of Grammatology* (1998), "under erasure" means "to write a word, cross it out, and then print both word and deletion. (Since the word is inaccurate, it is crossed out. Since it is necessary, it remains legible)" (xiv). In *Outside in the Teaching Machine* (1993), Spivak puts it this way: "One is left with the

useful yet semimournful position of the unavoidable usefulness of something that is dangerous" (5). Major, like Paul Gilroy, goes further than Derrida and Spivak, in this respect. In *Reflex* and *Emergency*, Major is attempting to "de-nature and de-ontologize 'race,' thereby disaggregating raciologies" (Gilroy 43). Major and Gilroy, who take a "postracial stance," choose to cross out race, *because* it is dangerous, and then not reprint it (42).

11 For a discussion of "blackness" defined as "continually being reconstituted as African Americans inhabit widely differentiated social spaces," see Anderson's *Beyond Ontological Blackness* (1995), 11.

12 When hooks and K hailed a cab that afternoon, the cabby refused to take them to the airport. Only when hooks threatened to report him did he agree to take them. It is interesting to note that when recounting this story hooks does not tell us the race of the cabby, though she never fails to remind us that the employees at the airport are "white." While hooks does say that the cabby's actions were racist, her emphasis shifts away from racist attitudes among people of color to racist attitudes among whites. In "Loving Blackness as Political Resistance" hooks suggests that black people, and, by extension, all people of color, cannot be racist because racism is a "system that promotes domination and subjugation," and black people are "in no way linked to a system of domination that affords us any power to coercively control the lives and well-being of white-folks" (15). The cabby's racism isn't racist in the same way, if it is racist at all, as the anonymous white man's. But as Guillermo Gómez-Pena argues, "dominance is contextual. We all, at different times and in different contexts, enjoy some privileging over other people and perform the ever-changing roles of victim and victimizer, exploited and exploiter, colonizer and colonized" (*New World* 13-4).

13 As Tate explains it, hooks' notion of "Postmodern blackness" "designates the complicated ways in which other positions—those of gender, class, sexuality, region, nationality, and so on—also determine the performance of African American identities" (6). "What this means," Tate writes, "is that different occasions and social contexts allow individuals to activate and to be perceived by one or more of the various constituents of their identities" (6). And yet, ironically, hooks does not allow the "white" man on the airplane to "activate" freely any one of the "various constituents of [his] identit[y]." She had already "perceived" the man as a white racist, and decided he was simply representative of a whole system of domination.

14 On the relationship between race and culture, see Walter Benn Michaels' *Our America: Nativism, Modernism, and Pluralism* (1995), 135-142. While critics like Gilroy "appeal to culture [...] to supplant the appeal to race" (139), Michaels argues that "what's wrong with the current conception of cultural identity is not that it developed out of racial identity [...]; what's wrong with cultural identity is that, without recourse to the racial identity that (in its current manifestations) it repudiates, it makes no sense" (142). Major's position, here, is closer to Gilroy's than it is to Michaels'. In an interview with Alexander Neubauer, for example, Major says, "I take the position that the cultural stuff is fairly superficial; all you can do is understand what it means. The stuff that truly counts [the human condition] is beneath it. I could think of dozens of examples of [writers writing outside there own cultural experience] happening. For instance, James Baldwin writing *Giovanni's Room* with depth and sensitivity, which has no black characters in it whatsoever. And Richard Wright's *Savage Holiday*, with no black characters, and it's a truly felt, deeply rendered story. There are dozens and dozens of examples, and not just across racial lines but in many, many different cultures" (Bunge 100).

15   Major's early work has more in common with Gertrude Stein, John Barth, Kurt Vonnegut, Donald Barthelme, and Ronald Sukenick than with Ralph Ellison, Richard Wright and James Baldwin. According to Major, the "obvious forerunners" to the kind of fiction he produces are "Laurence Sterne, James Joyce, Samuel Beckett. And Italo Calvino, Borges, Carlos Fuentes, Gabriel Garcia Marquez, Peter Handke. But Melville is still way back there as the ultimate forerunner [...] The digressive method works best for me. In this sense I am in the Melville tradition" (Bunge 29, 28).

16   Gates, here, seems to be conflating race and ethnicity. My position accords with Harold Abramson's in *Ethnic Diversity in Catholic America* (1973). There he argues, although "race is the most salient ethnic factor, it is still only one of the dimensions of the larger cultural and historical phenomenon of ethnicity" (175).

17   For a cogent argument about "the workings of the unconscious in language and its effects on black texts" (179), see Claudia Tate's *Psychoanalysis and Black Novels: Desire and the Protocols of Race* (1998), as well as Madhu Dubey's *Signs and Cities: Black Literary Postmodernism* (2003) and Phillip Brian Harper's *Framing the Margins: The Social Logic of Postmodern Culture* (1994).

18   By transcendental I mean ahistorical, beyond the reach of cultural change.

19   *Reflex*, in this sense, conforms to what Umberto Eco, in *The Role of the Reader: Explorations in the Semiotics of Texts* (1979), calls an "open work," which encourages readers to participate in the making of the text (63).

20   Cora's dialogue, here, suggests a tension between the modernist despair and the postmodern celebration of a fragmented world. On the one hand, she sounds like the persona in Eliot's "The Waste Land" who declares, "These fragments I have shored against my ruins" (2160), and, on the other, a postmodern woman who sees fragmentation as "an exhilarating, liberating phenomenon, symptomatic of our escape from the claustrophobic embrace of fixed systems of belief" (Barry 84), including those systems based on race-thinking.

21   On the "schizoid" and "schizoanalysis," see Deleuze and Guattari's *Anti-Oedipus: Capitalism and Schizophrenia* (1983). "Schizoanalysis," they write, "attains a nonfiguration ('abstract' in the sense of abstract painting), flows-schizzes or real-desire, apprehended below the minimum conditions of identity" (351). Cora, in this scene, is undergoing what Deleuze and Guattari call "deterritorialization," or "the journey through *ego-loss*" (Seem xix; emphasis original). For Deleuze and Guattari, this journey "serves to begin [...] a healing process" (xxii).

22   Major, through Cora, may be betraying his own anxiety about the "fragmentation" of the self and help explain his ambivalent turn toward humanism in *Emergency Exit* and his later novels. For a cogent discussion of the dangers of fragmentation, see "Against Fragmentation" in Charles Taylor's *The Ethics of Authenticity* (1991).

23   On the increasing inability to maintain stable racial categories in a hybrid world, see Paul Gilroy's "The Crisis of 'Race' and Raciology," in *Against Race* (2000), and Guillermo Gomez-Pena's "La Migrant Life," in *Dangerous Border Crossers* (2000).

24   In the Epilogue to *Skin Trade*, DuCille quotes Robert Kennedy quoting Martin Luther King, Jr.: "Some men see things as they are and ask 'why?'; I dream dreams that never were and ask 'why not?'" (171). Du Cille's pessimism shines through when she writes, "in the real world, however, it would seem that racism, sexism, and heterosexism are permanent features of the human condition" (173). The imaginative literature of writers like Clarence

Major, the theoretical work of critics like Paul Gilroy, and the prophetic visions and legacies of leaders like King and Kennedy, among others, serve as powerful counter-statements to such a pessimistic view.

25   Major dedicates *Emergency Exit* "to those people whose stories do not hold together." He then uses a line from Hemingway's *The Sun Also Rises* as an epigraph: "I mistrust all frank and simple people, especially when their stories hold together."

26   In *Tolerating Ambiguity* (1998), Wilson Neate argues that "domination consists of the denial of the self-representation of the other" (64). In *New World Border* (1996), Guillermo Gómez-Pena insists that "it just doesn't cut it anymore to pretend that the enemy is always outside. The separatist, sexist, racist, and authoritarian tendencies that we condemn others for perpetuating also exist within our own communities and within our own individual selves. We can't continue to hide behind the pretext that 'straight, white men,' or the all purpose 'dominant culture' are the source of all our problems" (13). Like Deleuze and Guattari, Gómez-Pena reminds us that there are forms of "fascism" within us all. See Foucault's Preface to *Anti-Oedipus*.

27   For a spirited critique of contemporary American writers who only write about "their mono-ethnic neighborhoods," see "Segregated Fiction Blues" in Stanley Crouch's *The Artificial White Man* (2004).

Works Cited

Abramson, Harold J. *Ethnic Diversity in Catholic America*. New York: John Wiley, 1973.

Anderson, Victor. *Beyond Ontological Blackness: An Essay on African American Religious and Cultural Criticism*. New York: Continuum, 1995.

Anzaldúa, Gloria. *Borderlands/La Frontera: The New Mestiza*. 2nd ed. San Francisco: Aunt Lute Books, 1999.

Barry, Peter. *Beginning Theory: An Introduction to Literary and Cultural Theory*.Manchester: Manchester UP, 2002.

Bell, W. Bernard.Introduction.*Clarence Major and His Art: Portraits of an African American Postmodernist*.Ed. Bernard W. Bell. Chapel Hill: U of North Carolina P, 2001. 1-9.

—. *The Afro-American Novel and Its Tradition*. Amherst: U of Massachusetts P, 1987.

Bradfield, Larry D. "Beyond Mimetic Exhaustion: The *Reflex and BoneStructure* Experiment." *Black American Literary Forum* 17 (1983): 120-123.

Bunge, Nancy, ed. *Conversations with Clarence Major*. Jackson: UP of Mississippi, 2002.

Crouch, Stanley. *The Artificial White Man: Essays on Authenticity*. New York: Basic, 2004.

Deleuze, Gilles, and Félix Guattari.*Anti-Oedipus: Capitalism and Schizophrenia*. Trans. Robert

Hurley, Mark Seem, and Helen R. Lane. Minneapolis: U of   Minnesota P, 1983.

Derrida, Jacques. "Structure, Sign and Play in the Discourse of the Human Sciences." *Writing and Difference*. Trans. Alan Bass. Chicago: U of Chicago P, 1978.

Dubey, Madhu. *Signs and Cities: Black Literary Postmodernism*. Chicago: U of Chicago P, 2003.

DuCille, Ann. *Skin Trade*. Cambridge, MA: Harvard UP, 1996.

Eliot, T.S. "The Waste Land." *The Norton Anthology of English Literature*.Vol. 2. Ed. M. H. Abrams, et al. New York: Norton, 1993. 2147-2160.

Eco, Umberto. *The Role of the Reader: Explorations in the Semiotics of Text*. Bloomington: Indiana UP, 1979.

Favor, J. Martin.*Authentic Blackness: The Folk in the New Negro Renaissance*. Durham: Duke UP, 1999.

Foucault, Michel. Preface.*Anti-Oedipus: Capitalism and Schizophrenia*. By Gilles Deleuze and Félix Guattari. Trans. Robert Hurley, Mark Seem, and Helen R. Lane. Minneapolis: U of Minnesota P, 1983.xi-xiv.

Fuss, Diana. *Essentially Speaking: Feminism, Nature and Difference*. New York: Routledge, 1989.

Gates, Henry Louis, Jr. "Canon-Formation, Literary History, and the Afro-American Tradition: From the Seen to the Told."*Falling Into Theory: Conflicting Views on Reading Literature*.Ed. David H. Richter. 2nd ed. Boston: Bedford, 2000.

--. *Figures in Black: Words, Signs, and the "Racial" Self*. New York: Oxford UP, 1987.

--. *The Signifying Monkey: A Theory of African-American Literary Criticism*. New York: Oxford UP, 1988.

Gilroy, Paul. *Against Race: Imagining Political Culture Beyond the Color Line*. Cambridge, MA: Harvard UP, 2000.

Goldberg, D.T. "Conversation: Facial Formation in Contemporary American National Identity." *Social Identities: Journal for the Study of Race, Nation and Culture* 2 (February 1996): 169-91.

Gómez-Pena, Guillermo.*Dangerous Border Crossers: The Artist Talks Back*. London: Routledge, 2000.

--. *The New World Border: Prophecies, Poemsand Loqueras for the End of the Century*. San Francisco: City Lights, 1996.

Harper, Phillip Brian.*Framing the Margins: The Social Logic of Postmodern Culture*.New York: Oxford UP, 1994.

Hogue, W. Lawrence.*Race, Modernity, Postmodernity: A Look at the History and the Literatures of People of Color Since the 1960s*. New York: State U of New York P, 1996.

hooks, bell. *Killing Rage: Ending Racism*. New York: Henry Holt, 1995.

--. "Loving Blackness as Political Resistance."*Black Looks: Race and Representation*. Boston: South End P, 1992.

--. "Postmodern Blackness."*Colonial Discourse and Post-Colonial Theory: A Reader*. Ed. Patrick Williams and Laura Chrisman. New York: Columbia UP, 1994.

--. "Representations of Whiteness in the Black Imagination."*Black Looks: Race and Representation*. Boston: South End P, 1992.

Hutcheon, Linda. *A Poetics of Postmodernism: History, Theory, Fiction*. New York: Routledge, 1988.

Klinkowitz, Jerome. "Clarence Major's Innovative Fiction." *Clarence Major and His Art: Portraits* of an African American Postmodernist.Ed. Bernard Bell. Chapel Hill: U of North Carolina P, 2001.

---. The Life of Fiction. Urbana: U of Illinois P, 1977.

Krupat, Arnold. The Turn to the Native: Studies in Criticism and Culture. Lincoln: U of Nebraska P, 1996.

Major, Clarence. All-Night Visitors. 1969. Boston: Northeaster UP, 1998.

---. Come By Here: My Mother's Life. New York: John Wiley & Sons, 2002.

---. Emergency Exit. New York: Fiction Collective, 1979.

---. Reflex and Bone Structure. New York: Fiction Collective, 1975.

---. The Dark and Feeling: Black American Writers and Their Work. New York: The Third P, 1974.

Michaels, Walter Benn. Our American: Nativism, Modernism, and Pluralism. Durham: Duke UP, 1995.

Miles, Robert. Racism and Labour Migration. London: Routledge & Kegan Paul, 1982.

Mosley, Walter. "Black to the Future."New York Times Magazine 1 Nov. 1998: 34.

Neate, Wilson. Tolerating Ambiguity: Ethnicity and Community in Chicano/a Writing.New York: Peter Lang, 1998.

Pérez, Emma. The Decolonial Imaginary: Writing Chicanas Into History. Bloomington: Indiana University P, 1999.

Roney, Lisa C. "The Double Vision of Clarence Major: Painter and Writer." Clarence Major and His Art: Portraits of an African American Postmodernist. Ed. Bernard Bell. Chapel Hill: U of North Carolina P, 2001.

Seem, Mark. Introduction.Anti-Oedipus: Capitalism and Schizophrenia. By Gilles Deleuze and Félix Guattari. Trans. Robert Hurley, Mark Seem, and Helen R. Lane. Minneapolis: U of Minnesota P, 1983.xv-xxiv.

Soitos, Stephen F. "Reflex and Bone Structure: The Black Anti-Detective Novel." Clarence Major and His Art: Portraits of an African American Postmodernist. Ed. Bernard Bell. Chapel Hill: U of North Carolina P, 2001.

Soper, Kate. Humanism and Anti-Humanism. Chicago: Open Court, 1986.

Spivak, Gayatri Chakravorty. Outside in the Teaching Machine. New York: Routledge, 1993.

---. Preface.Of Grammatology.By Jacques Derrida.Trans. Gayatri Chakravorty Spivak. Baltimore: John Hopkins UP, 1998. ix-lxxxvii.

Tate, Claudia. Psychoanalysis and Black Novels: Desire and the Protocols of Race. New York: Oxford UP, 1998.

Taylor, Charles. The Ethics of Authenticity. Cambridge, MA: Harvard UP, 1991.

Weaver, Hilary N. "Indigenous Identity: What Is It, and Who Really Has It?" American Indian Quarterly 25 (Spring 2001): 240-55.

West, Cornel. Race Matters. New York: Vintage, 1994.

"Isn't the whole point of writing to escape what people not me think of me": The Failure of Language and the Search for Authenticity in *Philadelphia Fire* and *God's Gym*

Ian Reilly

> One ever feels his two-ness, - an American, a Negro; two souls, two thoughts, two unreconciled strivings; two warring ideals in one dark body, whose dogged strength alone keeps it from being torn asunder. – W.E.B. Du Bois, *The Souls of Black Folk*

> History is better defined as an ongoing tension between stories that have been told and stories that might be told.
>
> Lynn Hunt

In "Twentieth-Century Fiction and the Black Mask of Humanity" (1953), Ralph Ellison urges African American writers to celebrate black culture on its own terms in the form of counter-narratives, in the hopes of dismantling racist stereotypes and cultural assumptions about African Americans propagated through the master narratives of America's most representative (white) authors. Ellison's critical project here, though not limited to preserving the interests of authentic African American representation in contemporary literature, stresses the need to "defin[e] Negro humanity" (148). The essay marks an important turning point in the treatment and subsequent reception of black characters in contemporary American literature because "the distortion of the Negro in modern writing," (147) Ellison argues, is no longer acceptable in a democratic society. In (in)direct response to Ellison's concerns, John Edgar Wideman's prolific body of work assumes the challenge of (re)defining "Negro humanity" and representing African American culture operating under the umbrella of conflicting ideologies. As an author whose work consistently points to the politics of incommensurable cultural and racial difference, whose voice struggles to reconcile what W.E.B. Du Bois calls "two warring ideals in one dark body," Wideman's fiction illustrates the difficulties in not only representing an authentic African American voice but also in legitimating the (male) black body in dominant discursive bodies of writing.

With the publication of *God's Gym* (2005), a collection of short stories that simultaneously invokes Ellison's project and distorts/challenges Du Bois' conception of "double-consciousness" (17), a reexamination of *Philadelphia Fire* (1990) will serve as an important point of departure from which to discuss Wideman's art because both texts actively engage with the dynamics of the political representation of the black body and how language shapes its ever-shifting signification. For Wideman, the politics of language figure prominently in both texts; therefore, a close reading of these texts will reveal how language at once engenders the collapse of interpersonal relationships in the domestic (i.e. private) space while it works toward building a communal voice with a political agenda to meet the concerns of an ever-changing black community. My work here also addresses how these texts illustrate the slipperiness of discourse, and how the appropriation of language is both a limited/limiting aesthetic practice and a political exercise that is problematized in the translation and performance of what might be called an "authentic" black language. Finally, this essay explores how language also complicates the question of authenticity precisely because for Wideman, identity is constantly (re)negotiated through language.

Ralph Ellison's *Invisible Man* provides an interesting starting point from which to discuss authenticity and language. The "blackness of blackness" sermon, Ellison's playful reconfiguration and reordering of the ur-creation myth in Western culture, challenges traditional notions of already established origins. In this sermon, Ellison describes the beginning as "blackness," as a counter-narrative to the white Eurocentric mythology of "whiteness." Here blackness, Kimberly W. Benston argues, is a performative act, "a construct of desire, mobilized at a site of struggle against various forms of closure. As interpretive respondents to its performative call, [the reader is] asked to accept the continuously unsatisfying and contradictory character of its enunciations" ("Performing Blackness" 173). Because Ellison's preacher takes on a performative role in the performance of his sermon, the text (and its "performative enunciations") opens up an "infinite realm of play" in which discursive practices are both revised and expanded, de-centered and re-centered, accordingly. Ellison's appropriation and refashioning of a foundational creation myth into a bold statement on the nature of "blackness" and its "ceaselessly elusive agency" (171) reveals as much about the instability of this construct as it does about the certainty of its subject: "Black will make you ... or black will un-make you" (*Invisible Man* 10).

In *Philadelphia Fire* and *God's Gym*, John Edgar Wideman engages with conflicting discursive strategies that frame the black body (the literary body as well as the "real" body) in problematic ways. Unlike Ellison before him, Wideman is interested in both the intellectual and political properties of the "blackness of blackness," of how black can either "make you or un-make you," how these tensions exist simultaneously, are mutually interconnected, and how they can be explored through the lens of postmodern fiction. Though Wideman's questions are framed differently, using different linguistic markers and literary techniques, some of Ellison's concerns are addressed in similar terms: "When your skin's gone, children / Are you black inside" (*Philadelphia Fire* 159). As we shall see, blackness here can only be measured through the performative enunciations in the text, most explicitly in the form of (mis)appropriated language and counter-narratives. These distinctions are important because they form the kernel of Wideman's understanding of the "the blackness of blackness," as a positioning of African Americans within a cultural framework that works against them despite their attempts to subvert oppressive forces through new language and politicized African American discourse. Importantly, Wideman's engagement with language in *Philadelphia Fire* (and much later in *God's Gym*) can be seen as an attempt to recuperate an authentic black voice in his fiction. Like Ellison, Wideman, in his early fiction (most notably in *A Glance Away* and *Hurry Home*), is conscious of his relation to canonical writers of the (white) Western European tradition. Whereas Ellison's conscious attempt to locate himself among these white writers is well documented, Wideman discusses his acculturation process in terms of a "value system [being] imposed upon [him]," ("The Black Writer" 28) a process that, he argues, did not signal a conscious rejection of his own "blackness" or black experience in the community. His subsequent de-centering of, or dislocation from, this Western European model of writing and his re-appropriation of African voice – history, culture, society – as both artifice *and* political commitment point to a notable shift not only in his writing but in his construction of an African (American) community in a chaotic and racist American culture.

James W. Coleman traces this marked shift in Wideman's writing (from *A Glance Away* through *Reuben*) as a slow, revelatory process in which the author's reintegration into the black community is fully realized through his depiction of the isolated black intellectual who, through countless failed (re)negotiations with black culture, ultimately re-immerses himself in black society. As Coleman notes, "Wideman [himself] is the writer-intellectual who has overcome his alienation and returned home" (9). Wideman's reintegration in the black community is significant, Coleman argues, because his "allegiance to the community [as writer-intellectual] dictates that [he] must seek to help it however [he] can" (7). Though Coleman's work does well to unpack Wideman's personal politics and the means through which he (re)appropriates a black voice, how Wideman's own political imperatives "help" the black community remains a contentious issue in Wideman's fiction. Wideman's shift from a Western European (read: modernist) model of writing to a progressively postmodern Afro-American model of narrative storytelling has progressively evolved, as has his full engagement with language and black consciousness. However, Wideman's deployment of the black body in his fiction is problematic because he is still engaging with two conflicting ideological representations of the body (Eurocentric and Afrocentric) and how these racially/ideologically marked bodies operate within prescribed cultural settings. In an interview with Jacqueline Berben-Masi, Wideman himself acknowledges the ongoing tension between these two conflicting ideologies in his work and how the narrative space they occupy frustrates any attempt at describing an "authentic" African American voice:

> If you're fighting for space, if you're fighting for voice, who knows what the final result will be. Because that space, once it's achieved, has a way of expanding, of incorporating, and you can't exactly make a distinction between the disciplined space and the larger space. They begin to bleed into one another. (Berben-Masi 584)

Doreatha Drummond Mbalia describes this tension in terms of the clash between Eurocentricity and Afrocentricity, and how writers like Wideman must undergo a re-education process of sorts that involves re-acculturation. More importantly, however, Afro-American writers and intellectuals like Wideman, Mbalia argues, must actively engage in what Fanon has called "decolonization," a process of rediscovery and reclamation of one's culture, which ultimately creates and champions "the African's own history, culture, and values as the foundation of self" (24). For Wideman, these (re)negotiations with African culture from within a dominant cultural order in America form the kernel of his aesthetic project in *Philadelphia Fire*. However, in *Philadelphia Fire* (and most recently in *God's Gym*) Wideman's political project remains ambiguous because the narrative spaces he creates for his characters – some of whom serve as surrogates for Wideman himself – "begin to bleed into one another." If, as Coleman suggests, Wideman's own re-acculturation is fully realized through his deployment of the (male) black body in his work, does his struggle to liberate strong African American voices in his work point to an authentic representation of the African American community or does Wideman as writer-intellectual show how far removed he is from a fixed understanding of his own culture? To answer these questions, an examination of Wideman's language is needed. That Wideman himself acknowledges the problematic nature of describing an "authentic" African-American voice, of "fighting for voice," points to the writer's ongoing (re)negotiations with language and culture. That language problematizes the notion of authenticity in Wideman's writings is significant because he sees authenticity as a process through which identity is potentially defined and secured through language. The search/quest for authenticity, then, is both frustrated and pushed forward through the construction and dissemination of appropriated language. Wideman's choice of narrative tropes will serve to unpack some of these problems.

As a writer looking to recuperate an African voice in his fiction, Wideman employs postmodern writing strategies as a potential means to "reclaim[ing an] African Personality[1]" (Mbalia 27). Because postmodern narratives are committed to producing subversive counter-narratives, though not exclusively in the form of socially responsible and politically progressive texts, postmodernism engages with a number of rhetorical strategies that serve to de-centre and re-contextualize different realms of subjective experience. Postmodernism's flirtation with nihilism and its refutation of logic and objective realities enable (if not assist in) the re-ordering of power structures, make possible shifts in a community's cultural positioning, and allow for reconsiderations of master narratives of the dominant culture. Even so, postmodernism's nihilistic tendencies would seem to foreclose any possibility of authenticity. In this light, any discussion of authenticity as a fixed construct from which to theorize cultural positioning would necessarily be at odds with the postmodern concerns of the author. Rather, this opening up of the infinite realm of play that postmodernism affords enables its author to reconsider how notions of authenticity are valued and understood. Paradoxically, it is postmodernity's very nihilism that signals new ways of understanding the term authenticity: as a process through which language complicates, challenges, and organizes how identity – individual, cultural, ideological – is negotiated.

Wideman's experimentation with language in *Philadelphia Fire* in the form of disjointed narratives, multiple reconfigurations of self, self-reflexive dialogue, intersubjectivity, and his appropriation of *The Tempest* all shape his artistic revisionary practices. These postmodern markers provide the groundwork for Wideman's musings on African American experience in the chaotic city. As Fritz Gysin observes, Wideman's use of postmodern narrative strategies is significant because they point to the author's "'recentering' of [his] culture's focus on issues that have always concerned marginalized [i.e. African American] constituencies" ("From Modernism to Postmodernism" 141). At the same time, postmodernism, though liberating in these respects, could be seen as a "white" construct that does not unlock the same liberating potential for black writers. "Black writers," Coleman states, "do not start from a position of equality, and to realize postmodern potential, they must generate the voice to construct black liberating fictions *against* the hegemony of Western discourse" (*Black Male Fiction* 5). Because Wideman's writing is concerned with the "recentering" of his community's political agenda in *Philadelphia Fire*, an examination of how depoliticized language fails to elicit a tangible individual response in the figure of Cudjoe will serve to illustrate how agency is achieved most often when language takes shape in the form of political protest and subversive historical revision.

Some critics like Jerry Varsava have pointed to the novel as a "recourse to history," one that "engages in historiographical revisionism" (428). Because Cudjoe's cultural positioning in the narrative is informed by geographical markers, much of the narrative's "historiographical revisionism" hinges on his location within a culture and his understanding of the hegemonic mechanisms in place. In other words, this recourse to history is important because it engages in the production of subversive narratives in an attempt to de-centre already established notions of culture. However, the dissemination of historically revised, subversive narratives is frustrated in the novel for two reasons: the protagonist's inability to decode language and his lack of agency in "staging" or "enacting" these counter-narratives. *Philadelphia Fire*'s first narrative voice belongs to Cudjoe, a de-centered, marginalized figure who embodies failure, but more specifically, a form of failure that is as related to "blackness" as it is to manhood. His failure is tied to his abandonment of his family (a white woman and two half-white kids), and the community. In the process, he becomes "a half-black someone who couldn't be depended upon" (10). His failure at home and in the community is rooted in his inability to understand the power of – and behind – language: "He knew them not at all. They spoke another language" (69). Cudjoe's failure as father and family man results in his self-imposed exile and isolation that takes him to the island of Mykonos. In search of new language and identity, he divorces himself from both the poverty of "[the] people dump[s]" and the promise of "[m]odern urban living in the midst of certified culture" (78). As Timbo notes, "he copped the education and ran" (81). Several critics have pointed to Cudjoe's self-imposed exile as a means of recuperating the self, of moving out of the bastardization of being labeled "a half-black someone" and recuperating an African personality. I would argue, however, that Cudjoe's dislocation from society is complete when he immerses himself in a Mykonosian society in which "[he isn't] required to do a goddamn thing. Cool out. Day after day of nothing and nobody g[ives] a fuck." He becomes an "institution," an "[i]nvisible man," an existential afterthought who, at his most productive, "[writes] a lot of bullshit poems and unfinished essays" (87). Cudjoe's shift in geographical location or cultural positioning does little in terms of rehabilitating the ambiguous "wound" he feels.[2] His need to (un)dress, suture or close this ambiguous wound is symptomatic of the growing anxiety he feels which stems from his cultural isolation and his ambivalence toward returning home to a deteriorating, conflict-ridden Philadelphia. Here Wideman's treatment of the both the city and Cudjoe point to "the history of an intricate hurt" (113), a juxtaposition that ultimately broaches the personal and the political.

If, as Mbalia argues, Wideman's aesthetic project is the recuperation of an African personality in *Philadelphia Fire*, how does Cudjoe's narrative problematize this view? If Wideman's novel hinges on historiographical revisionism, how successfully does the text reclaim the African personality in its treatment of Cudjoe? Because Cudjoe's cultural positioning is problematized by his ten-year assimilation in Greek culture, how effective is Wideman's construction of a counter-narrative? Cudjoe's expatriate life in Mykonos is significant because it serves as an important bridge between Eurocentric and Afrocentric concerns. As Varsava notes,

> It is symptomatic of the de facto acculturation of African Americans after centuries in the New World that Cudjoe has fled not to black Africa but to the shores of the Mediterranean, that sea of the "middle-of the-earth" that paradoxically separates and joins white Europe and black Africa. (430)

The quest for authenticity is problematized in Cudjoe's straddling of two ideological/geographical spheres. Wideman sheds light on how notions of authenticity are easily complicated but also how constructing an authentic black voice is problematized in ways that are not always exclusively tied to language. Any rejection of, or refusal to participate in African American culture necessarily complicates how authenticity is perceived. However, this tension between two conflicting ideologies only reinforces the notion that authenticity is negotiated through ideological exchange. Cudjoe's *nostos* is triggered by news of the MOVE tragedy and the possibility of finding Simba Muntu, the only boy who survived the great fire. In his search for the boy, Cudjoe's sense of social responsibility is heightened, as is his revitalization of paternal concern. The quest for the lost boy Simba is not merely the search for the "subject," but a committed engagement to recuperating an African narrative: "[I'm writing] [a]bout the fire, but about us too" (82). Simba, then, represents the possibility of subverting and escaping the master narratives of the dominant culture, and of legitimating/liberating the voice of African culture, especially given the Afrocentric world view of MOVE. At the same time, Cudjoe sees in Simba the opportunity to re-imagine his place in a legitimating role as father and saviour. Crucial to our concerns here, however, Cudjoe's lack of agency and his inability to decode language, impede any reconciliation between master narrative and marginalized voices or between survivor and would-be paternal benefactor.

Cudjoe's failure once again is reflected in his inability to legitimately engage with language. Just as his estrangement from his family stems from their failure to understand each other ("they spoke another language"), so too is his subsequent isolation in Mykonos and Philadelphia related to his failure to grasp the fundamental components of language. The problematics of language at work here are intrinsically tied to what Wideman sees as a disconnect between politics and discourse: the sense of entrapment Cudjoe feels at home in a cramped apartment serves to distance himself from his family and the community; his self-effacing status as the "[o]nly splib" in Mykonos obliterates any thought he might have had to take up political action or assume a politically-minded role on the island. Instead, he engages unsuccessfully in the acquisition of a new language (Greek words for the female anatomy), words that, he confesses, "escap[e] him even as he hears them" (6). For Cudjoe, the process of acculturation and the assimilation of new language is futile because "[he] doesn't know what to make of the exchange," or to use Wideman's basketball metaphor, "[his words are] on line but [with] not enough arch" (76, 35). In Wideman's own self-reflexive meditations on language in part two–the narrative doublet for ruminations on paternal failure and the limitations of language–he is incapable of engaging in even the most basic of linguistic exchanges with his son. He states, "I don't know what words mean when he says them. I don't know if he knows what they mean or knows why he says them [...] Words have become useless" (99). In this respect, Wideman's postmodernist concerns come to light in his epistemological questioning of the currency of (de)politicized language.

In his most recent publication, *God's Gym*, a collection of stories that fuses the personal and political concerns of its author, Wideman's narratives raise similar epistemological questions related to language. Though Wideman's appropriation of different voices through gender and race shift one's view of how he engages with these questions, he continues to grapple with how language is constructed, received and interpreted. These stories are about "scribbled words in the wrong language" (146), about reading and writing, presence and absence, the distance between speech and silence, understanding and misunderstanding. As in his novel, Wideman's stories suggest how language stripped of political context results in the breakdown of interpersonal relationships; they also point to how language fails the black male. In "What We Cannot Speak About We Must Pass Over in Silence," Wideman's treatment of paternal failure and surrogate fatherhood once again figures prominently. Upon receiving notice of his friend's death, a nameless fifty-seven year old bachelor attempts to locate his friend's son, incarcerated somewhere in an Arizona prison. What begins as the narrator's modest goal to notify the son of his father's death develops into a series of correspondence through letters–letters to lawyers, prison boards, paralegals, and finally, to the incarcerated son – and grows into his desire to visit the son. These matters are complicated when the narrator learns that the man he finally locates in an Arizona prison may or may not be the son of his deceased friend. The son's response to the narrator's first letter is unambiguously clear: "Some man must have fucked my mother. All I knew about him until your note said he's dead. Thanks" (100). The son's reply potentially dissolves the relationship between both men in that the narrator assumes his search for the son ends in "[a] case of mistaken identity" (100). In fact, the narrator's commitment to corresponding with the son dissolves following the son's initial response: "His answer enough to cure me of letter writing forever" (106). In this context, writing serves as a bridge between two people from two different realms of experience but also shows how language complicates interpersonal narratives through the (mis)interpretation of language itself. The narrator's note informs the son of his father's death; the son's response in turn problematizes the narrator's position in relation to both men–the deceased friend and the son. Despite his suspicions that the experience is nothing more than a "hallucination" and a "fabrication," (100) the narrator's resolve to visit the son and assume the role of surrogate father is strengthened when he is unable to recall his dead friend's face. His attempt to reconstruct the absent face is described in terms of "milk[ing] the friend's features from [his own]" (108). Because he is unable to recuperate a palpable image of his friend's face, the narrator reconfigures his friend's face to be indistinguishable from his own. In his refashioning of his friend's physicality through his own, his shift from mere emissary to surrogate father is complete and his revitalized commitment to visiting the son is sealed with another letter. Even here, Wideman implicitly affirms the idea that authenticity, as a process, must always be negotiated – through language as much as through the construction of self – because there is no fixed point from which to describe authenticity.

Importantly, the narrator's relationship with the son is based purely on the written word, on letters both written and received. Writing becomes the means through which interpersonal relationships are forged, but writing not only facilitates but also strengthens the relationship between two strangers. The dynamic of their relationship changes once the narrator receives his visiting form, upon which the "son instruct[s him] to check the box for family and write *father* on the line following it" (109). The inclusion of the word father on the form, the son urges, is nothing more than a formality that will "cut red tape and speed up the process," (109) but the letter strengthens the bond between both men and the narrator's resolve to visit the son is fixed. This search for the missing son and the symbolic inscription of the word *father* echo Cudjoe's search for Simba and how his attempt to find the boy represents his longing to reassume a paternal role. Language here, which exists solely in epistolary form, reinforces the bonds between men. In these exchanges, two strangers forge an ambiguous relationship that stems from the narrator's need to connect with the narrative of his friend's life. It is significant that the story culminates in the nameless narrator's first and only visit to the unknown prisoner that ultimately ends in the cancellation of the visit. The story's abrupt, unresolved narrative reveals as much about Wideman's consistent problematic constructions of fathers and sons as it does about the failures of language. Narrative frustration here reinforces how language dismantles interpersonal relationships in the community as easily as it creates them. Their meeting is aborted in the text's final paragraph so as to pre-empt any attempts at dialogue. Language expressed in written form remains, in this context, a private, personal exercise. Similarly, during a prolonged period of isolation on Mykonos, Cudjoe, the isolate black male, turns to writing as a form of consolation, if not survival; however, once Cudjoe engages with language outside of his writing, his consistent inability to understand language leads to the disintegration of his interpersonal relationships. The nameless narrator's late arrival to the prison (he arrives two days late) and his general sense of foreboding upon arriving in Arizona signals to the reader that a meeting is unlikely, if not ill fated. The threat of (performing) language~and the implication for Wideman that spoken (not written) language frustrates and ultimately breaks down relationships in the community~is averted, and as the story's title suggests, what cannot be spoken must be passed over in silence.

Personal failure in personal relationships in turn translates to the black male characters' commitment to political action. In *Philadelphia Fire*, language takes on greater meaning when the text plays with political markers. Nowhere is Wideman's wordplay more pronounced (and his political intent more focused) than in his appropriation of *The Tempest*. Mbalia points to Wideman's examination of the "cause" of African exploitation and oppression (topics pregnant with meaning in his reworking of Shakespeare's text), evincing that Wideman's "answer revolve[s] around the Prosperos, those early European capitalists, or agents of capitalists, who went around 'discovering,' exploiting, and oppressing other people for   profit   (114).   Cudjoe's former ambivalence about place and political commitment has been remedied by his (re)discovery of (his own) politicized language. The end of the book's first section anticipates his attempt to forge an authentic black identity. In a dream, he hears

> "a bunch of kids singing. The words are unintelligible. Another language. But the singing gets to me anyway, right away. I can feel what they're singing about. Doesn't matter that I can't understand a word. It's a freedom song. A fighting song (93).

Though the language barrier still challenges Cudjoe's understanding of the relevance of their singing, he comes to appreciate the political virtues as well as the performative enunciations of the "fighting song," two crucial components in his own future performance. The song itself serves as a call-and-response to the narrative concerns addressed in the novel's second section, invoking the distinct characteristics of African music and jazz. In Cudjoe's revisionist meta-narrative/loose adaptation of *The Tempest*,[3] he fashions his own response to the children's fighting song. Here Cudjoe's politicized rhetoric addresses the need to subvert the language of oppressive Euro-capitalist culture he associates with "Earl the Pearl Shakespeare" whose play "about colonialism, imperialism, recidivism, the royal fucking over of weak by strong, colored by white" operates under the umbrella of political discourse that determines "[w]ho's in, who's out, [and] who says so" (127, 140). These inclusionary/exclusionary practices of seminal/canonical texts, Wideman suggests, call for authentic revisions. What makes Cudjoe's/Wideman's brilliantly conceived play so engaging is the text's experimentation with language, voice, perspective, persona, and history. At the same time, what makes Wideman's attempt to stage "real guerrilla theater" (143) so problematic is Cudjoe's inability to pull it off: "Was it ever performed? Nope" (149). Cudjoe's subsequent failure to stage the play ultimately points to the slippery nature of claiming a legitimating authentic identity; more specifically, Wideman's novel can be read as a text that negotiates two realms of discourse (Eurocentrism and Afrocentrism) that ultimately complicate his representation of an authentic African identity in his treatment of black men. In "The Black Writer and the Magic of the Word," Wideman (1988) attributes some of the difficulties of learning the dominant culture's language to the alien characteristics of writing as opposed to the oral traditions of African culture: "You learn the language of power, learn it well enough to read and write but its forms and logic cut you off, separate you from the primal authenticity of your experience" (28).

The disconnect between learning "the language of power" and achieving the "primal authenticity of [black] experience" is central to Wideman's concerns in *God's Gym*: neither can be achieved in relation to the other. These revisionary practices are also invoked and frustrated in similar fashion in "Who Invented the Jump Shot." The story begins at a conference centre in Minneapolis where the narrator's "noncolored colleagues will claim [...] a white college kid [...] proved by such and such musty, dusty, documents [...] launched the first jump shot."[4] By the end of the seminar, through the efforts of white scholars, "they'll own the jump shot" (71). In his refusal to participate in this "pissing contest," (71) the narrator engages in his own form of historical revision as he tries to recuperate the story of who invented the first jump shot, a story beginning on January 27, 1927 with the first incarnation of the Harlem Globies. The narrator's counter-story is meant to establish an alternative version to what, he imagines, will soon become dogmatic lore once they've "[r]ewrit[ten] history, planting their flag on a chunk of territory because no native's around to holler, Stop, thief" (72). What begins uneventfully as a recounting of the Globies' initial trip to Hinkley, Illinois, where they will play the town's best for money, slowly degenerates into a meditation on black oppression and the failure of language. The team is chauffeured by an entrepreneurial driver, a white man who will profit from his exploitation of the black bodies he will lead from town to town, accepting money from white people who have come to "[w]atch Jim Crow fly" (73) on the basketball court. The narrator's attempt to "seek the origins of the jump shot elsewhere, in the darkness where [his] lost tribe wanders still" (72) is frustrated by his inability to continue the story in his own words. Despite his obvious identification with the young black men in the Studebaker en route to Hinkley, the narrator himself identifies an unmotivated shift in his positioning when he appropriates the voice of the driver. Central to this slippage is the narrator's inability to summon his own language to tell the story, and that the struggle implicit in his telling of the tale is engendered by the hegemonic discourse to which he is subjected to at the conference. Because black voices are suppressed by "the enemy's narrative" (76) even the speaker's own narrative unwittingly aligns itself within a hegemonic power structure.

> Please. If you believe nothing else about me, please believe I'm struggling for other words, my own words, even if they seem to spiral out of a mind, a mouth, like the driver's, my words, words I'm trying to earn, words I'm bound to fall on like a sword if they fail me. (76)

Here Wideman is interested not only in how these master narratives come to insinuate themselves in the resistance narratives of the black community, but also how narratives are frustrated by his black male characters to access/decode/construct language. Narrative frustration is complete when the narrator points to his own shortcomings as a writer whose "gray matter [is] hopelessly whitewashed" and whose work is stripped of its political motivations in the act of creating counter-narratives: "Isn't the whole point of writing to escape what people not me think of me" (75). When language fails to sustain his political agenda, he is "bound to fall on [his words] like a sword." The question of agency once again figures prominently here because Wideman's thematic dramatization of counter-narrative is undermined by what he sees as African Americans' relationship to the English language. What could have been a significant moment for the narrator to assert the importance of a subversive counter-narrative to what will remain (in the story at least) an uncontested master narrative is reduced to a plea for understanding. Agency for this black male character, then, remains out of reach, as does the legitimating power of language. Here Wideman's dramatization of the narrator's inability to articulate his own story once again illustrates how any attempt to describe authenticity is problematized to great effect in the construction of language and the creation of stories about black culture.

Both the nameless narrator and Cudjoe's failure to appropriate and redirect the language of power~not the power of language (their language is powerful)~jeopardizes the efficacy of their respective political projects. It is worth noting that although Cudjoe's adaptation of *The Tempest* is never staged and the nameless narrator in "Who Invented the Jump Shot" never completes his own story, the articulation of their political projects register on many levels with the reader because their words~*Wideman's words*~belong to each text. In publishing *Philadelphia Fire* and *God's Gym*, Wideman himself becomes the agent through which these narrators reach an audience: "While revealing that language is the source of black male oppression, [Wideman's fiction] also thematizes the postmodernist possibilities of changing the Calibanic [hegemonic] story by controlling language" (*Black Male Fiction* 5). These metafictional properties of the narrative, however, are problematized by what Coleman calls "Calibanic discourse" (or the demonization of the black male), a hegemonic discourse that frustrates the creation of counter-narratives and puts limits on black male subjectivity. Whether the black male figures that populate Wideman's narratives here are ineffectual or languageless, in the end their counter-narratives are pitched to the reader who is left to make sense of the import of their collective struggles against hegemonic power structures. In other words, the liberation of black voices, to some extent, is left solely in the hands of the reader. Benston's earlier remarks on how the "interpretive respondent" (i.e. the reader) is asked "to accept the continuously unsatisfying and contradictory character of [the text's performative] enunciations" are useful here in terms of describing the agency the reader enjoys in his/her generation of meaning of Wideman's texts. From this perspective, the reader is also perpetually engaged in the process of negotiating and defining authenticity. If readers go on to stage Cudjoe's adaptation of *The Tempest* or lend a voice to the disenfranchised characters in *God's Gym*, perhaps Wideman's attempts to re-center his community's interests will be further realized. If Cudjoe's appropriation of Shakespeare (a questioning of oppressive/colonial discourse) and the search for Simba (the attempt to liberate an oppressed black male voice) suggest a working toward a better understanding of the black male characters in African American literature, perhaps Lynn Hunt's definition of history will gain even more currency: "History is better defined as an ongoing tension between stories that have been told and stories that might be told" ("History as Gesture" 103). Wideman's voice continues to negotiate the "ongoing tension between stories that might be told" against stories that have been told, and in so doing, works toward the liberation of his community's voice and forging a better understanding of what authenticity means.

Notes

1   Mbalia borrows the term from Kwame Nkrumah who defines the term as "the cluster of humanist principles which underlie the traditional African society" (quoted in Mbalia 23).
2   References to wound(s) appear on 5, 54, and 172.
3   What Wideman elsewhere calls "[an] authentically revised version of Willy's con" (131).
4   For a brief discussion of the jump shot debate, see Caponi's (1999) introduction to *Signifyin(g), Sanctifyin' & Slam Dunking* 3-4.

Works Cited

Benston Kimberly, W. "Performing Blackness: Re/Placing Afro-American Poetry." *Afro-American Literary Study in the 1990s.*Ed. Houston A. Baker Jr. and Patricia Redmond. Chicago: U of Chicago P, 1989. 164-193.

Berben-Masi, Jacqueline. "From Brothers and Keepers to Two Cities: Social and Cultural Consciousness, Art and Imagination: An Interview with John Edgar Wideman." *Callaloo: A Journal of African-American and African Arts and Letters* 22.3 (1999): 568-84.

Caponi, Gena Dagel. *Signifyin(g), Sanctifyin' & Slam Dunking : A Reader in African American Expressive Culture.*Amherst: University of Massachusetts Press, 1999.

Carden, Mary Paniccia. "'If the City is a Man': Founders and Fathers, Cities and Sons in John Edgar Wideman's Philadelphia Fire."*Contemporary Literature* 44.3 (2003): 472-500.

Coleman, James W. *Black Male Fiction and the Legacy of Caliban.* Lexington, KY: UP of Kentucky, 2001.

~~. *Blackness and Modernism: The Literary Career of John Edgar Wideman.* Jackson: UP of Mississippi, 1989.

Du Bois, W.E.B. *The Souls of Black Folk: Essays and Sketches.* New York: Fawcett Publications, 1961.

Ellison, Ralph. *Invisible Man.* New York: Vintage, 1995.

~~."Twentieth-Century Fiction and the Black Mask of Humanity."*Within the Circle: An Anthology of African American Literary Criticism from the Harlem Renaissance to the Present.* Ed. Angelyn Mitchell. Durham, NC: Duke UP, 1994. 134-148.

Gysin, Fritz. "From Modernism to Postmodernism: Black Literature at the Crossroads." *The Cambridge Companion to the African American Novel.*Ed. Maryemma Graham. Cambridge, England: Cambridge UP, 2004. 139-155.

Hunt, Lynn. "History as Gesture: Or, the Scandal of History."*Consequences of Theory.* Ed. Jonathan Arac and Barbara Johnson. Baltimore: Johns Hopkins UP, 1991. 91-107.

Mbalia, Doreatha D. *John Edgar Wideman : Reclaiming the African Personality.* London: Associated University Presses, 1995.

Varsava, Jerry. "'Woven of Many Strands': Multiple Subjectivity in John Edgar Wideman's Philadelphia Fire."*Critique: Studies in Contemporary Fiction* 41.4 (2000): 425-44.

Wideman, John Edgar. *God's Gym.* New York: Houghton Mifflin Books, 2005.

~~. *Philadelphia Fire.* New York: Mariner Books, 2005.

~~. "The Black Writer and the Magic of the Word."*New York Times Book Review*(1988): 1, 28-29.

ROCHELLE BROCK &
RICHARD GREGGORY JOHNSON III,
Executive Editors

Black Studies and Critical Thinking is an inter-disciplinary series which examines the intellectual traditions of and cultural contributions made by people of African descent throughout the world. Whether it is in literature, art, music, science, or academics, these contributions are vast and far-reaching. As we work to stretch the boundaries of knowledge and understanding of issues critical to the Black experience, this series offers a unique opportunity to study the social, economic, and political forces that have shaped the historic experience of Black America, and that continue to determine our future. Black Studies and Critical Thinking is positioned at the forefront of research on the Black experience, and is the source for dynamic, innovative, and creative exploration of the most vital issues facing African Americans. The series invites contributions from all disciplines but is specially suited for cultural studies, anthropology, history, sociology, literature, art, and music.

Subjects of interest include (but are not limited to):

- EDUCATION
- SOCIOLOGY
- HISTORY
- MEDIA/COMMUNICATION
- RELIGION/THEOLOGY
- WOMEN'S STUDIES

- POLICY STUDIES
- ADVERTISING
- AFRICAN AMERICAN STUDIES
- POLITICAL SCIENCE
- LGBT STUDIES

For additional information about this series or for the submission of manuscripts, please contact Dr. Brock (Indiana University Northwest) at brock2@iun.edu or Dr. Johnson (University of Vermont) at richard.johnson-III@uvm.edu.

To order other books in this series, please contact our Customer Service Department:

(800) 770-LANG (within the U.S.)
(212) 647-7706 (outside the U.S.)
(212) 647-7707 FAX

Or browse online by series at www.peterlang.com.